POWER IN WASHINGTON

Douglass Cater

POWER IN WASHINGTON

A Critical Look at
Today's Struggle to Govern
in the U.S.A.

Collins

ST JAMES'S PLACE LONDON
1965

c

To S.D.C. and N.C.C.

INTRODUCTION

The reporter who spends his time in Washington gains special perspectives. He is member of a sizable intelligence apparatus whose allegiance is to authority outside the official government. He concentrates on watching government in moments of crisis, on witnessing the tests of men and institutions. He has certain privileges over more leisurely observers. While he may be barred from the inner council chambers, at least he has a chance to catch policy-makers while their defenses are down, and before their policies and passions can cool.

Yet the reporter also runs risks as an observer. His temptation is to see and describe government as a marathon drama whose lively actors strut in meaningless succession across the stage. If his convictions are strong, he may create for his readers a melodrama in which the good guys are constantly engaged with the bad, or in which the special interest lurks behind the papier-mâché figure of each politician. But the reporter has trouble with the larger story of government. While the political scientists tend too often to cram their observations into theory's convenient pigeon-holes, the reporter usually avoids theory in sorting out the fast moving events that cross his vision.

I cite this both to explain and to qualify a book which offers one reporter's perspective on government in Washington today. After more than twelve years of watching at close hand, I felt a need to stand back and try—to borrow the youthful ambition of Woodrow Wilson—"to catch its present phases and to photograph the delicate organism in all its characteristic parts exactly as it is today. . . ."

This, I recognize, is an immodest ambition. Government

has become an infinitely larger and more complex mechanism than it was when Wilson wrote. The fragmented power structure he described has grown more fragmented, despite the efforts at co-ordination. Merely to encompass all parts of the power structure requires a treatment more systematic and scholarly than is possible here. Important areas of the Washington scene—for example, the courts and the regulatory agencies—are treated cursorily in my text, simply because they have remained largely beyond my reportorial experience. It has been my more limited purpose to record the particular experiences and insights which had meaning for me in seeking to penetrate the mysteries of the struggle to govern.

My debts are numerous: to Max Ascoli who has been my editor on *The Reporter* throughout this book's long period of gestation; to Hannah Arendt, Paul Horgan, John Macy, Justice Arthur Goldberg, Rowland Evans, Richard Neustadt, John Maguire, Sidney Hyman, Congressman Richard Bolling, and Member of Parliament Roy Jenkins who have read and criticized various drafts of the manuscript; to the Wesleyan University Center for Advanced Studies which provided time for reflection, and to President Victor Butterfield and the late Sigmund Neumann for inviting me to be a Fellow; to Walter Pincus who was a collaborator in probing the foreign lobbyists and the subgovernment of defense; to Betty Posniak and Jill Gibbons, skilled translators of my penciled copy; and, finally, to my Libby Cater who, besides lending research assistance, freely gave that vital margin of faith.

CONTENTS

VI.   THE STRUGGLE TO GOVERN

I

The Constitution

THE CONSTITUTION: THE LIVING VERSUS THE LITERAL

". . . The Constitution of England is so exceedingly complex that the nation may suffer for years together without being able to discover in which part the fault lies. . . ."

THOMAS PAINE, 1776 [1]

". . . The Constitution is now, like Magna Carta and the Bill of Rights, only the sap-centre of a system of government vastly larger than the stock from which it has branched—a system, some of whose forms have only very indistinct and rudimental beginnings in the simple substance of the Constitution, and which exercises many functions apparently quite foreign to the primitive properties contained in the fundamental law. . . ."

WOODROW WILSON, 1884 [2]

At least since de Tocqueville's time, the observer arriving in Washington finds himself engaged in a search for the sources of power. Who holds power in the American system of government? According to the dictionary definition, power means "ability to act" or, more pertinent, "the possession of controlling influence over others." Of course, all power in this democratic nation ultimately is vested in "the people." But such knowledge does not help much in defining and describing how power is exercised.

Before residing long in the nation's capital, the observer begins to suspect that there are a great many possessors of power. He watches the vast power of the President, even one reviled as weak and insecure. He sees the stubborn power of the committee chairman in Congress, the artful power of the lobbyist, the specialized power of the business leader or the labor chieftain, the durable power of the bureaucrat. He observes the members of the press and finds that they, too, hold power.

Power in Washington has many guises. It can be statutory, its limits specified with verbal nicety; or it can be nowhere written down but every bit as specific. It can be derived from tenure—and Congress is not the only place where seniority counts. It can be a sturdy product of massive organization. It can be mobile and transitory. It can be derived from reason or from unreasoning passion, from expert knowledge or lack of it. It can be silent and secretive; or, in an age of publicity, it can be a phenomenon based almost exclusively on noise.

The trappings of power are equally varied. They are measured superficially by the color and depth of the bureaucrat's office rug, the sleekness of his limousine. For the chief executive, in a democracy supposed to eschew ceremony, symbols can be seen and heard in the scurry of secret service agents, the bombast of motorcycle and helicopter cavalcades, the split-second timing of his schedules. One fairly good yardstick for most officials is the number of reporters attending their briefings—a measure that caused concern in the early days of the Kennedy Administration when U. N. Ambassador Adlai E. Stevenson was consistently outdrawing Secretary of State Dean Rusk.

There are other trappings. On Capitol Hill, power is often enshrouded in musty offices with brass spittoons and ancient leather armchairs. Patriarchal power may walk or ride the bus to work without being diminished. It cannot be reckoned by the number of secretaries in the outer office, but by who keeps whom waiting there.

Power of sorts flaunts itself at fancy dress events in a city which vies increasingly with New York to be social as well as political capital of the nation. It can be studied in the pecking order of the hostesses, the line-up of the place cards, the tense lines of anxiety around the eyes of those who pursue entertainment almost as a vocation. Power also lodges in unparty-like places. It is found at the shirt-sleeved drafting session stretching into the wee morning hours, and at the secretive hotel room conference where only a bottle and a bucket of ice ameliorate the blunt confrontations.

The observer learns that he must rely on all his senses if he is to identify power in all its manifestations. Watching the kaleidoscope of power in Washington, he tends to grow confused. He has read the Constitution and he dutifully makes the rounds of the three great branches of government to watch the exercise of Constitutional powers. But he soon discovers that American government operates under a living, not a literal, Constitution. He must read that document differently from the way a hardshell Baptist reads his Bible.

Nowhere in the text of the Constitution is it stipulated that the denizens of the Third Branch shall serve as final interpreter of its meanings. This was a power asserted by early occupants of the Supreme Court which has so far withstood time's testing. Each desegregation crisis raises the question of whether the Court's power as interpreter will survive, and it demonstrates how fragile that power would be without the sustaining power of armed deputies from the Second Branch of Government.

"This political role of the Court has been obscure to laymen—even to most lawyers," wrote Robert H. Jackson before he became a Justice. "It speaks only through the technical forms of the lawsuit, which are not identified with politics in its popularly accepted sense. Yet these lawsuits are the chief instrument of power in our system. Struggles over power that in Europe call out regiments of troops, in America call out battalions of lawyers. When the Court decides where power will be recognized, it often thereby settles whether that power can ever effectively be exercised. A given power held to reside in the states becomes at once power subdivided into forty-eight sections, each circumscribed by a state's boundaries—a power which can easily be defeated, evaded, or cancelled by playing one state against another. The same power held to reside in the nation is quite another matter in its effectiveness. So, too, serious practical consequences wait upon the distribution of power between the President and the Congress." [3]

"We are under a Constitution, but the Constitution is what the judges say it is. . . ." This truism enunciated by Charles Evans Hughes, later to become Chief Justice, has almost daily proof. The Supreme Court has parsed the written words of the Constitution to accommodate a dynamic nation, stretched the Commerce Clause to bind together a union whose state boundaries long ago lost most of their meaning, discovered belatedly in the Fourteenth and Fifteenth Amendments the authority to make that union satisfy the urgent demands of an uneasy social conscience.

Since the celebrated Court-packing fight of 1937, the cumulative thrust of the Third Branch has been to enlarge the concentration of power in Washington. But the Court has not played such a major role in parcelling out power within the federal government. The more significant power struggle inside Washington takes place outside the jurisdiction of the Court. The contest between the Executive Branch and Congress is vastly different from anything contemplated by the drafters of the Constitution. Article I specifies: "All legislative power herein granted shall be vested in a Congress of the United States, which shall consist of a Senate and House of Representatives." Congress was to make the laws and hold the purse strings. The President was to have only a limited power of veto over the legislative process.

Consider the situation today. Whether guided by the more active or passive concept of the job, the President is now the central figure in the legislative process. The President's program occupies the dominant place on the congressional agenda. Most of the major laws are drafted in the President's office; the budget is put together there and presented to Congress as a packaged entity. A bill initiated by the individual congressman faces giant obstacles unless it has been submitted first to the President's Budget Bureau for "legislative clearance." Yet as recently as 1937, such initiatives on the President's part provoked bitter talk in Congress of "Roosevelt's dictatorship."

The turnabout has not been entirely in one direction, for Congress has found countervailing powers. Article II of the Constitution states: "The executive power shall be vested in a President of the United States of America." There is no allocation—except in the Senate's ratification of treaties and confirmation of appointments—of a congressional power to investigate, review, or veto. Today, Congress regularly asserts this power without serious challenge.

This congressional "oversight" of the Executive goes on without any pretense of legislative purpose. It is continuous and contemporaneous. We are accustomed to news stories of this variety: "A House subcommittee is investigating whether prolonged delays in the development of the Centaur rocket have resulted from poor management by industry and the government. The investigation, by a unit of the Committee on Science and Astronautics, was prompted in part by the failure of the high-priority Centaur on its first flight test last week. . . . Even before the test flight, members of the House subcommittee on advanced research and technology, raised questions about the project." [4]

Or, when the Secretary of Defense cancelled construction of a nuclear aircraft carrier, the Chairman of the Joint Atomic Energy Committee went on television to declare,

B

according to one news account, that the Secretary "would have been wiser had he waited for the committee's advice before making his decision. [The Chairman] stressed that the committee had long experience on atomic matters and that it had a record of being right regarding military applications of atomic energy." [5]

Congress is prepared to advise and consent at each stage of executive decision-making. Its committees are organized to act as boards of review over the everyday work of the executive agencies, regularly asserting their claim of jurisdiction before an issue has reached the President's desk. Their capacity for conducting post mortems is so swift that frequently a program can be eviscerated before it has gone through the birthing process. Critical issues of farm or foreign policy—a revision of crop supports, a new approach to Red China—provoke elaborate investigations in Congress even when the Executive Branch has made no pronouncements and submitted no legislative requests. With increasing frequency, Congress has sought to penetrate the Executive by means of a "legislative veto," sometimes to be exercised by a single committee or committee chairman.

This extra-constitutional thrust and counter thrust does not end there. Congress regularly attaches "riders" containing legislative edicts to appropriation bills in happy certainty that the President dares not risk delay and distemper by exercising his constitutional power of veto. On the other hand, the recent President has not hesitated to "impound" funds duly appropriated by Congress which exceeded his budget requests. While the Constitution does not grant him this authority, neither does the Constitution indicate a way to prevent him from exercising it.

By a literal reading of the document, the House of Representatives was not intended to share the "advice and consent" power in the area of foreign policy. But the present conduct of foreign policy today costs money and, according to tradition, all appropriation measures originate in the House. It can lead to the situation when, during the

Eighty-seventh Congress, House conferees doggedly insisted on imposing strictures against use of aid funds for Communist-oriented countries, thereby substantially altering the President's foreign policy.

The power struggle in Washington can scarcely be described simply as a clash between the two great branches of government, each cohesive and concerted in its purpose. In Congress, as Woodrow Wilson made clear over a half-century ago, "Power is nowhere concentrated; it is rather deliberately and of set policy scattered amongst many small chiefs." The "disintegrate ministry" he depicted is no more integrated today. Most programs of substance must clear the four committees of the authorizing and the appropriating process as well as, in the House, the highly autonomous Committee on Rules, before the general membership has a voice. Nothing in the Constitution can explain the way Congress allocates its power or authorizes its committee hierarchs to rule so undisputedly.

Between the two Houses, neither prepared to grant precedence or privileges to the other, open warfare is ever threatening to erupt. The feuding can provide opportunities for a President to shape his legislative strategies by playing off one House against the other. But it can also raise hazards. During a recent session, action on vital money bills was frustrated because of a petulant squabble between the two chairmen of the Appropriations Committees, both octogenarians. The Chairman of House Appropriations, who has been in Congress since 1923, believed his committee was being slighted. But the Chairman of Senate Appropriations, who has been in Congress since 1911, was equally adamant. For nearly three months, progress halted and the executive payrolls ran short while the conferees debated when to meet, who should hold the gavel, and similar minuscule matters of prerogative.

After winning overwhelming approval in both Houses, aid to higher education was killed in 1962 because of a conflict in conference. The President would have accepted gladly either the House or Senate version, but it was not up to him. The conference—a strictly extra-Constitutional device for reconciling differences between the two Houses —wields *de facto* power of tremendous proportions. The ordinary congressman, supposedly *pare inter pares*, has little recourse when his legislative wishes are thwarted there even though they may be shared by a majority of his colleagues. He even has difficulty learning what happened, for the sessions are held behind closed doors.

The Executive, despite a President's best efforts at coordination and control, has its own problem of integration. Each great department has a life force of its own, each has its own constituency quite distinct from that of the President. Tucked away within the vast bureaucracy are countless chiefs, many vested with statutory authority, who have closer ties to key members of Congress than to their department heads or to the President.

On election night, candidate Kennedy asked two close friends dining with him for an assessment of FBI Director J. Edgar Hoover. Both offered unfavorable verdicts. Next morning, as the first order of business at his first press conference as President-elect, Kennedy announced his intention of reappointing Hoover to his long-time job. Everyone understood that it was a shrewd and power-conscious move on Kennedy's part.

Other career servants hold persuasiveness with a President: the Joint Chiefs of Staff, with their tremendous political power both as a group and individually; the head of the Army Corps of Engineers who presides over the pork barrel projects dear to the congressman; the chieftains in the Bureau of Reclamation and the National Guard. In recent years, bureaucrats in the National Institutes of Health, by favor of two strategically placed members of Congress, have regularly been able to override the President's estimate of their budget needs.

Fierce rivalries for funds and functions go on ceaselessly

among the departments and between the agencies. A cunning bureau chief learns to negotiate alliances on Capitol Hill that bypass the central authority of the White House. The senior civil servant senses a power in his tenure able to withstand transient whims. "Some of these bureaucrats are absolutely frank about it," Presidential Assistant Lawrence O'Brien remarked. "They tell us, 'We're going to be running things in Washington after you've gone. . . .' " For a President, working his way with the Executive can be as difficult as working with Congress.

"The constitutional convention of 1787 is supposed to have created a government of 'separated powers,' " one perceptive observer has written. "It did nothing of the sort. Rather, it created a government of separated institutions sharing powers." [6] As government has grown and the problems it deals with have become more and more complex, the sharing of power has proliferated. New institutions have sprung up. Unique to American government, the independent regulatory commissions arrived on the scene, exercising power that is executive, legislative, and judicial, yet not clearly belonging to any of the three branches. They exist in a Constitutional limbo. They are the subject of repeated lamentations such as the one voiced by a former member of the Civil Aeronautics Board: "Responsible to no one, divided within themselves on matters of basic policies, swamped under a burden of detail, the agencies are not effective instruments of government today." [7]

This and other pleas for reform go unheeded. The regulatory commissions developed in response to urgent necessities of government never envisaged by the draftsmen of the Constitution. Despite their obvious inadequacies, their dilemma goes deeper than mere administrative ineptitude. They represent an unresolved problem of how to distribute power in areas where the constitutional "separation" would be completely unworkable.

The political parties are repositories of power, extra-con-

stitutional and extra-governmental, and figure large in the
Washington rhetoric. Traditionally, parties are supposed to
serve as ways of organizing power to bridge the gulf between the Executive and Congress. But the growth of the
party role has not kept pace with the growth of big government. Power in the two-party system is still largely decen-
tralized in state and local groupings. Despite vigorous efforts at cohesion, national party headquarters are hardly
central command posts. In control of finances and selection
of congressional candidates, Democrat and Republican are
pretty much national parties in name only.

This shortfall in role, and consequently of power, should
not be overstated. The party does provide the machinery
for staging elections and appealing to common loyalties.
In Congress, party preference does exercise a vital first
option on a member's voting habits. Yet, while organized
on the two-party system, Congress operates on a multi-party
system. The great issues, foreign and domestic, have riven
both the major parties. As a result, the quest for majority
mandate on a critical issue usually gets down to the business of building coalitions that transcend party allegiances.

Even while paying lip service to his party, a President
finds himself obliged to bypass it. With the help of modern
communications, he has more direct means of contact with
his public than the party's many-layered relay system. On
the compelling issues of foreign affairs and defense, he inevitably seeks to clothe his policies in the respectable robes
of bipartisanship. Toward such matters as fiscal and mone-
tary policy and even civil rights legislation, he makes constant efforts to maintain an un-partisan posture. His ap-
pointees to high office often bear little relation to the party
which elected him.

Still other non-governmental agents share in the exercise
of power. Washington has become a mecca for organizations in search of a role. Private and quasi-public, domestic
and foreign, they set up their headquarters in the city and

go to work. Some operate behind vast façades of plate glass and marble; others in cramped basement rooms with only the essential typewriter and mimeograph machine. Some have substantial bureaucracies; others, one or two part-time operatives. Business, industrial and trade associations, labor and farm unions, church, education, and welfare councils—all are present and accounted for. The larger cities of the nation are no longer content to rely on their congressional delegations but send additional special emissaries to pry and prod. Research and intelligence operations mounted by private groups run competition with the organized intelligence of the Executive. Washington lawyers and public relations advisers are specialized in the technique of applying persuasion at the right time and place.

All this organizational life constitutes, in effect, an extra branch of government with powers of initiative and veto. The activity is not to be compared to that of the old-fashioned lobbyist who hung around Congress and sought to influence, by hook or crook, the legislative process; it is not confined to the halls of Congress. A whole new approach to the art of applying pressure has developed. The modern lobbyist, as a recent survey showed, spends only ten per cent of his time in discourse with the congressmen, another ten per cent with legislative assistants. He finds that the most effective way of communing with the politicians is by circuitous routes. He has developed formidable apparatus for cultivating and collecting support among their constituents.

No one who has been inside government doubts the power belonging to these outsiders. They command a communication system that is frequently swifter and more effective than that of the government. They also command financial rewards that can attract men away from government. Not long ago, a congressman from Texas quit a ranking position on the House Ways and Means Committee to become Washington representative for the American Petroleum Institute. The Director of Legislative Relations for the AFL-CIO is also an ex-congressman. Both are able, aggressive men who know their way around Washington. They are hardly less influential for no longer being able to vote on the roll calls.

The role of outsiders on the inside in Washington has not been lost on foreign governments, particularly those in need of assistance. The newborn nations of Africa and Asia soon discover that it is not enough to dispatch an ambassador to the United States or to confine their representations to the Department of State. The Washington lawyer and the public relations adviser are also agents of modern diplomacy. The size of this American retinue of the foreign government working in our nation's capital often appears to be in inverse ratio to the size and importance of the particular country. The late Trujillo dictatorship of the Dominican Republic maintained one of the largest and best paid of all time.

The great diversity of the power operators in Washington lends added role to still another group who figure prominently: the communicators—members of the press and other media—who swell the city's population and have a keen sense of their own importance. The anxiety about press relations exhibited by everyone from the President down attests to this importance, and only the Supreme Court remains fairly aloof.

The press, bearing a loosely drawn mandate to probe and pry, exercises first of all an intelligence function within the government. No ordinary member of Congress has the same opportunity to pose a pertinent question to a President or a bureau chief with expectation of an answer. No Presidential aide is quite so free to ferret out the intimate intentions of members of Congress. No other outside agents can wander so freely through the corridors of the State Department or the Pentagon to detect the murmurs of policies aborning.

There is good cause for the privileged position of the press. It is indispensable as the independent conveyor of news to the various possessors of power, none of whom is willing to trust the other's propaganda. That is why American government never has found it convenient to adopt, in the manner of the British parliamentary system, an Official Secrets Act restricting the reporter's enterprise.

Beyond the Washington community, the press serves as the most regular informant of the larger publics that may be attentive to government. Because power is so dispersed, public opinion in America must play a continuous role as arbiter among the contestants. The ability to make public policy depends to a large extent on the capacity to capture public attention. It gives a separate power to the communicators. The priorities they establish—*i.e.*, their definition of "news" and their diligence in pursuing it—affects the course of politics and can even contribute to more massive shifts of power within the government.

The business of government has grown gargantuan. It involves programs of vast speed and momentum. It requires decision-making that is daily and enormously varied. "Mr. Speaker," declared one congressman not long ago in a burst of candor, "our Committee is about to present to the House one of the most complicated pieces of legislation that the House has ever been called upon to consider. It is something you are almost forced to accept on faith." But very little in Washington is accepted on faith by those who have the power to affect it.

How does all the wheeling and dealing among the power merchants produce government? Eighty years ago, while still more reporter than politician, Woodrow Wilson addressed himself to this question. "The leading inquiry in the examination of any system of government must, of course, concern the real depositories and the essential machinery of power," he wrote. "There is always a centre of power; where

in this system is that centre? In whose hands is self-sufficient
authority lodged and through what agencies does that authority speak and act?" [8]

Wilson's first book, *Congressional Government,* published in 1885, concluded that Congress was the central
and predominant power in the American system and that
the Presidency had become an ineffectual office. But less
than three decades later, Wilson wrote another book, *Constitutional Government in the United States,* concluding
that the President was once again at the front of things:
"His office is anything he has the sagacity and the force to
make it." It was a conviction shared by another future President. In early 1960, only a year before his inauguration,
candidate John F. Kennedy declared, "We will . . . need
what the Constitution envisioned: a Chief Executive who
is the vital center of action in our whole scheme of government."

Whatever the Constitution envisioned, history does not
give assurance that the President always is the *vital* center
in American government. Walter Lippmann, writing in
1955 an introduction to a new edition of *Congressional
Government,* remarked, "The fact is that at times the
system works as [Wilson] describes it in this book and at
other times it works as he describes it in the second book
. . . There exists, one might say in limbo, a third book
describing the American system in its ups and downs."
Lippmann felt that if Wilson had written such a third
book he might have taken a new view of the balance of
power. Wilson's own experience as President, according to
Lippmann, showed "that it is not a stable balance, that the
tendency of the system is to become unbalanced—and
especially after wars when Congress is, for a time, predominant."

An examination of power in Washington today requires
a somewhat different model of government. Wilson depicts a tilt mechanism whose balance seesaws back and
forth between the President and the legislature. But if the

experience since the Second World War offers any guide, the mechanics of the power system has become more complicated.

In the first place, the central position of the Presidency *vis-à-vis* Congress during all three postwar administrations has never been in serious doubt. Even during the fanatic outcropping of McCarthyism, President Truman waged a war and conducted a far-flung foreign policy without threat of congressional take-over. Under the more diffident leadership of Eisenhower, Congress had a capacity to sabotage Presidential priorities but not to substitute priorities of its own. One serious observer of the Washington scene was led to speculate: "We may be witnessing such a profound shift in the division of Congressional and Presidential power that in the future any Presidential incumbent, no matter how strong or weak he is, can prevail in a test of wills . . . It scarcely matters any more whether the President is weak or strong. The office itself upholds his hands, like those of an aged Moses during the battle against the Amalekites." [9]

But the President is challenged other than frontally from Congress. In one important area of policy after another, substantial efforts to exercise power are waged by alliances cutting across the two branches of government and including key operatives from outside. In effect, they constitute subgovernments of Washington comprising the expert, the interested, and the engaged. These subgovernments are not to be confused with factions. Within them, factions contend to greater or lesser degree. The power balance may be in stable or highly unstable equilibrium. But the subgovernment's tendency is to strive to become self-sustaining in control of power in its own sphere. Each seeks to aggregate the power necessary to its purposes. Each resists being overridden.

As an overly neat example consider the tight little subgovernment which rules the nation's sugar economy. Since

the early 1930s, this agricultural commodity has been subject to a cartel arrangement sponsored by the government.
By specific prescription, the sugar market is divided to the
last spoonful among domestic cane and beet growers, and
foreign suppliers. Ostensibly to insure "stability" of supply,
the U. S. price is pegged at a level considerably above the
competitive price in the world market. It has been in fact a
way to subsidize domestic sugar growers who are not genuinely competitive with producers abroad. For Latin American countries able to secure quotas, it has provided a bo-
nanza of sizable proportions.

Political power within the sugar subgovernment is largely
vested in the Chairman of the House Agricultural Committee who works out the schedule of quotas. It is shared
by a veteran civil servant, the director of the Sugar Division
in the U. S. Department of Agriculture, who provides the
necessary "expert" advice for such a complex marketing
arrangement. Further advice is provided by Washington
representatives of the domestic beet and cane sugar growers, the sugar refineries, and the foreign producers.

All these experts are notably skilled in technical and
political persuasion. For the foreign sugar producer, necessary Washington representation has enlisted some of the
ablest and highest paid talent in the city including at least
one former Cabinet officer. Their emoluments, as declared
under the Foreign Agents Registration Act, are often on a
percentage basis in ratio to the quotas awarded their clients.

There are good and sufficient reasons why so much power
has accumulated in the hands of a single committee chairman—in recent years, Harold Cooley, Democrat of North
Carolina. Because the Sugar Act contains an excise tax,
Cooley asserts the Constitutional prerogative of the House
of Representatives to initiate all revenue measures. Because
the legislation is highly technical, he claims that only his
committee is able to cope with it. Within the committee
itself, whose thirty-five members compete in their concerns

for cotton, tobacco, wheat and the other commodities, a skillful Chairman dominates by playing off one interest against another.

It permits him remarkable discretion. In reviewing the sugar quotas, Chairman Cooley has had the habit of receiving the interested parties one by one to make their presentations, then summoning each afterward to announce his verdict. By all accounts, he has a zest for this princely power and enjoys the frequent meetings with foreign ambassadors to confer on matters of state and sugar.

Until recent years, nothing disturbed the hegemony of this little subgovernment, though a few lonely voices were raised in Congress against the disregard being shown for the consumer. In the Executive, as long as order prevailed in the sugar market, high officialdom was otherwise preoccupied. But in 1958, the equilibrium was rudely shaken when Cuba, a major quota recipient, was taken over by the forces of Fidel Castro. As relations between the two countries continued to deteriorate, it became necessary to redistribute Cuba's quota. Chairman Cooley wished to award a large share to the Dominican Republic then under the rule of Generalissimo Trujillo. The Secretary of State, as part of a policy of sanctions against Latin American dictatorships, was even then negotiating a boycott of Trujillo within the Organization of American States.

Quite a struggle ensued. For a period, it remained doubtful whose foreign policy would prevail—the U. S. government's or the sugar subgovernment's. Chairman Cooley forced a temporary increase of the Dominican quota, but the U. S. Treasury slapped a special tax on it. With the change of Administrations in 1961, extra Executive resources were wheeled into the battle. Attorney General Robert Kennedy made it known that he was examining the spending habits of the affluent Dominican lobbyists for evidence of "improper" efforts at persuasion.

At long last, Mr. Cooley retreated, and soon afterward General Trujillo fell. But in yielding the particular battleground, the Chairman still clung resolutely to his accustomed power. Despite President Kennedy's desire to move toward a "global quota" purchased at non-premium prices, the old arrangement whereby Mr. Cooley deals country-by-country with the lobbyists had been preserved largely intact.

The subgovernment of sugar cannot be considered the perfect prototype; it is too small and tightly ordered. But it does illustrate certain essentials of subgovernment: a complex problem to be dealt with and the coalescing of power among those who have the interest or the yen to deal with it.

Other subgovernments may leave more to extragovernmental control. Oil, an intricate power arrangement, is largely manipulated outside the formal offices of the federal government. Yet, as one critic has remarked, "The highly developed private government of oil seeks the support of public government wherever its own political and economic machinery is inadequate for fulfilling industry objectives . . . Through taxes and related subsidies the American government supports the industry in developing its productive capacity. At the same time, through the whole complex conservation system the government backs the planned withholding of products." [10]

One could scarcely learn much about the role of the government in the affairs of oil by studying the formal legislative process. Congress has passed no basic laws on the subject since the Connally "hot oil" Act of 1935. Despite numerous fierce battles, the congressional attempt to define the limits of federal regulation of natural gas has come to naught. The agencies of the government have played competing roles. The Supreme Court, by interpretation, broadened the Federal Power Commission's mandate over regulation; the FPC, caught between conflicting pressures, has steered a confused course; the Office of Emergency Planning weighs the pleas of domestic producers for limitations on the international ones; the State Department's Middle East diplomats are continually caught up in the foreign politics of oil; the Justice Department, as administrator of the anti-trust laws, brings entirely different principles to play. Finally, the Senate Finance and the House Ways and Means Committees have a definitive say in the tax policy of the oil depletion allowance. As any oil lobbyist knows well, the places where decisions are reached in Washington are many and the decisions are often contradictory. No one, certainly not the President, has the time and the power to coordinate all the decision-makers. This very fragmentation of government power adds to the subgovernmental power of those outside the government who are interested in oil.

But the power arrangements of Washington are not limited to commodities. The coalitions have a tendency to form in almost every area in which the power of government gets involved—from foreign aid to veteran benefits, resource conservation to the conquest of outer space. President Eisenhower spoke of an immense combination of power when, in his farewell address in January, 1961, he warned that ". . . in the councils of government, we must guard against the acquisition of unwarranted influence, whether sought or unsought, by the military-industrial complex. The potential for the disastrous rise of misplaced power exists and will persist. We must never let the weight of this combination endanger our liberties or democratic processes."

The subgovernment of defense is far-flung, comprising a vast Executive bureaucracy, numerous committees in Congress, and a formidable representation in the wider Washington community. Its quest for men and materials stretches to every community in the country, its involvements to almost every nation in the non-communist world; its priorities affect the nation's allocation of brain and muscle power. Still, it is a loosely knit power system. Within it, factions are constantly at odds—air vs. army vs. navy, strategic vs. tactical forces, nuclear vs. conventional. Their disputes are of a size and technicality to baffle the average citizen and even the average Secretary of Defense.

Some subgovernments, such as those dealing in certain agricultural products, are highly self-sufficient; others, as the one dealing in foreign aid, have great difficulty achieving a viable power base. Though their outlines may not always be distinct, this is the system of power contemplated by those who operate in Washington as they determine how they can get things done. It is this system with which a President, looking down on government from his special eminence, must reckon.

The President and the other operators learn to be exceedingly realistic in their appraisals. For each subgovernment, special account must be taken of the distribution of power: is the congressional committee chairman purposeful or weak, the regulatory commission strict or compliant, the bureau chief entrenched or insecure, the pressure group expert or inept, the press interested or bored, the Court touchy or timid? Finally, is the President's concern incessant or intermittent?

It would be a mistake to describe this subgovernmental system—in the fashion of Charles Dickens' Fat Boy—simply to make the reader's flesh crawl. To describe the system is not automatically to condemn it. In large part, it has been the result of an increasingly fragmented power structure trying to cope with increasingly big and complicated problems. These are working arrangements for the effective exercise of governmental power. In modern government, that power must be exercised.

"In whose hands," Woodrow Wilson asked eighty years ago, "is self-sufficient authority lodged and through what agencies does that authority speak and act?" [11] The question is relevant today. More urgently than when Wilson wrote, the problems confronting government cannot be adequately handled by "disintegrate ministries." Since Wilson's time, there has been increased attention to the Presidency as the energizing center of government. There has been enormous development of the President's office as the agency through which his authority speaks and acts. Once a small, mostly clerical adjunct to the White House, the Executive Office of the President has become a sizable bureaucracy on its own, teeming with staff aides, experts, and specialists intended to assist the President.

But the President's authority can hardly be described as "self-sufficient." He is challenged on all fronts: by the hierarchs on Capitol Hill who, heeding other voices and other votes, are disposed to bargain with him on more or less equal terms; by the mammoth Executive departments in which at times even his cabinet officers become his competitors; by the extra-governmental groups who on particular issues can often stimulate greater grass roots reaction than he can; by the leaders of the press who can shout longer, if not louder, than he about what government ought or ought not to be doing. Finally, the President is even challenged by his own bureaucracy whose rituals and routines may tend, it has been noted, to make him clerk rather than leader in his own office.

A President sits at the top of government's power structure. No one else in government views things from quite the same elevation; no one is completely answerable to the man who sits there. He is endowed by the Constitution with far greater responsibility than authority and, contrary to popular myth, the gap between responsibility and authority has expanded as the burden of his job has grown. To make his office operable, the President often finds himself serving as broker among the power groups rather than as banker drawing on his own limited reserves of power.

A decade ago, Justice Robert Jackson described the most pressing aspect of government's dilemma: "We face the rivalry, which may break into the hostility, of concentrated governments that can decide quickly and secretly on their

c

policies. Our power is so dispersed that nothing can be decided quickly or secretly." [12] In periods of narrowly defined "national emergency," the government has acted with dictatorial dispatch. But what about the extended period of national emergency in which the nation lives and prospectively will live for the indefinite future?

The problem of organizing effective power is formidable even on the domestic front. There are vital areas in which the coalitions necessary to claim priority for clearly determined needs simply do not exist. The long stalemate over federal aid to education is a case in point. Inattention to the desperate demands of the exploding metropolises, lack of care for the aged, neglect of the depressed areas of the country and the chronically unemployed—all stem from failures of power more than from basic conflict of ideology.

According to some political purists, stalemate in these areas is both inevitable and proper as long as a clear public "consensus" is absent. This amounts to a curious philosophy of immobilism. It means not only failure to grapple with the pressing needs of this era; it means also a helpless perpetuation of the programs of an earlier era, grown oversize and often irrelevant to their original purpose. Some, as in the case of the farm program, continue to create the conditions they were meant to cure. Others become pawns of the special power groupings that have grown up to manage them. These—the untouchables—are responsible in large part for the corruption of government.

The inability to bury the old or take new initiatives represents a crisis of institutions that goes deep in the Constitutional system. It raises the spectre of Tom Paine's indictment of another system: "But the Constitution of England is so exceedingly complex that the nation may suffer for years altogether without being able to discover in which part the fault lies. . . ." President Kennedy declared to a group of students gathered in Washington, ". . . [our] Constitution has served us extremely well, but all its clauses

. . . had to be interpreted by men and had to be made to work by men, and it has to be made to work today in an entirely different world from the day in which it was written. . . ." Hostile critics are quick to claim that in this direction lies tyranny, fearful that any change will alter the traditional checks and balances. But the traditional checks and balances have already been vastly altered. Compared to what the founding fathers envisaged, power has grown infinitely more fragmented. There are many more checks—although they do not always balance one another.

The central problem confronting government today is how to make power in Washington more cohesive. The solution does not lie in dumping vast grants of arbitrary power in the lap of the President. A good case can be made for strengthening Congress, provided that Congress can resolve its frustrated search for role. But Congress and all the other institutions of government need to be examined as they now exist, not as they were once supposed to exist.

The clear and present danger, more than in Wilson's time, is that government becomes disintegrate. It is not that the balance of power tilts toward the Legislative branch —that is no longer likely any more than a major shift back toward the sovereign states. What does happen is that the subgovernments flourish and grow autonomous. They become arrogant in their jurisdictions, defiant of efforts to form a larger consensus than each finds sufficient to its needs. Like princely states, jealous and contentious, they would substitute a new confederation for the "more perfect union" which the Constitution sought to form.

ON THE NATURE OF SUBGOVERNMENTS: THE MILITARY-INDUSTRIAL COMPLEX

"I'd rather run the Pentagon from up here."
CONGRESSMAN CARL VINSON [1]

President Eisenhower's warning in his farewell message about the "conjunction of an immense military establishment and a large arms industry" was perhaps purposefully vague. Yet the sinister ring of his words—"The potential for the disastrous rise of misplaced power exists and will persist"—has given wide scope to interpreters, each to summon his own fears. Two Washington newspapermen, writing a best-selling novel about a military cabal in the Pentagon which came within an inch of capturing the government, afterward sought to lend legitimacy to their plot by the argument, ". . . there would be no reason for men like Eisenhower to fear a 'military-industrial complex' unless they fear military control of the government, either overt or covert, and unless they believe that such control would be an evil thing." [2]

Still another interpreter made the chilling comment about our present situation that "No power in our country's history has posed so black a threat, been so inimical to our traditions, or so menacing of our future, as the military-industrial alliance that has fostered 'The Warfare State.' " [3]

Eisenhower, though sorely aggravated by pressures on his defense budgets, would not be likely to accept either of these elaborations. But by making the 'military-industrial complex' part of the political vocabulary, he has aroused public consciousness of what is the largest of the subgovernments in Washington. Both in size and complexity, it is of a different order of magnitude from the tiny subgovernment of sugar discussed in the last chapter. The two, in fact, run the gamut of the power arrangements for dealing with the business of government. Few are so tightly ordered as sugar; no other is so pervasive as defense. By examining the two extremes, we can obtain better perspective on the problems connected with the exercise of power in Washington. It will then be appropriate to make a more detailed examination of the traditional institutions of government involved in that exercise.

The defense establishment in the United States has changed vastly since that distant day in 1796 when a French visitor called upon Mr. James McHenry, the Secretary of War:

> It was about eleven o'clock in the morning when I called. There was no sentinel at the door, all the rooms, the walls of which were covered with maps, were open, and in the midst of the solitude I found two clerks each sitting at his own table, engaged in writing. At last I met a servant, or rather *the* servant, for there was but one in the house, and asked for the Secretary. He replied that his master was absent for the moment, having gone to the barber's to be shaved. Mr. McHenry's name figured in the State Budget for $2,000, a salary quite sufficient in a country where the Secretary of War goes in the morning to his neighbor, the barber, at the corner, to get shaved. I was as much surprised to find all the business of the War Office transacted by two clerks, as I was to hear that the Secretary had gone to the barber's.[4]

A few years later, in 1801, the central office staff of the War Department numbered, in addition to the Secretary and the accountant, fourteen clerks and two messengers. The field staff consisted of eleven agents and clerks in the quartermaster's department, two armories (at Springfield, Massachusetts, and Harpers Ferry, Virginia) with seven officials, a superintendent of military stores with twelve civilians, two agents for fortifications, and several employees in the Indian Department. A beginning of the military-industrial complex was the recording on March 6, 1791, of a contract between the Secretary of War and William Duer who was to supply the troops en route to Fort Pitt for which Duer posted a bond of $4,000 and received advances of $15,000. Early failures in supply and accounting prompted Secretary of Treasury Alexander Hamilton to offer the first of a long series of plans for military reorganization, afterward complaining in a letter to President Washington, "The utility of the thing does not seem to be as strongly impressed on the mind of the Secretary at War as it is on mine." [5]

The U. S. Navy got its start after a bitter fight in 1794 between the Federalists and the Republicans over a bill to provide six ships to protect American commerce against the Algerine corsairs. Abraham Clark, arguing the Republican cause in the House of Representatives, had objected to the establishment of a fleet on the grounds that "when once it had commenced, there would be no end of it. We must then have a Secretary of the Navy, and a swarm of other people in office, at a monstrous expense." [6]

The Federalists had their way—though construction on three of the ships was later cancelled when peace was achieved with Algeria—and in due time, as Clark predicted, there was clamor for the establishment of a separate Navy Department. A Federalist argued, ". . . it was a thing impossible for one man to undertake the business of the War and Navy Departments. As well might a merchant be set to do the business of a lawyer; a lawyer that of a physician.

. . ." [7] And a Republican replied, "To carry this idea to its full extent, it would not only be necessary to have separate d̓epartments, but also a great variety of subdivisions." There would soon be proposals, he chided, for "commissioners of gunbarrels and of ramrods." [8]

When the new Department was at last established, U. S. Minister William Smith in Lisbon wrote Secretary of War McHenry inquiring whether he would preside over Army or Navy: "are you to be Mars or Neptune? are you to wield the Truncheon or the Trident? God prosper you in whatever capacity; you have an arduous task and sad Devils to deal with. . . ." [9]

The devils with which Defense officials must deal today are sadder and more numerous. The vast five-sided building on the Potomac, which serves as headquarters, houses twenty-five thousand workers within its seven thousand offices and seventeen and a half miles of corridors. These are only the central staff for over three and a half million military and civilian personnel serving under the Secretary of Defense, and another four million who are employed by defense industries in America. It has been calculated that the total approximates the entire population of Sweden. The Defense Department's fifty-billion-dollar budget is bigger than the combined governmental budgets of Great Britain, Italy, West Germany and France. The military owns real estate in the U. S. equivalent to a land area the size of the state of Tennessee; its holdings abroad are equal in area to Rhode Island and Delaware.[10]

A statistical recital of the men and weaponry of our modern peacetime forces is hardly adequate to describe the change since Secretary McHenry's day. Military might, no longer measurable in pure bulk, has also moved cataclysmically in the direction of smaller packaging. Recently, in memory of the Revolutionary War hero, the nuclear submarine *Lafayette* was commissioned as the eleventh of our Polaris fleet. This slim black vessel, resembling a slightly oversized whale, carries greater destructive firepower than all the bombs and shells of the Second World War. By 1965, according to one wry estimate, U. S. defenses will have the equivalent of thirty-five tons of TNT for "the personal containment of every human then living on the globe." [11]

The military establishment now consumes approximately fifty per cent of the federal budget, fifteen per cent of the nation's durable goods, ten per cent of the gross national product. Defense installations exist in nearly two out of every three congressional districts, averaging two and a half per each. The defense dollar is universal. During the decade of the fifties, over a quarter of a trillion were spent, involving thirty-eight million purchases.

Back in the 1840s, a Secretary of the Navy advocated as a reason for building metal ships that it would "foster the domestic iron industry." [12] Today, vast components of American industry have not only been fostered but have become utterly dependent on defense contracts. The aircraft manufacturers rely on non-military production for only a margin of their output. The fast growing missile industry has no private market.

Regularly the politicians in Washington inquire anxiously, as they did in recent Joint Economic Committee hearings, about "Progress made by the Department of Defense in Reducing the Impact of Military Procurement on the Economy." One of their particular concerns in trying to make this goliath tread lightly is the plight of "small business," which nowadays is defined to include enterprises of considerable size. But the demands of defense are not so readily adaptable. In 1960, a study found that twenty-five per cent of military procurement dollars went to five corporate giants; fifty per cent was shared by only twenty-one companies; the top one hundred defense contractors and their subsidiaries accounted for nearly three-fourths of all prime contracts over $10,000.[13] Whatever else, big defense seems destined to deal mainly with big business.

Other aspects of military "impact" also raise worrisome

questions for the economy. The transition from the manned aircraft to the missile has created fast changing demands for industrial plant and expertise. Planes were built in huge factories, involving great numbers of skilled and semi-skilled workers on assembly-line production. Missiles, with their electronic components, are assembled by smaller crews of highly skilled technicians in air-conditioned and automated insularity. On Long Island, in Baltimore, and in Southern California, the advent of the missile can be witnessed in stark conditions of unemployment even as defense expenditures continue to rise. This is one reason for the urgent appeals that echo through the Congress on behalf of the B-58, the RS-70, and other species of manned aircraft.

Even starker problems appear to loom ahead. As the conquest of space—for combined reasons of defense and national prestige—takes an increasing bite of money and brainpower, there is evidence that it is leading science and technology ever further into remote realms of achievement. What will be the economic impact? *Science*, a magazine published by the American Association for the Advancement of Science, has declared editorially, "The problems of space are different from the problems of the earthly tax-paying economy. Not more than a small fraction of the cost of the moon program will be recovered through technological fallout." [14] Thus, the ironic complaint of those who question our space program is of too little rather than too much "impact" on the economic life of the nation.

Even the barest sketch of the physical anatomy of the defense-industrial complex can provoke grave concerns. It is big on a scale not even imagined by the organization men only a few years ago. It is far-reaching, affecting men's lives and thoughts to a degree that we perceive only vaguely. One of Eisenhower's specific complaints, uttered at his final Presidential news conference, was what he called "an almost insidious penetration of our own minds that the only thing this country is engaged in is weaponry and missiles." Though he alluded specifically to magazine advertisements on behalf of weapon systems sponsored by their manufacturers, this is only a small part of the far-flung communications focusing public attention on military matters. The annual funds for research and development have grown from $750 million in 1940 to $12 billion two decades later. This sum is purchasing brainpower not merely for government laboratories but for the independent, defense-oriented centers of cerebral activity such as the RAND Corporation. Defense projects are buying time and attention in countless universities; they account for well over half the operating budget of one of the best, the Massachusetts Institute of Technology. According to one gloomy analysis, "By now, there are fourth and fifth generations of scientists who have never worked on anything but weaponry and who view their careers as lifelong. They are permanently dedicated to the fascinating invention and construction of what may appear to be a succession of weapons systems stretching through foreseeable time. In a real sense, these men are institutionalized: captive to their narrow specialities and to the paymaster, the grant and the contract." [15]

Overseas, the Defense Department maintains a communication chain which includes two hundred and five radio and thirty-four television stations. At home, such government-owned facilities are forbidden by law but there are still fairly direct channels for the "penetration" of our minds. "Public Affairs" in the Pentagon commands a budget several times the amount spent for that purpose by the State Department. In the quantitative flow of news releases and speeches, the contest between these two bureaucracies is not even close.

The Pentagon has other advantages in this publicity contest. For one thing, the military drama is more visible than the diplomatic. Planes can be made available to transport the press to distant beachheads along the news front; the correspondent covering the Pentagon soon grows accustomed to these gratuitous services. Resources in men and guns, ships and planes and missiles can be supplied for television and films. The Pentagon's Audio-Visual Division has estimated that it is continually assisting private producers on at least thirty-five major film projects and ten television serials. *The Longest Day*, a dramatic account of the Normandy landing produced by Twentieth Century-Fox, received the Audio-Visual Division's blessing and its generous assistance. But the power to bestow is also the power to withhold. Stanley Kramer was denied permission to film scenes aboard a U. S. submarine for *On the Beach*, the story of the aftermath of an atomic war. "It was neither patriotic nor inspiring," explained the Division's Director to reporter William Manchester. "Its message was that nuclear war is hopeless—and that's absolutely contrary to fact." [16]

Pentagon-produced film footage depicting advances in weaponry goes directly into the nightly network news programs, usually without identifying marks of origin. It can influence even the experts, as demonstrated during the hearings in 1962 of the House Armed Services Committee. The second ranking committee Democrat, Representative Paul Kilday, made the plea for additional funds for the B-52 bomber program: "Of course our hearings here show that there was quite a change in [Air Force] concept, that I don't think we have paid enough attention to. And it was accentuated in my mind by watching a newscast on television the other day with a B-52 flying on the deck, with automatic pilot. . . ." [17] Not infrequently such promotion of weapons begins before their design has left the drafting board.

Cooperation between Pentagon and communicators extends from documentaries prepared for school use to cartoon strips in which certain characters, like *Steve Canyon* and *Terry and the Pirates*, show a consistent partiality for Air Force doctrine. It extends to the field of books. A pub-

lished guide prepared by the Air Force indicates the variety
of aids given the prospective author: "Official help is offered
in planning a book project, developing the subject, arranging access to the Air Force Archives and other sources of information (including personal interviews), locating and
making available research materials, providing pictorial doc-
umentation, advising on content, reviewing for accuracy
and security, and guiding in placement for publication.
When travel is essential to the project, the author is given
authority to fly (space available, via military air) wherever
necessary in the Air Force to do research and gather background color."

This succor does not terminate upon date of publication.
Afterward, the Air Force Guide notes that a favored book
may receive large-scale promotion, including reviews in the
five hundred Air Force Base newspapers, in the Office of
Information Service newsletter distributed world-wide to
all Public Information officers and Air Force Commanders,
and in the official *Retired Personnel Newsletter*, circulation
thirty thousand. There can be spot announcements and
brief reviews on the Air Force radio and television stations
around the world. Selected books may be sent to all base
exchange officers, carried in the listings of the Air Force
mail order book program, sold in base exchanges, considered for the Air Force Association's "Aerospace Book
Club," and purchased for use in Air Force libraries.

Over a five-year period, the Air Force Book Branch has
claimed credit in the spawning of more than four hundred
air and space books. As of recent date, more than one hundred and fifteen volumes were under commercial contract.
One such project, *The Manned Missile, The Story of the
B-70*, was written by Ed Rees, former military correspondent for *Time* Magazine, at the suggestion of the Chief of
the Air Force Book Branch. Rees became an enthusiast for
the aircraft, the object of considerable political controversy in Washington, and subsequently went to work for
its manufacturer.

. . .

In the continuing dialogue on defense, it is often difficult to tell exactly where the official spokesmen leave off and the unofficial ones begin. The Pentagon has considerable overlap in both membership and activities with the service associations which are headquartered in Washington and dedicated to building a bridge between public and private interests in defense. They range in size and purpose, from the Association of the U. S. Army with sixty-three thousand members and a $290,000 annual operating budget, to the Aerospace Industries Association with only seventy-nine members—all large corporations—contributing $1.4 million in dues. A principal occupation for most of them is publication (*Army, Navy—the Magazine of Sea Power, Air Force and Space Digest, Ordnance*) in which the line between official and unofficial becomes blurred. Their articles are highly authoritative statements of a military position, often written by experts within the service. Advertising, providing financial support for these magazines, comes predominantly from defense contractors. Not infrequently, as in *Army*'s promotion of the Nike-Zeus anti-missile system, the message is directed less to the general public than to the President and his Secretary of Defense.

The roster of these associations reads like a *Who's Who* of the military command, active and retired, of defense contractors, and even of members of Congress. They can be quite explicit in their purposes—for example, the Navy League, "the civilian arm of the Navy"; the Air Force Association, "To support the achievement of such air power as is necessary." But they deny that they engage in anything as opprobrious as "influence-peddling." The former President of Aerospace Industries Association, a retired general, testified, "We believe we do not operate according to the classic definition of a lobbyist . . . We don't even dream of buying any influence of any kind." Rather, the argument is offered that the modern age of defense makes necessary these interlocking relationships with the Pentagon. As a former president of the Air Force Association explained, "The day is past when the military requirement for a major weapons system is set up by the military and passed on to industry to build the hardware. Today it is more likely that the military requirement is the result of joint participation of military and industrial personnel. . . ." [18]

Suspicion crops up that this "joint participation" involves more than meets the eye. In 1959 a House Armed Services subcommittee spent considerable time probing what has become a significant sinew in the military-industrial complex—the flow of high military officers, on retirement, into high paying jobs with defense contractors. The hearings revealed that more than fourteen hundred retired officers of the rank of major or higher—including two hundred and sixty-one of general or flag rank—were in the pay of the hundred biggest defense contractors. General Dynamics, the largest of this group, had employed one hundred and eighty-seven.

According to the testimony, none of these retired officers was involved directly in negotiation of defense contracts. But fairly subtle distinctions were made between what was considered proper and improper. Admiral William M. Fechteler, former Chief of Naval Operations, who went to work as consultant for General Electric's Atomic Products Division (then involved in the nuclear plane project) explained the way in which he had arranged appointments in the Pentagon for a visiting GE vice-president: "I took him in to see Mr. Gates, the Secretary of the Navy. I took him in to see Admiral [Arleigh] Burke [Chief of Naval Operations]. He had not met Admiral Burke before. And then I made appointments with him with the Chief of the Bureau of Ships. But I did not accompany him there, because those are matériel bureaus which make contracts. And I studiously avoid even being in the room when anybody talks about a contract." [19]

Although the House subcommittee managed to dig up

abuses in the defense contractor expense accounts (the Martin Company, for example, entertained twenty-six high ranking officers on a weekend party in the Bahamas), it found no evidence that contracts had actually been bought or sold. The most that could be concluded, in the tart comment of Vice Admiral Hyman G. Rickover, was that retired officers frequently leave their jobs to men "who are their dear friends, or . . . whom they have been influential in appointing, and naturally they will be listened to." [20]

The subgovernment of defense involves Congress in more ways than investigating other people's influence on the Pentagon. Congress is a locus of power, intimately involved in the military-industrial complex. Even as with industry, the day is past when the Pentagon's requirement for a weapon system is determined by the experts and simply passed along to Congress. There is "joint participation" which extends into the most meticulous consideration of weapons and contract allocations. As an official for Boeing testified during the latter years of the Eisenhower Administration in defending his company's propaganda campaign on behalf of the Bomarc missile against the Nike-Hercules, "Many of the most important decisions . . . are not made by military technicians. They are made in the Congress of the United States." [21]

Congress is not a single entity in its approach to military matters. Its members have varying degrees of effectiveness in this field. By a recent count, forty of them are reserve officers, including six generals. One hundred and twenty-four members of Congress sit on the committees dealing with defense—the Armed Services and the Defense Appropriations of both Houses, the Senate Aeronautical and Space Sciences, the House Science and Astronautics, and the Joint Committee on Atomic Energy. Even within the committees, of course, members are vastly disparate in interest and influence. One Senator, Richard Russell of Georgia, is Chairman or ranking member on Armed Services, Defense Appropriations, Aeronautical and Space Science, and Atomic Energy. Carl Vinson, also of Georgia, a Representative with nearly five decades' service in Congress, is Chairman of House Armed Services.

Power is clustered in other ways. By geographical grouping, for example, southern Democrats constitute nearly three-fifths of the majority party membership on the Armed Services and Defense Appropriations Committees of the two Houses; Mississippi holds a place on all four. It is possible to discern naval strength in the fact that thirty-eight of the fifty-four members of the Armed Services committees presently come from coastal states.

The role played by the barons in military and other areas will be discussed at greater length in a later chapter. The ordinary congressman, not a member of these committees, displays ambivalence in military matters. Though he has been remarkably passive about many of the major issues of defense policy, he is unabashed about promoting what he regards as his own constituent interests in the defense economy. Senator Jacob Javits of New York complained lustily when statistics revealed that his state was receiving only 9.9 per cent of military procurement while California was getting 23.9 per cent. Representative Ken Hechler of West Virginia rose to announce in the House of Representatives, "I am firmly against the kind of logrolling which would subject our defense program to narrowly sectional or selfish pulling and hauling. But I am getting pretty hot under the collar about the way my state of West Virginia is shortchanged in Army, Navy, and Air Force installations . . . I am going to stand up on my hind legs and roar until West Virginia gets the fair treatment she deserves." [22]

This parochial pressure for the defense dollar has become part of a member's accustomed duties, and he neglects it at his peril. In 1962, when Senator Wayne Morse, Democrat of Oregon, was a candidate for reelection, the Portland *Oregonian*, one of the state's leading newspapers, chided him editorially for his shortcomings in the defense procurement field: "Washington State's *working* senators won a billion dollars in military spending in one year for their people . . . Oregon's *talking* senator has won only 6½ per cent of what Washington received." [23]

The congressman's efforts on behalf of his constituency can go far toward making a military expert of him. A not atypical example is that of Congressman James Wright, a young Texas Democrat, whose district encompasses Fort Worth which in turn encompasses the Convair Division of General Dynamics. Convair, with approximately eighteen thousand employees, has been the city's largest employer. In Wright's view, the company has brought "nothing but good" to his district—not merely jobs, but managers and technicians to raise the educational level, plant and equipment, and, as an accidental byproduct, even a president for the local college. When the Kennedy Administration came to power, Convair was in serious financial trouble. It was facing further losses because of the Defense Department's decision to taper off procurement of the B-58 Convair produced.

Though not a member of any relevant committee, Congressman Wright became a self-appointed advocate for the B-58, making elaborate appeals to both the Executive officialdom and Congress. In private audience he even sought to convince the Air Force Chief of Staff, General Curtis LeMay, of the strategic necessity of the B-58. In Congress he testified before House and Senate committees. Convair officials collaborated by supplying facts and figures and, according to one critical observer, by "using Wright's office as their Capitol Hill headquarters." The numerous subcontractors rallied to join the campaign. Due at least in part to these efforts, the House added an extra $448,840,000 for procurement of "long range bombers," but President Kennedy flatly refused to spend it for the B-58. Convair, later, was mollified by a defense contract for the TFX fighter plane, which, in turn, roused the

D

wrath and the rearguard opposition of those members of Congress who have a rival bidder, the Boeing Company, as a constituent.

This self-afflicted lobbying in Congress can have other stimuli. Congressman Melvin Price, Democrat of Illinois, the ranking House Member on the Joint Atomic Energy Committee, was inspired by his specialty to become Washington's leading advocate of the nuclear plane. During the eleven-year period in which this ill-fated project was under development, Price sponsored more than forty sets of hearings for the purpose of prodding it along. When funds for the plane were reduced during Eisenhower's later years in office, Price made a trip to the Soviet Union and returned warning publicly that the Soviets were on the verge of another Sputnik-type triumph by pioneering nuclear flight. In an effort to bypass Defense Department opposition, Price's subcommittee sought unsuccessfully to get the project transferred to the Atomic Energy Commission which, it was felt, would be more amenable. Finally, after more than one billion dollars had been invested, President Kennedy ordered the project terminated. In the terse words of one review, "An airplane had never been flown on nuclear power nor had a prototype airplane been built." [24]

A senior member of the House subcommittee on Defense Appropriations testified, "I am convinced defense is only one of the factors that enter into our determinations for defense spending. The others are pump priming, spreading the immediate benefits of defense spending, taking care of all services, giving all defense contractors a fair share, spreading the military bases to include all sections, etc. . . . There is no state in the union and hardly a district in a state which doesn't have defense spending, contracting, or a defense establishment. We see the effect in public and Congressional insistence on continuing contracts, or operating military bases though the need is expired." [25] These eco-political involvements are nowhere more clearly visible than in the status of the National Guard and Reserve programs. Rooted in the deep aversion felt by the drafters of the Constitution toward standing armies and, more recently, in the political mythology of states' rights, they now constitute a multi-billion dollar annual commitment for which the federal government must pick up 97 per cent of the bill. Maintaining separate identities for the fifty state programs has become a colossal waste of money and battle readiness in the age of the missile and the airborne strike force. Yet these citizen soldiers are so solidly entrenched politically that no one in Washington dares challenge them frontally. Congress has fixed a mandatory "floor" for the National Guard which President Eisenhower, after a three year effort, despaired of ever changing.

Similar forces, if not so well embedded, are constantly grouping and regrouping around the weapon systems. Each one acquires a political anatomy—often before it has acquired a physical one. For years, controversy has raged around the Army's Nike-Zeus anti-missile system with Congress eagerly appropriating funds to push it into production while the President has held back, arguing, in Eisenhower's words, that "funds should not be committed to production until development tests are satisfactorily completed." The political power drive of the Nike-Zeus was evident when, on February 1, 1961, *Army* devoted an entire issue to the weapon system. Four of the seven articles praising it and urging a speed-up of the program were written by army commanders on active duty. Full page advertisements by Western Electric Company, prime contractor for the missile, and eight of its subcontractors appeared. A map conveniently detailed how much of the $410 million initial contract was being spent in each of thirty-seven states. Commencing the very next day after publication, a procession of Senators and Representatives began to reiterate *Army*'s appeal. *Congressional Quarterly*, which keeps non-partisan watch on Capitol Hill, found it appropriate to correlate the enthusiasms of various congressmen with the expenditure chart.

Like his predecessor, Kennedy balked at giving the go-ahead for a weapon that could eventually cost between five billion and twenty billion dollars. His Secretary of Defense, Robert S. McNamara, postponed a decision by shifting planning to the more advanced Nike-X. But even if it should prove 100 per cent effective in intercepting enemy missiles, McNamara has voiced grave doubts about its value unless Congress is willing to support a Civil Defense program capable of protecting the populace from its radioactive fall-out.

It would be wrong to regard the subgovernment of defense as a secret conspiracy of malefactors. The greater problem arises because of its wide array of competing factions—because of the ever shifting coalitions of politicians, pressure groups, and military professionals striving to assert dominancy for a service, a doctrine, or a weapon. The fact that defense has become a gargantuan governmental activity does not automatically bring increased risk of a military cabal capable of seizing power. On the contrary, the job of running anything as complicated as the modern defense establishment makes such seizure probably less likely than in the past. The missile *cum* nuclear warhead does not facilitate the staging of a *coup d'Etat;* nor is there convincing evidence that the man in uniform is less disposed to civilian government than is the man in mufti. The wise and the fanatical exist in both ranks.

There is little use in taking a doom-and-gloom view of "the warfare state" since the need for large-scale military preparedness during the foreseeable future is likely to continue. Too much of the literature on the subject—including Eisenhower's vague farewell admonition—begs the question of how to maintain military power while dealing with the political power that accompanies it.

More than other subgovernments, the subgovernment of defense has created a situation altering the traditional power arrangements of our Constitutional system. It has, in fact, led to a reversal of the relationship in military matters envisaged by the founding fathers. In their zeal to guard against martial aggrandizement by the President who was to be Commander-in-Chief, they securely lodged with Congress the power "to raise and support armies." They stipulated that no money for this purpose could be appropriated for a term longer than two years as further check on an overly ambitious President.

Since the end of the Second World War, however, the check has worked mostly in the opposite direction. The President, abetted by his Secretary of Defense and his budget officers, has exerted the more consistent constraints on the military budget. In Congress, urgent pressures to break through these constraints have been regularly generated. The facts and figures vary from one administration to the next, but the pattern remains familiar. Confounded by the rising cost of defense, the President has shown greater discipline in cancelling obsolete weapons and holding back on new ones until their need can be proven. Though relentless in pruning the non-military budget, Congress displays greater willingness both to perpetuate the old and to innovate the untried.

This constitutional turnabout is not without logic. Still, it can be questioned whether the new system of checks and balances has worked as well as it ought. During the Eisenhower Administration, even with a famous general serving as Commander-in-Chief, there were discouraging signs that the subgovernment of defense had gotten out of control. Despite the incessant efforts to economize in the Pentagon, there were repeated instances of wasteful expenditure, of proliferation of weapon systems without regard for military necessity, of failure to cut losses on projects such as the nuclear plane even after they had demonstrably failed. Anxiety for dollar savings led to a military doc-

trine based, in the immortal phrase of one Presidential
assistant, on "a bigger bang for a buck." This meant the
unbalancing of our nation's military strength by starving
the conventional warfare forces even while the forces for
total war were developing a capacity for "overkill."

It was not a very encouraging picture of military management when Secretary of Defense Neil McElroy, upon
being queried about two duplicatory missiles, expressed
the fervent wish that Congress would "hold our feet to the
fire" in order to force a choice. Gradually the conviction
developed in Washington that no mere Defense Secretary
was capable of ruling over the defense establishment.

There was widespread jubilation when Defense Secretary McNamara, on taking over in 1961, showed signs of
having both the mental and intestinal fortitude for the
job. During his first years in office, McNamara proved to be
a man of unusual energy and decisiveness. Combining aca-
demic background as a teacher at the Harvard Business
School and executive experience as President of the Ford
Motor Company, he came closer than any of his predecessors to demonstrating mastery over the Department.
Though he rejected proposals for reorganization requiring
congressional action, he moved deliberately to accomplish
much the same objective by fiat. The three services were
allowed to remain formally intact, but they have been re-
grouped and reoriented not simply for fighting purposes
but to serve in combined forces for intelligence, research,
procurement, and various other functions. Secretary Mc-
Namara has sought to make the defense establishment better serve national strategy objectives, building forces adaptable to a wide variety of situations rather than simply to
all-out nuclear war. His goal, as he has emphasized, has been
to provide "options" for the President in responding to military challenge. He has startled a good many politicians by
his bravado in cancelling weapons and installations no
longer deemed necessary. He has displayed a ruthless de-

termination to compare costs of competing weapon systems and to get rid of the waste and duplication of allowing each service to go its isolated way.

If this brand of leadership in the Pentagon can prevail, a good many qualms provoked by the military-industrial complex will be dispelled. Yet it is well to inject a cautionary note. So far the Secretary has been operating under conditions of an expanding defense economy. Despite curtailments, the overall impact of McNamara's program has been to provide a bigger pie for the slicing. A more serious test of his—and the President's—capacity to withstand the pressures of the military-industrial complex will arise when defense spending levels off or even declines.

There have been forewarnings that this testing will not be gentle. Congress has twice tried to override McNamara's veto on the RS-70 (the supersonic bomber redesignated a reconnaissance-search craft) by appropriating funds which the President was then obliged to refuse to spend. Even more ominous, McNamara stirred bitter antagonism on Capitol Hill by his decision on the TFX, an experimental tactical fighter plane.

The TFX controversy deserves special consideration. Both the Air Force and the Navy were eager for an advanced fighter plane, and the Secretary had assented, while stipulating that they must come up with a single model acceptable to both services. From McNamara's point of view, the insistence on "commonality" meant a potential savings of one billion dollars as well as a reversal of the trend toward endless proliferation of weaponry. But this also meant a great deal of agonizing within the two services and among the nine defense contractors anxious to be selected to design and produce the prototype models.

Competition for the TFX contract—worth an estimated $7 billion in eventual production—stimulated a desperate struggle in an industry feeling the pinch of cutbacks in manned aircraft. That there were political factors not far beneath the surface in this struggle was evident in a Douglas Aviation executive's comment to a reporter: "The only place where politics is important is if two contractors are neck and neck—then subcontracting has political advantages and can swing to the best political merchandiser." [26] According to this executive's assessment, Douglas has tried to locate a substantial portion of its subcontracts in Missouri and Oklahoma, whose Senators Stuart Symington and the late Robert Kerr have been powerful participants in military matters. Following its usual strategy, the Boeing Company had chosen dependable subcontractors from politically important distressed areas. General Dynamics, combining forces with Grumman Aviation in the competition, had kept politically flexible by having two or three alternatives for each subcontracting category and postponing final selection.[27]

Dark allegations that politics had played an even more direct role began to circulate when it turned out that McNamara and his top deputies had rejected the verdict of the TFX Sources Selection Board awarding the contract to Boeing and had assigned it to the General Dynamics-Grumman team. Chief beneficiary was General Dynamics' Convair Division located in Texas, home of then Vice-President Lyndon Johnson and the Secretary of the Navy Fred Korth. A Senate Committee began a probe of the contract which soon turned into an angry effort to overturn McNamara's decision. A key member on the committee was Democratic Senator Henry Jackson of Washington, the headquarter state of Boeing.

Though no evidence of political favoritism was turned up, the TFX investigation became a stubborn test of will between the Pentagon heads and the Senate Committee. In overriding the experts, McNamara argued that the Boeing bid did not meet his standards either in its cost estimates or its design of a common model for the two services. The Senate Committee, digging up alleged discrepancies in McNamara's data, sought to prove that Boeing's bid was superior and less costly than that of General Dynamics. One newspaper columnist, direly predicting McNamara's resignation if he were defeated on the issue, argued that, ". . . the rights and wrongs of the TFX affair are very much less important, in any case, than the rights and wrongs of the attack on McNamara, for which the TFX affair is merely the vehicle. If this vehicle had not served, another one would have been made to serve. That was inevitable in view of the nature of McNamara's effort." [28]

Whatever the particular rights and wrongs, this controversy points to the fantastic difficulties that confront even the best of Secretaries in trying to govern the defense establishment. How can he possibly master the myriad technical details to make judgments which challenge those of the experts and the interest groups? How can he afford to spend the time and energy necessary to fight rearguard actions which threaten to drag on indefinitely at the discretion of a few members of Congress?

The TFX affair raises even more fundamental questions about the subgovernment of defense. McNamara's reasoned effort to resist the wasteful proliferation of weapons resulted in a single contract of leviathan proportions which was predestined to have shattering impact on the contractors. The Defense Department's Office of Economic Adjustment, after examining the effect of military procurement on sixty cities across the nation, concluded that the community consequences for either Boeing or General Dynamics in losing the TFX job would be equally severe.[29] Can the defense dollar, vitally affecting the employment and well being of millions, be allocated without regard for the fate of companies and communities? As the weapons systems continue to get bigger in size and more selective in number, feast or famine conditions in various parts of the country inevitably result unless there is economic as well as strategic planning. Yet this could lead to new political troubles.

·   ·   ·

Future dilemmas are even more serious than the present ones. With man's knowledge, by estimate, doubling every ten years, what priorities are to be placed on the military effort? Projection of the potential advances in the art of war spirals military costs right off the top of the budget chart. Should the Pentagon keep pace with this fantastic race of science? In the long run, there are other cost factors to be accounted in measuring the nation's strength—the education of its children, the conservation of its resources —that are more important than McNamara's cost accounting for comparative weapon systems.

To pose an alternative, it is always conceivable that the protracted negotiations with the Soviets will lead to more meaningful steps toward arms control than a test-ban treaty. What will be the political consequences for the military-industrial complex? Powerful alliances, motivated by a variety of doctrinal and economic interests, will find reason for resisting such a development and, judging from past experience, one can predict ugly in-fighting. When Secretary of State Rusk sought merely to discuss with Secretary of Defense McNamara how to prevent a war in Europe from escalating into nuclear holocaust, Air Force zealots leaked a distorted version of Rusk's memorandum to the press in the effort to sabotage any shift in strategy.

The subgovernment of defense presents in macrocosm— as the subgovernment of sugar presents in microcosm —a challenge to the traditional institutions of American government. The question is raised whether these institutions—the Presidency, Congress, the party system, the press, and pressure groups—are adaptable to new problems in the organization of power. Can they continue to provide proper checks and balances and still exercise effective power? Or are these institutions in danger of becoming as obsolete as the military weaponry of a few years ago?

II

The Presidency

3

THE SHAPING ROLE OF
THE SELECTION PROCESS

"An eminent American is reported to have said to friends who wished to put him forward, 'Gentlemen, let there be no mistake. I should make a good President, but a very bad candidate.'"

JAMES BRYCE, 1888 [1]

"It is not only the unit vote for the Presidency we are talking about, but a whole solar system of governmental power. If it is proposed to change the balance of power of one of the elements of the solar system, it is necessary to consider the others."

SENATOR JOHN F. KENNEDY
in 1956, opposing electoral college reform [2]

In Tibet, upon the death of the Dalai Lama who is both spiritual and temporal leader, the priests commence a search for the infant boy to whom his soul has migrated. This weird and wonderful quest may go on for years. To the Westerner, it is a highly mystical way of selecting a new head of government. Yet one might wonder whether a truly impartial observer would judge the American method of choosing a President any less mystical.

The subject is not irrelevant to a study of power in Washington. For the way our leader is chosen reveals a great deal about the forces that shape and condition his leadership. Beyond the manner of the man, the basic strengths and weaknesses of the office are affected by the selection process.

That process has changed radically from what the founding fathers thought it would be. In the Constitution, they provided that the President is to be chosen by electors which each state shall appoint "in such manner as the legislature thereof may direct. . . ." Alexander Hamilton explained that such a system was desirable in order that "the immediate election should be made by men most capable of analizing the qualities adapted to the station, and acting under circumstances favourable to deliberation and to a judicious combination of all the reasons and inducements, which were proper to govern their choice. A small number of persons, selected by their fellow citizens from the general mass, will be most likely to possess the information and discernment requisite to so complicated an investigation."

"It was also peculiarly desirable," Hamilton added, "to afford as little opportunity as possible to tumult and disorder . . . the precautions which have been so happily concerted in the system under consideration, promise an effectual security against this mischief." [3]

Consider, by way of contrast, our latest experience in picking a President. For no less than two years, the contest was actively pursued. Its initial stages consisted of trial by public opinion poll—a unique custom requiring the American people to pass judgment on their political leaders before those leaders have formally offered themselves. Dr. Gallup and his fellow pollsters served as arbiters of a ritual that eliminated a good many men with "qualities adapted to the station." Others survived this test by means of skillfully conducted publicity campaigns which kept them in the public eye.

Then came the period of the party primaries during

which a few states, usually remote and rural, undertook a further winnowing of the candidates. Commencing in the dead of winter many months before the election, the politicians and the press journeyed to the farthest out-reaches of Wisconsin and West Virginia where costly bat-tles were waged to win a comparatively small number of voters. In the final outcome, the primary verdict proved to be crucial.

Next, there was the traditional celebration of the party nominating conventions—nowhere mentioned in the Con-stitution. Amid the greatest possible "tumult and disorder," thousands of delegates gathered in cavernous halls and made manifest each party's choice.

But this was only the beginning. The formal contest had only started and, for the nominees, the modern miracles of communication in no way lessened its ordeal. On the con-trary, their itineraries took them in great jet-assisted leaps across the nation. The objective was to maximize publicity impact by staying in the same place for the barest possible time. Yet they did not dispense with the old-fashioned inter-course of the handshake. Both nominees showed a grim determination to set marathon records in the solemn ritual which Henry Adams once described as "the dance of de-mocracy." Mr. Kennedy, despite an ailing back, proved himself capable of standing hours at a time, unflinching, while passers-by exercised the inalienable right to press flesh with a prospective President. Mr. Nixon issued stern instructions to accompanying guards not to protect him too zealously from the crowd's crush. Neither was willing to challenge custom by refusing—as Senator Taft once re-fused during the New Hampshire primary campaign in 1952—to sign autographs. Taft had reasoned, with excellent logic, that it took twice as long to sign his name as to shake a hand. He lost the primary.

In the 1960 contest, one more hurdle was added to the obstacle course over which we run our prospective Presi-dents. Television turned the nation into a vast agora of democracy where the citizenry could examine the candidates before casting their ballots. The "Great Debates" of that year brought the two contenders face-to-face in a discussion of the issues that was meant to be extemporaneous and unrehearsed. An estimated seventy thousand Americans witnessed one or more of the famous Lincoln-Douglas debates a century ago; over one thousand times as many viewed Kennedy-Nixon.

Only at the end of the process did the electoral college play its constitutional role. Though not the deliberative assembly envisaged by Hamilton, it imposed a higher mathematics on the contest having a powerful effect on both Presidential politics and politicians.

The way we select our Presidents inspires the awe if not the admiration of politicians the world over. The late British Labour Party leader, Hugh Gaitskill, voiced a widespread concern when he spoke to a meeting of American newspaper editors about the candidates: "I find it astonishing how you survive physically. To me, frankly, three weeks of electioneering in England is sufficiently tiring. But you have nine months, each and every day . . . I suppose what it amounts to is that in your system you go through such an ordeal beforehand that if at the end of it you ever do come out as President it must seem a completely restful holiday." [4]

Substantial numbers of people share Gaitskill's concern about our Presidential election process. Their suggested remedies are varied and contradictory. Some propose getting rid of the primaries; some would extend them to all the states. Some would abolish the party nominating convention; some agree with Lord Bryce that it is "so exactly conformable to the political habits of the [American] people that it is not likely soon to disappear." Some seek reform of the electoral college system; some would eliminate it as a Constitutional anachronism.

As a reporter who has watched the campaigns at each

successive stage, I find it difficult to approach these institutions arbitrarily. On the matter of party primaries, I sympathize with neither the abolitionists nor those who would extend them nationwide. For the public, they serve as a useful measure—but only one measure—of a candidate's virtues. For the candidate, they permit a certain freedom to chart his moves, just as in a well calculated game of chess. He ought not to be forced—as he is statutorily forced in the Oregon primary—to meet his opponent on a terrain not of his own choosing. Such selective competition offers an opportunity for an underdog candidate to challenge the cozy arrangements of the professional politicians. But to extend the primary to all states would be to destroy the role of the professionals and strengthen the already excessive influence of the pollsters and the publicity-mongers. A nationwide primary would give an added advantage to those in public life who disport themselves with flair if not with finesse. It would eliminate all reason for holding the political conventions. Once the public had spoken, how could the politicians say nay?

I do not believe the conventions ought to be eliminated. As long as organizations—call them bosses, machines, and pressure groups, if you like—play a substantial role in the nation's politics, they need to get together in search of a common candidate and, hopefully, a common purpose. As long as the American melting pot continues to hold unassimilated chunks—religious, regional, and ethnic—the party convention provides one place where they can be stirred around and brought to a slow boil. Working at its best, the convention serves to strengthen the party's ties far better than any scheme allowing the primaries to take its place. It provides a semblance of a national party to compete with the more parochial party in Congress.

But the convention does have a major public relations problem. Today's politicians parley before television when once they would have retreated to smoke-filled rooms. This reached *reductio ad absurdum* at the 1960 Democratic con-

E

vention, when a delegate rushed before a camera on the convention floor and, while millions eavesdropped, pleaded with the party's Presidential nominee to reconsider his Vice-Presidential choice. It is disconcerting for the delegates to go about their business with a knowledge that the whole nation is looking over their shoulders. But reform of the convention must be sparing. Many of the ill-considered suggestions for speeding up the schedule and giving more "viewer appeal" would quickly destroy the old-fashioned purpose of arriving at a consensus. As it is now, the delegate often wonders if he would not have done better to stay home with his TV set.

Has television radically altered the entire election process? The opening series of Great Debates in 1960 was only partially indicative of their potential; they were launched without a great deal of public forethought. First suggested in 1952 by Blair Moody, a Michigan newspaperman then serving out the unexpired term of the late Senator Arthur Vandenberg, the idea of the debates, according to the testimony of one network head, "quickly seized the imagination of the broadcasters." But it failed to interest the candidates in 1952 or 1956. Stevenson reportedly felt that to challenge Eisenhower would be regarded as a gimmick. A more basic obstacle lay in Section 315 of the Federal Communications Act requiring equal broadcast time for all candidates, even those of the fringe groups.

In August, 1960, Congress temporarily suspended Section 315 on a trial basis. The legislative deliberations, however, showed little concern for how the election contest was to be programmed. Certain members, including Senator Mike Monroney, Democrat from Oklahoma, argued that Congress ought to commandeer prime viewing hours from the networks for whatever use the candidates might wish to make of them. Network officials resisted, asserting that the First Amendment was a guarantee of their right to determine matters of format and scheduling. But they promised generous cooperation with the candidates. One broadcaster felt that an hour weekly could be ventured without risk of "overexposure, oversaturation, and redundancy."

Among the witnesses at the congressional hearings, Adlai Stevenson, who had by then acquired enthusiasm for the idea, attempted to sketch out a more detailed plan for the debates. He favored a ninety-minute program each week in which the candidates could deal, one at a time, with such issues as "disengagement or containment, farm policy, disarmament. . . ."

With Congress failing to be more specific, the new venture was caught up in the strategies of networks and candidates. On the night of Nixon's nomination, NBC Board Chairman Robert W. Sarnoff got the jump on his competitors by offering eight hours of prime evening time for what he dubbed "The Great Debate." Kennedy, the challenger and the lesser known of the two candidates, promptly accepted. Four days later, Nixon wired his agreement, stipulating only a "full and free exchange of views without prepared texts or notes and without interruption."

During preliminary conferences there was a great deal of bargaining about the number of debates, the times and places, and the cutoff date. Whether to hold a final one after the pre-arranged four remained in bitter dispute almost until election day. But on one important matter there was agreement: both candidates desired to have a panel of reporters serve as interrogators. A Nixon aide explained to this reporter shortly before the first program that the panel would serve to increase viewer interest. He feared that the candidates would be "too polite" if they questioned each other. A Kennedy aide remarked that since the role of prosecuting attorney is essentially unsympathetic, it was better to turn this thankless task over to others.

The result was to achieve neither the relentless interrogation of the "Meet the Press" variety nor the clash that can occur during a genuine confrontation. Not once did either candidate ask a question directly of the other. The bulk of the time was carved into two-and-a-half-minute responses to questions and ninety-second rejoinders. As one of those chosen by lot to participate, I found my role somewhat baffling. Beforehand, I had entertained Walter Mitty dreams of posing a question so trenchant that neither candidate could attempt circumlocution. Both the candidates had mastered the program's special form of gamesmanship, and no matter how broad—or how specific—the question, each extracted his last second of allotted time. The panel's purpose was hardly more than to designate categories—animal, vegetable, or mineral—on which the two men might or might not discourse.

The networks, while sparing neither expense nor effort in staging this venture, recognized the potential hazards involved. High network officials personally supervised the painting and furnishing of stage sets, ordered and reordered changes in backdrop color, drapery texture, and the like. The third debate—carried on split-screen with one candidate in New York, the other in Los Angeles—presented a particular challenge, as evidenced by a report of its production problems:

Set construction itself was not complicated, but an incredible amount of effort was expended to be sure that each set, studio, light unit, camera, microphone, and transmission element of the broadcast was absolutely identical. ABC bought the cloth for the background from the same mill run in an amount large enough to cover both sets. All of the paint used for both sets was mixed in New York. After the New York set had been painted, Fred Schumann, Director of Production Services for ABC, carried the same can of paint, by plane, to Los Angeles and delivered it personally to the west coast set painters. At Los Angeles, the 80 by 90-foot studio was equipped with lighting instruments manufactured by the Mole Richardson company. The east coast studio had Kliegl Brothers instruments. Adhering to the quality dictum, the lighting director ordered the Mole Richardson instruments removed and Kliegl instruments, identical with those used in New York, installed in their place. An even more sophisticated refinement concerned the lamps used in the lighting instruments. The west coast bulbs, regardless of their wattage, were rated at a slightly higher Kelvin temperature than the bulbs used on the east coast. The lighting director ordered the bulbs in the east coast instruments removed and replaced with the higher Kelvin temperature units.[5]

Such fastidiousness was not unwarranted. After the first debate, a public storm threatened to arise over the fact that candidate Nixon looked, as one newspaper account reported, "tired, drawn and appeared to be ill." A Republican leader claimed Nixon's make-up must have been applied by someone with Democratic leanings. The *Chicago Daily News*, in whose city the telecast occurred, ran the headline, "Was Nixon Sabotaged by TV Make-up Artist?" Fortunately, the Columbia Broadcasting System, producer of this debate, was in the clear since Nixon had turned down the network's offer of a make-up expert. One of his aides had applied Max Factor's "Lazy Shave," a pancake cosmetic, over the candidate's heavy beard.

Television presented new concerns for the candidates and their handlers. Before the first debate, Nixon aides took pains to get studio technicians to avoid "modeling" when lighting the Vice-President, insisting that two 500-watt spotlights be added to shine up into his eyes. Nixon TV specialist Ted Rogers explained this particular torture for his boss: "He's critical on television; there's an enormous contrast between his very pale, white translucent skin, and his jet black hair."

Kennedy, though not requiring make-up, still showed keen consciousness of the requirements of television politics. A production report on the second debate has recorded:

> About 6:30 P.M. Friday, Kennedy arrived in the studio for the preshow check, preceding Nixon by previous agreement . . . shortly after Kennedy reached his place

on the set, he walked over to the Nixon podium, then back again, and asked why there were more lights on his part of the set than on Nixon's. Robert Kennedy, standing in Nixon's place, complained contrarily that there were more lights on Nixon's set. Both made several trips to the control room to view each other in the Kennedy portion of the set, carrying on a running discussion of the light with their advisers, demanding lighting changes replete with such comments as "did 'they' arrange our lights too?" [6]

One fact was quite clear: as they approached this brave new frontier of television, the two candidates were far more concerned about their images than their arguments. Both proved remarkably adaptable to the new art form. They were marvels at extemporization, wasting none of their precious time by reflective pauses, never having to grasp for the elusive word, always able in the peculiar alternation of reply and rebuttal to switch topics without a hitch. Each showed a willingness to discuss or rebut anything within the allotted time. The flowering of television in politics had coincided with the flowering of politicians peculiarly adapted to its special demands.

Thirty-one separate public opinion samplings, it has been reckoned, were taken of the Kennedy-Nixon debates. Beyond that, Sam Lubell conducted his own brand of selective interviewing.[7] The results are edifying: altogether, some 70 million of the 107 million adult Americans—and perhaps another 10 to 15 million younger ones—watched or listened to the first debate. At least fifty-five per cent of the total adult population saw all the debates and over eighty per cent saw or heard at least one. The average viewer tuned in for approximately two and one-half hours. In both the United States and Canada, more than two-thirds of those interviewed who had viewed the debates responded "positively" to the idea of holding them.

But what was learned from the debates is less clear. Lubell found that among those he interviewed, "The overwhelming majority responded in terms of how the candidates looked and handled themselves rather than in terms of the issues that were argued about. Many voters explained that they tried to make sense of the arguments of the candidates, 'but the more we listened the more confused we got.' " Data gathered by Elmo Roper indicated that the style of presentation was more important than the content or even the personality of the debaters. A survey held in Canada, where the viewers were not directly involved in making a choice, concluded that the mass audience was left with "some very distinct impressions of the capabilities of the two men as debaters and as persons, but . . . with very little idea of what the debate was all about." [8]

Who won the debates? The surveys were remarkably consistent in awarding the first to Kennedy, calling the second a tie, awarding the third to Nixon, and finding the fourth, again, very close. (A survey among New Yorkers gave Kennedy both the second and third by a large margin.) But in judging the debates as a whole, Kennedy came out well ahead—far more than his slim plurality on election day. One elaborate sampling technique for rating the candidates as "An Ideal President" found that Kennedy moved ahead most sharply after the first debate on the quality of "experience"; Nixon's ratings were inconclusive. "Both men moved away from Ideal by the end of the debates but Nixon moved away more decisively than did Kennedy." The conclusion was that "Kennedy did not necessarily win the debates, but Nixon lost them. . . ."

Did the debates affect the outcome of the election? A disconcerting fact is that, according to one survey, a larger percentage of viewers than non-viewers remained unchanged in their commitment. Perhaps this can be explained by the fact that non-viewers were less interested in the contest. But whether the final verdict was determined by the debates, the surveys' only report is that "Apart from strengthening Democratic convictions about their candidate, it is very difficult to say conclusively." [9]

No one with experience in politics should be unduly surprised to discover that voters form their judgments on factors other than the pure logic of the candidate's argument.
Still, a careful rereading of the transcripts of the debates is a
depressing experience. The dialogue was largely a paste-up
job containing bits and snippets from campaign rhetoric
already used many times. As the series wore on, the protagonists were like two weary wrestlers who kept trying to
get the same holds. What stands out is how limited the vocabulary of the debates really was and how vaguely specified were the candidates' notions of what they wanted to
do. Kennedy, we were told over and over, wanted to get
America moving again. Nixon argued that it was moving
but "We can't stand pat."

Not even the trained political observer could keep up
with the rapid cross fire of fact and counterfact, of grazing
references to Rockefeller Reports, Lehman Amendments,
prestige polls, G.N.P., and other miscellany. Some of these
facts uttered so glibly are startling in post mortem (for
example, Nixon on Indo-China: "Now, as a result of our
taking the strong stand that we did, the civil war there was
ended and today, at least in the south of Indo-China, the
communists have moved out and we do have a strong free
bastion there."). The controversy over defending the off-
shore islands of Quemoy and Matsu which extended for
three debates was both ludicrous and dangerous. Kennedy
began by speculating vaguely that the islands should not be
included in the U. S. defense perimeter, then proceeded to
back vigorously away from this position. In riposte, Nixon
enunciated a far more sweeping commitment to the islands' defense than Eisenhower's, then also backed away.
The public was not edified nor was U. S. foreign policy
strengthened.

In light of subsequent revelations, the debate over Cuba
was even more ludicrous. Kennedy suggested helping exiles
and groups within Cuba who were in opposition to Fidel
Castro—a program even then actively being promoted by

the Central Intelligence Agency. Nixon, responding indignantly, called Kennedy's recommendations "the most dangerously irresponsible recommendations that he's made during the course of the campaign . . . if we were to follow that recommendation . . . we would lose all of our friends in Latin America, we would probably be condemned in the United Nations, and we would not accomplish our objective . . . It would be an open invitation for Mr. Khrushchev to come in, to come into Latin America and to engage us in what would be a civil war, and possibly even worse than that. . . ."

In his autobiographical *Six Crises* published in 1962, Nixon relates that, having been a strong advocate within the Eisenhower Administration for the covert operation against Castro, he found himself in a personal dilemma when Kennedy suggested it as a new proposal. But his explanation for his handling of the dilemma was, to say the least, peculiar. He states in *Six Crises:* "There was only one thing I could do. The covert operation had to be protected at all costs. I must not even suggest by implication that the United States was rendering aid to rebel forces in and out of Cuba. In fact, I must go to the other extreme: I must attack the Kennedy proposal to provide such aid as wrong and irresponsible because it would violate our treaty commitments." [10]

How Nixon as President would have dealt with the CIA operation he so vigorously denounced remains to be speculated. For President Kennedy, this loose discussion of a critical foreign policy issue undoubtedly was a cause of embarrassment. One can wonder whether his campaign commitments handicapped the ruthless appraisal of CIA-invasion plans that a new President should have been prepared to make. Evidently the President, though feeling grave doubts about the Bay of Pigs venture, felt unable to order its abandonment.

Candidates have said foolish things long before the birth of television. But a noteworthy achievement during

and after the Second World War was the self-restraint,
consciously accepted by Presidential candidates, in critical
areas of foreign policy. Even Eisenhower's "I will go to
Korea" was a campaign pledge of implicit rather than
explicit rashness. The dialogue of the Great Debates
showed a dangerous tendency to depart from such restraint.
Exhilarated by the size of the audience, compelled to be
both brief and lively, shrewdly aware that the real verdict
was being based not on what they said but how they said
it, the candidates were egged into arguments that neither
enlightened the public nor elevated themselves.

Perhaps a saving grace is that it could have been worse.
A great many politicians, ordinarily wise and skillful, would
have committed more grievous excesses before such severe
challenge. The capacity to utter well-chosen words on abbreviated time schedules before the glare of the floodlights
is not granted to all men; historians have speculated about
how well Lincoln or Jefferson might have done.

I have dwelt overlong on the portent of television debate because it is the newest hurdle in the race for the
Presidency. But it is time to come to the final hurdle, the
only one in fact set forth in the Constitution—the electoral college. When the founding fathers turned to the
problem of how to choose the President, they showed curious indecision. Three times they considered and then rejected the notion of allowing the two Houses of Congress
to make the choice. Also rejected was the suggestion of reliance on a direct popular vote. "It is as unnatural to refer
the choice of a proper character for Chief Magistrate to the
people as it would be to refer a trial of colors to a blind
man," argued George Mason of Virginia. In the end, the
Constitution drafters agreed on the electors who would be
chosen for "their wisdom and character," but failed to add
a single word defining their discretionary powers. Even
the question of distinguishing between Presidential and
Vice-Presidential choices was overlooked and had to be

rectified by the Twelfth Amendment after the embarrassing tie vote between Thomas Jefferson and Aaron Burr in 1800.

Independent electors or automatic agents for the popular majority in each state? Since the rise of the political parties, tradition has ruled in favor of the latter role. But it is only tradition. In 1912, a number of electors pledged to Theodore Roosevelt announced that they would switch to President William Howard Taft if it developed that their votes were pivotal. In 1948, all eleven Alabama electors who had been nominated in the Democratic primary made known in advance that they were going to vote for the Dixiecrat nominee, and one Tennessee elector switched to him after the election.

The case for the independent elector has been argued for the most part by the strategists of southern reaction. By preventing either of the major party candidates from getting an electoral majority they hope to throw the election into the House of Representatives where, according to Constitutional edict, the President would be chosen on the highly unrepresentative basis of one vote per state. In 1960, after a great effort to foster an independent elector movement, fifteen of them cast their votes for Senator Byrd.

Other critics of the electoral college claim that it is unrepresentative to allot a state's entire electoral vote to a nominee who wins only a bare plurality of the popular vote. By capturing a few key states, a candidate can win with fewer popular votes than his opponent. John Quincy Adams, Rutherford B. Hayes, and Benjamin Harrison won the Presidency while losing the popular election. Woodrow Wilson, Harry Truman, and John F. Kennedy received more votes than their chief opponents, yet won by less than fifty per cent of the total.

The debate over electoral reform in Congress makes it abundantly clear that members are concerned not so much with violating the will of the people as with the fact that the President's mandate differs from their own. Many are anxious to rearrange the system so that the political pressures causing him concern are identical with those affecting them. The object of electoral reform is to redefine how the man who is elected will behave as President— mainly, of course, how he will behave toward Congress.

Examine the situation that confronted the Democratic and Republican nominees last time. Seven states—New York, California, Pennsylvania, Illinois, Ohio, Texas, and Michigan—controlled 205 of the 266 electoral votes necessary to win. Realistic campaign strategy meant that getting a margin of only one popular vote to make a plurality in each of these seven became an all-absorbing goal. The nominees had been chosen primarily for their prospective appeal in these key states. Their speeches, personal appearances, and general campaign positions were influenced of necessity by this strategy.

This has led to a reversal of Constitutional intent. The electoral college was deliberately weighted in favor of the small states. But in practice the system has been far over-weighted by the pivotal power of the big two-party states. New York's forty-five electoral votes constitute a swing of ninety to the Democratic or Republican nominee—often on the basis of a few thousand popular votes. The fierce competition for the key states tends to focus attention on certain groups and interests within those states which may hold the margin. It helps account for the fact that nominees of both parties become suddenly solicitous of minority group issues—civil rights, immigration, and an assortment of ethnically inspired stands on foreign policy.

Among the approaches to reform, one, sponsored by Senator Karl Mundt, Republican of South Dakota, would select electors in each state by congressional districts, with two running at large, in exact conformity with the state's delegation to Congress. Supporters of Mundt's proposal talk of achieving "balance and symmetry in the political roots of the government of the United States." But what they would really do is to fix the same bias in the Presidency that exists in Congress, giving added strength to the rural-agricultural populations now over-represented in the House of Representatives. Instead of the power now belonging to the key "swing" states, this system would allocate power according to the gerrymandering of the state legislatures. Presidential nominees would probably end up vying over the size of the farm subsidy.

A second proposal for reform is to apportion each state's electoral vote in accordance with its popular vote—an idea which at various times has attracted both liberals and conservatives in Congress. Former Senator Henry Cabot Lodge of Massachusetts, who ran as the Republican Vice-Presidential nominee in 1960, was a sponsor of such a Constitutional Amendment. The late Senator Estes Kefauver, liberal Democrat from Tennessee, argued that it would contribute to progress in the South by invigorating the two-party system. Former Representative Ed Gossett, a conservative Democrat from Texas, predicted flatly that the Civil War would have been avoided had the amendment been in effect since, by his estimate, its effect would be to subdue extremists. Except for Gossett's predictions, the amendment might be in effect today. It passed the Senate over a decade ago and was headed for passage in the House when he publicly extolled the curbs it would impose on the National Association for the Advancement of Colored People and other agents of minority groups. As a result, Northern congressmen in droves turned against the amendment.

When the Lodge-Gossett reform came before the Senate a second time, Senator John F. Kennedy was among the principal opponents who succeeded in defeating it. His was a prophetic fight. If the amendment had been in effect in 1960, according to one careful estimate, Kennedy would have won 286.871 electoral votes and Nixon (with his running mate Lodge) 265.036. But the tabulation does not account for the likelihood that a third party movement in the South, with the added hope of success, would have drawn a great many additional electoral votes away from the Democratic ticket. Even had Kennedy not lost, the outcome might have been in doubt for a considerable period of time. As one analyst commented shortly after the election, "The country might drift in torment and indecision for weeks while handfuls of votes were counted and recounted and the electoral vote then recomputed." [11]

One other proposed reform keeps recurring: the substitution of direct popular elections for the electoral college. But this stands little chance of serious consideration since the less populous states would never ratify an amendment giving added weight to the mass vote of the big cities. Probably this is for the best, since a nominee soliciting a purely popular mandate might be less concerned about reconciling the nation's sectional differences. The demagogue playing to the mob would have new incentives.

Contemplating the possibilities of the various electoral reforms leads this writer to a spirited defense of the status quo. There need to be curbs on the elector's capacity to disregard his mandate, but to alter the system radically in a misguided effort to create "balance and symmetry in the political roots" would be Constitutional quackery. A President has reason to draw his inspiration from somewhat different roots than the Congress. It is fitting that he be obliged to show special concern for the underdog groups of the nation who congregate in our cities. His efforts to reconcile the treatment of these groups with the nation's ideals has seldom failed to contribute to the public well-being. The politics of the electoral college is useful education for Presidents.

Lord Bryce, describing *The American Commonwealth* seventy years ago, thought it proper to include a chapter inquiring "Why Great Men are not Chosen Presidents." He raised the question without much feeling of distress since, as he explained, "Four-fifths of [the President's] work is the same in kind as that which devolves on the chairman of a commercial company or the manager of a railway, the work of choosing good subordinates, seeing that they attend to their business, and taking a sound practical view of such administrative questions as require his decision." [12] Few American or foreign observers would adopt such a complaisant attitude today. We live in an age when the hourly judgments of the man who holds that office can shape the future of all mankind—even determine whether mankind has a future.

It is not susceptible of proof that "great" men are regularly being eliminated by the selection process. Those who go along on the campaign trail do sense a rationale in the way a President is picked. For one thing, the various hurdles demand of the man who would be leader that he prove himself equipped physically and temperamentally to sustain the rigor of that job. As Woodrow Wilson once remarked, "Men of ordinary physique and discretion cannot be Presidents and live, if the strain be not somehow relieved. We shall be obliged always to be picking our chief magistrates from among wise and prudent athletes—a small class." The strain of the Presidency has certainly not been relieved since Wilson's day.

There is logic in the campaign's testing of how well a candidate can mobilize the men and money that are essential. A President must become accustomed to dealing with men and money in large quantities, and must also be capable of winning the kind of loyalty from his following that money alone cannot buy.

Finally, one detects amid all the hurly-burly of campaigning, a mysterious communion which establishes for the President-to-be ties with the people. Many witnessed the communion at work in the West Virginia primary when Candidate Kennedy, rich, Catholic, and of urban background, was faced with a combination of poverty, Protestant suspicion, and rural scepticism. The candidate himself appeared surprised by his ability to make contact with people and situations totally alien to any he had known previously.

Even in retrospect, it is hard to see how Kennedy survived the obstacle course. Beside youth and religion, he had other handicaps to overcome. He was not a born politician with a natural affinity for men and issues; rather, he was a self-made political entrepreneur who advanced by a rigorous discipline together with an uncommon share of good fortune. But his success points the way of the new-style politician in America. The tireless concentration on planning, polling, and publicity provides a case study for Presidential politics of the future.

The system for picking Presidents has changed vastly from that envisaged by the founding fathers. If the best man has not always prevailed, it would be difficult to point to better choices who have been conspicuously eliminated. Still, the verdict of 1960, made by a margin of 113,238 votes out of more than 68 million cast, provides ample cause for speculation about the future of our selection process. The optimist can discern in the advent of television politics the opportunity by which a Catholic candidate could overcome prejudices of the past. The pessimist, on the other hand, may wonder whether the "very pale, white translucent skin" of the Republican nominee, more than any issue, brought about his defeat. It is possible that the two men's handling of the crisis arising from the election eve arrest in Georgia of the Negro leader, Dr. Martin Luther King, made the vital difference. Was Kennedy's public intercession on behalf of King evidence of greater resourcefulness or greater cunning?

The sidelines observer must raise other questions. How well does the selection process work not only in selecting the wise and able leader but also in conditioning him for the job ahead? The increase not merely in cost but in the "tumult and disorder" of the modern campaign is leading to a preposterous situation. The tempo has become so frantic that genuine doubt arose last time whether the two nominees, both abnormally healthy young men, could stand the pace. Panic stirred Kennedy strategists when his voice, overstrained by the West Virginia primary, showed signs of failing. There was alarm in Republican quarters when Nixon, because of an infected knee, was obliged to postpone campaign activities for a fortnight.

This is not a condition to be remedied simply by statute. The greater restraints must be imposed by a public philosophy that frowns on the excesses and penalizes those who commit them. There must be wider recognition of what we are trying to accomplish as we run the candidates over the hurdles. We must be aware that the way in which we select a President not only determines who he will be but also helps decide the talents, temperament, and even the fundamental philosophy brought to that high office.

F

THE DO-IT-YOURSELF NATURE OF PRESIDENTIAL POWER

"As a rule, there is far more danger that the president of the United States will render the office less efficient than was intended, than that he will exercise an authority dangerous to the liberties of the country."
JAMES FENIMORE COOPER, 1838[1]

"All Presidents start out pretending to run a crusade, but after a couple of years they find they are running something much less heroic, much more intractable: namely, the Presidency."
ALISTAIR COOKE, 1963[2]

As a people, we continually apply yardsticks to our Presidents and call out the measurements. Even while the man is fresh in office we commence solemn deliberations about what his rating will be according to the Gallup poll of history. We have established all sorts of indices for determining, of an instant, whether a President is "strong" or "weak," "great" or "mediocre." We seldom bother about contradictions; it is an old American tradition to accuse one of being despot and weakling in the same breath.

The trouble is that we have never been very precise about defining what we expect of the President. It is extraordinarily difficult to describe his job. We know from reading our newspaper that the man residing at 1600 Pennsylvania Avenue gets a great volume of mail, meets politician and miscellaneous publicity seekers, approves or vetoes laws, commands millions of military personnel along with countless tanks, planes, and missiles, and generally "runs the government." He is expected also to boss his party, inspect floods and other disasters, greet kings and sundry heads of state, and occasionally pay visits abroad. He is the nation's top strategist and its chief public relations man.

Theodore Roosevelt once described the President as "almost . . . a king and prime minister rolled into one." Certainly he suffers the adversities of both. His every move outside the White House stirs a public celebration, more impromptu but scarcely less regal than the British monarch's. On the other hand, his every act receives scrutiny in Congress more persistent and critical than a prime minister might expect in Parliament. A President cannot resolve his differences by dissolving Congress, nor can Congress, except by use of the unlikely weapon of impeachment, dismiss him.

Political scientists are accustomed to breaking down the Presidency into neat functions—referring colloquially to the hats the man in that office wears. But this, too, deals inadequately with the complex and overlapping nature of his job. The President does not always recognize when he takes off one hat and puts on another.

Not all the professional measurers apply the same yardstick. Some talk about the President in managerial terms, others in charismatic, still others in purely aesthetic. Sidney Hyman has described one role of the President as that of "an artist"—certainly an important perspective. But all the yardsticks have had one thing in common: they were outsiders' standards for taking the measure of the man in the White House. It remained for Richard Neustadt, a professor at Columbia University who once served as President Truman's assistant, to try to look at the job through a President's eyes. His book, *Presidential Power: The Politics of Leadership,* which delves into the official lives of Roosevelt, Truman, and Eisenhower, is an intriguing exercise in scholarly transmigration.

To begin with, Neustadt remarks on a paradox of Presidential leadership in recent times: "We tend to measure Truman's predecessors as though 'leadership' consisted of initiatives in economics, or diplomacy, or legislation, or in mass communication. If we measured him and his successors so, they would be leaders automatically. A striking feature of our recent past has been the transformation into routine practice of the actions we once treated as exceptional. A President may retain liberty, in Woodrow Wilson's phrase, 'to be as big a man as he can.' But nowadays he cannot be as small as he might like."[3]

The paradox is that the growth of the President's role as the central agent of government is by no means the same thing as leadership. His role has grown largely because no one else—neither Congress nor the courts nor the bureaucracy—can supply the services he is called on to provide. The White House is the only place where the competing claims on government can be brought into some sort of adjustment.

"In form, all Presidents are leaders nowadays. In fact, this guarantees no more than that they will be clerks." Neustadt's study of power is in reality a penetrating examination of the chronic weakness afflicting the modern President. Truman summed it up as well as any when he remarked, "I sit here all day trying to persuade people to do the things they ought to have sense enough to do without my persuading them. . . . That's all the powers of the President amount to." [4] Kennedy echoed the theme when, in response to a query whether he had encountered any problem he had not anticipated, he mentioned the difficulty of getting decisions carried out effectively, "It's easier to sit with a map and talk about what ought to be done than to see it done," he said.

A President has to have an acute awareness of the resistances that exist to any step he takes. The elements of his essential knowledge can be picayune: that he must communicate with a certain committee chairman in the mornings because he is too drunk by afternoon—any afternoon —to be coherent; that a certain bureaucrat is so buttressed by interest-group support that he can regularly defy the occupant of the White House, Democrat or Republican; that a certain issue has grown so mired in lobbyist intrigue that it is irredeemable. If he is to be any good, a President must have a mental catalogue of the movers and shakers in the Washington community, their habits and habitats. He needs to know the crotchets of M. De Gaulle of France, Mr. Meany of AFL-CIO, Mr. Reston of the *New York Times*, and many, many others.

How does the President save himself from merely serving as clerk to other people's priorities? The "commands" he can give with reasonable expectation that they will be carried out are fairly few and limited in scope. Neustadt delves particularly into three instances of the power to command: Truman's firing of General MacArthur, his seizure of the steel mills, and Eisenhower's dispatch of troops to Little Rock. All three were self-executing in the sense that the President's order was obeyed—though the Supreme Court later reversed the steel seizure. But all three were forced on a President as acts of last resort. Whatever their necessity, they represented failures rather than successes in Presidential leadership. The consequences flowing from them were a severe drain on the President's power.

For a graphic description of a President's dilemma, it is useful to read the Inter-University Case Study, *The Steel Seizure of 1952*. Its conclusion is that, ". . . while the White House was convicted by public opinion of the crime of grasping for unchecked power, its troubles in the steel crisis had come from its lack of influence—over public opinion, over labor and industry, and, in the critical early stages of the controversy, over some of its own stabilization agencies." [5] A decade later, President Kennedy resorted to persuasion rather than command when confronted by a sudden price rise in the steel industry.

Persuading people to do things, as Truman remarked, is the principal way Presidents get things done. Truman's own experience with the inception of the Marshall Plan offers vivid evidence of how Presidential persuasion really works. Viewed in the context of the times—Truman being otherwise engaged in bitter warfare with the Republican Eightieth Congress—it was a miraculous venture. It required skillful use of Presidential power, but it also required borrowing on the power and prestige of everyone in sight. One wonders whether it would have been possible at all except for the cast of supporting actors: General Marshall, Senator Vandenberg, Under Secretary Acheson, the Harriman Committee, Bevin and Bidault, and finally Joseph Stalin himself. Each provided help—Stalin, by opposition—which a politically embattled President could not provide. The result of the successful venture undoubtedly added to the President's power to deal with foreign policy.

The President has certain advantages in the game of persuasion. He commands publicity as does no other politician. He acquires added persuasiveness from the awesome elevation of his office and because few politicians wish to offend him unnecessarily. He has indirect ways of punishing offenders which, though cumbersome, can be cruel. It is necessarily a subtle business.

"The essence of a President's persuasive task with congressmen and everybody else," Neustadt writes, "is to induce them to believe that what he wants of them is what their own appraisal of their own responsibilities requires them to do in their own interest, not his . . . That task is bound to be more like collective bargaining than like a reasoned argument among philosopher kings." This interpretation runs counter to widely held views about Presidential power. A good many Americans seem to think that only folly or knavery on the part of the President prevents him from getting his views accepted. President Eisenhower paid indirect lip service to such an idea at the time he announced his intention, despite ill health, to run for a second term. Because there had been a "public clarification" of a number of important issues during his first term, Eisenhower argued, he could now safely delegate them to close associates. Four years later, Eisenhower was still working hard to clarify those issues and, if anything, was delegating less.

The press adds to the mythology of Presidential leadership when it suggests a process by which all the business of government, on reaching the stage at which a decision must be made, passes through the White House "in" and "out" baskets. In reality, nothing could be further from the truth. Even assuming that the government's business could be channeled so rigidly, there are finite limits to a President's time—to the number of associates he can see, the documents he can read, the decisions he has the physical endurance to make. Decision-making goes on at all stages and levels of government; important policies and programs bloom or wither often without a deliberate act by the President.

The chief executive must try to impose his will by more selective means. He does it, consciously or unconsciously, by his "choices"—a word more precise than "decisions": the choice at his press conference of the appropriate words to stimulate or squelch someone else's decision; the choice of whether to shortcut channels and reach down through officialdom to grasp a problem requiring attention; and, most important, the occasional choice not to make a difficult choice.

Neustadt's thesis is that a President builds up or tears

down his power by the choices he makes. He should make them with a constant awareness of his personal power stakes, for building power through his choices is the only way he can find to make his job operable. This is the unique contribution he must offer to policy-making after his experts have offered their contributions. A President must be an expert in building power.

We have been accustomed for so long to thinking about Presidents in the more lofty concepts of nation-building that the above thesis comes as a rude shock. This argument for a shrewd and power-conscious President seems Machiavellian. But, in the tradition of Machiavelli, Neustadt is convinced that only an expert in power can bring together the princely states of American government. He also believes that such an expert can best assure a "viable" public policy. In the decade ahead, comprised of a "snarly sort of politics with unstable parties and unruly issues," the Presidency will be no place for political amateurs.

By such a yardstick, Neustadt rated the three Presidents: Roosevelt, high; Truman, medium; Eisenhower, low. It remains to apply that measure to Kennedy, who completed less than three years in office.

President Kennedy's early career offered few indications of that zestful love of power which Roosevelt exhibited. The eldest son, Joseph Kennedy, Jr., was slated to be the politician in the family. Only after Joe Jr.'s death in World War Two did the second son, as his father has noted, feel obliged to take over the legacy. Kennedy's record in both the House of Representatives and the Senate showed him to be a tough campaigner, but not one of the power-conscious elite of those two bodies. He neither sought nor was invited to join the so-called inner clubs. Until near the end of his career in Congress, he did not exhibit much concern for legislative achievement.

Close friends differ about the origins of Kennedy's Presidential ambition. As late as 1956, he was remarkably in-

different to the efforts of his associates to promote him for
Vice-President on the Democratic ticket. He took stoically
his narrow defeat at the Chicago Convention in 1956.
Three years later, when he had already commenced the
sustained drive for first place, he still managed to convey a
certain dispassion about his high ambition. Asked bluntly
by reporters why he *ought* to be President, he answered
simply that he thought he could do as good a job as anyone
else available. To the question of why he should *want* to
be President, he quoted an ancient Greek proverb he had
learned from Dean Acheson: "Happiness lies in the exercise
of vital powers along lines of excellence in a life affording
them scope." Kennedy admitted he found in politics, as in
no other pursuit, a purely personal happiness. This seemed
hardly a driving motivation for seeking power.

Kennedy's writings provide a few clues to his notions
about leadership. His first book, *Why England Slept*,
an expansion of his college thesis written in 1940, gave an
impressive analysis of the British government's failure to
keep pace with German rearmament. The chief villains
were not the politicians but the unthinking British public
which, he felt, refused to support forthright leadership
and then sought "to make scapegoats for its own weaknesses."

Fifteen years later, while recuperating from an operation,
Kennedy drafted his *Profiles in Courage* which took quite
a different approach to the problem of leadership. This
time he paid glowing tribute to the politician who, in time
of crisis, stood staunchly against the prevailing sentiment
of colleagues and public. The book was a testament to a
leadership prepared to sacrifice power for the keeping of
conscience.

There were to be further shifts in Kennedy's perspective.
Almost a year before his inauguration, he delivered a
speech to the National Press Club which drew heavily
on the charismatic school of Presidential interpretation.
(A short time before the speech, one of his aides had bor-

rowed Sidney Hyman's book.) "In the decade that lies
ahead," Kennedy declared, "the challenging, revolutionary
Sixties, the American Presidency will demand more than
ringing manifestos issued from the rear of the battle. It
will demand that the President place himself in the very
thick of the fight, that he care passionately about the fate
of the people he leads, that he be willing to serve them at
the risk of incurring their momentary displeasure." Referring to Woodrow Wilson's assertion that a President is
at liberty to be as big a man as he can, Kennedy argued,
"But President Wilson discovered that to be a big man in
the White House inevitably brings cries of dictatorship. So
did Lincoln and Jackson and the two Roosevelts. And so
may the next occupant of that office, if he is the man the
times demand."

During the spring or summer of 1960, Kennedy read
Neustadt's book. That it struck a responsive chord is evident from the thinly veiled account of its author's experience as reported by Richard Rovere in *The New Yorker* a
month after the election:

About a month ago, the President-elect asked a man
from an eastern university to advise him on a wide but
clearly defined range of current problems and to give him
the name of people competent to deal with them in the
new administration. A day or two earlier, the newspapers
had reported that Mr. Kennedy had asked another man
—one whose background was more practical than theoreti-
cal—to do a job that sounded to the new recruit very much
like, if not identical with, the one he was being asked to
undertake. The scholar, who has a fluent command of the
local patois, asked Mr. Kennedy how he should "relate" to
the other appointee. The answer was crisp and categorical:
"Don't." The President-elect went on to say that it would
suit him down to the ground if the two men never saw
each other; he supposed, though, that they would have to
confer, and he only hoped that they would do as little con-
ferring as possible before they reported, as he wished each
of them to do, directly to him. With his eyes on the ceiling

and the merest hint of apology in the voice that is noted for its rather narrow emotional range, he said, "I simply cannot afford to have just one set of advisers." Far from being offended, the scholar left with a spring in his step and a firmer conviction than he had had up to then that the republic was in good hands. . . .

Mr. Kennedy, he felt, had already mastered the beginning of Presidential wisdom. "If he had not made that remark," he said, "I should have gone directly to my hotel room and got to work on a memorandum pointing out the weaknesses of the command system and urging him not to be afraid of a little administrative untidiness. If a President has only one set of advisers, the advisers take over the Presidency."

The attempt to measure Kennedy leadership presents a number of bafflements. At times there appeared to be a conflict between the "passionate" President of the Press Club speech and the power-conscious President of Neustadtian analysis. Or, using Kennedy's earlier writing, there was a tension between the politician of conscience depicted in his second book and the politician constrained by an apathetic public of his first.

Critics have found evidence of this conflict on all sides. The politics of foreign aid provides a clear example. In the first Inaugural Address, the Alliance for Progress proposals, and numerous other pronouncements, the President promised eloquently to assist the underdeveloped countries along the road to progress. Foreign aid was to be rescued from its former stereotype as simply a way of supporting the defense effort. Impact programs to stimulate basic growth in Latin America, Africa, and Asia were to be given the highest priority.

The results were hardly in accord with all these high hopes. The progress of the new AID agency was frustrated by frequent delays as well as a rapid succession of three directors during its first three years. The President's legislative proposal to finance development aid on a long-term basis finished with a hastily negotiated compromise which left power intact in the hands of the obstinate lords of the congressional appropriation subcommittees. With foreign aid subjected to ever increasing re-examination, its political future looked increasingly dark. Members of Congress who have sought to fight for the program, complained bitterly of being abandoned by the White House.

On other foreign fronts, critics have also pointed to a dualism between "vigorous" and "realistic" Presidential leadership:

Laos: The President held a televised press conference to emphasize, with use of maps, the threat to southeast Asia of a communist takeover of this little country. The settlement in Laos, negotiated not long afterward, promised at best that if the communists kept their word the country would remain neutral;

Berlin: Kennedy voiced repeated determination not to yield Allied rights. Yet he did not make a passionate protest when the Soviets erected a wall dividing that beleaguered city, and lesser officials tried to characterize "the Wall" as a psychological defeat for the Soviets;

Cuba: Kennedy accepted the "tunnel vision" of his CIA advisers by agreeing to the ill-fated invasion in the Bay of Pigs. Yet a cautious concept of power caused him to eliminate plans for U. S. air "cover" of the refugee invasion force which was sadly under strength for such a mission. Only a year and a half later, with Soviet missile-sites under construction in Cuba, did he pick up the challenge.

On the domestic front, there were similar contrasts between courageous expectations and cautious operations. In Congress, President Kennedy offered quiet support to Speaker Sam Rayburn in the fight to enlarge the House Rules Committee. But enlargement was a timid and, in retrospect, not wholly effectual way of trying to tame that recalcitrant group, and when Rayburn died, Kennedy remained fastidiously aloof from any show of preference in the short-lived struggle for leadership in the House. There was little evidence that the President was willing to take risks to obtain congressional reforms that might lessen the legislative stalemate. The very narrowness of the margins of defeat—on Medicare, on the Administration farm bill, on the Urban Affairs Department—revealed a discouraging inability to supply the necessary inducement to shift the balance.

The legislative struggle took on a quite different character from the trail blazing of the New Deal era. It is more reminiscent of the dogged trench warfare of the First World War than of the swift panzer movements of the Second. The item-by-item fight on Kennedy's tax reform proposals was more typical of the massed confrontation of forces that frustrated spectacular gains.

In a number of major battles Kennedy appeared to make a display more for the record than for anticipated results. There was the frantic and futile effort to push the Urban Affairs plan through the Senate before it received an inevitable veto in the House. Similarly, Medicare was hurried before the senators in hopes of diverting attention from the slow strangulation it was receiving in the House Ways and Means Committee. Bills for federal aid to lower and higher education went down to defeat in a way that obscured party responsibility.

Despite his campaign promises to "get America moving," Kennedy's actions in the economic field created the image of a President whose primary role was to adjust and balance the delicate mechanisms of the economy instead of stoutly exhorting it to new furies of movement. The effort to stem the gold flow, to correct the adverse balance of payments, and to spur industry through sizable tax concessions gave evidence of this cautious preoccupation with balance and adjustment. As he declared somewhat impatiently to criticism, "What we need is 'not more labels and more clichés' but more basic discussion of the sophisticated and technical questions involved in keeping our mighty economic machine moving steadily ahead." [6]

The President was equally impatient with criticisms that his policies in the foreign field appeared to lack a "grand design." After one background session, the *New York Times* reported that "President Kennedy believes that the grand design of his Administration's foreign policies derives from what he thinks has been a generally consistent United States course since 1945. As he sees it, the long-range purpose of himself and the nation is to work toward a world in which free states can develop sufficient internal resources to maintain their independence." [7] Of course, the critic could respond that this was a concept so grand that it was entirely lacking in design.

It must be admitted that the vantage point of a Washington reporter is not the best for gauging leadership. Trevelyan wrote of the first Queen Elizabeth, "Her bold decisions were few and can be numbered, but each of them began an epoch." Yet a scribe attending Elizabeth's court might well have had difficulty perceiving which ones were epochal. The press corps in Lincoln's capital did not discern greatness in the President's often irresolute behavior. Hindsight tends to etch deeply the sharp lines of leadership that appeared blurry close at hand.

Unlike Queen Elizabeth, a modern President must feel content not to begin any epoch if only he can maintain prosperity and avoid a war. Conceding his many difficulties, Kennedy enthusiasts found promising portent in three decisive acts during his early years in office: the challenge and rebuff to the steel industry's attempt to raise prices; the dispatch of federal deputies and troops to enforce the court-ordered enrollment of a Negro, James Meredith, in the University of Mississippi; and the confrontation of Khrushchev with the "quarantine" of Cuba. All three were successful in accomplishing short-term objectives. Steel reduced its prices; Meredith was enrolled; Khrushchev withdrew his missiles and bombers from Cuba.

In staging the showdowns, the President displayed a

capacity to mobilize the strength of his office speedily and efficiently. Particularly in the second Cuban crisis, he acted in such a way that sustaining strength was drawn from other holders of power, at home and abroad. By Neustadtian analysis, he showed keen awareness of the stakes and came through these crises with his personal power not only intact but enhanced.

Yet, it must be pointed out that the three episodes had other factors in common. None started as acts of the President's own volition, but were forced upon him—by U. S. Steel President Roger Blough, by Mississippi Governor Ross Barnett, and by Soviet Premier Nikita Khrushchev. All three had been attempts to call the President's bluff; he had to respond or be counted a coward. In each case, his opponents grossly overplayed their strength. Blough lacked the economic conditions to sustain a price rise; Barnett had no troops to back him up once the President federalized the National Guard; and Khrushchev was without conventional military capacity to break a blockade.

Those who participated most intimately with the President during the Cuban crisis—dramatically described as the prototype war of the thermonuclear age—are cautious about drawing lessons from it. One White House participant has pointed out privately that certain conditions made the situation unique. First, for nearly a week the government had possession of documented intelligence—evidence of the missile sites—about which no one in the press knew, or knew that the government knew. This permitted remarkable facility in planning the response, catching the enemy by surprise, and forewarning friendly allies. In marked contrast, for example, the building of the Berlin Wall was known simultaneously to government and press and was accomplished before government officials could confer with one another or consult the Allied powers in Berlin.

Secondly, the military phase of the Cuban quarantine was directed, quite literally, from a telephone on Secretary

McNamara's desk, providing tight control against the accidental or the unexpected. The chief anxiety in Washington was whether Soviet communications were as foolproof as those of the U. S. Doubt on this matter prompted the decision to allow the first Soviet ship, the tanker *Bucharest*, to pass through the blockade uninspected.

A third condition set the course of the Cuban crisis. In responses to questions at his press conference the previous month, the President had flatly committed himself to act in the event of aggressive build up in Cuba. Would he have acted had he not made that public commitment? Having experienced the awful loneliness of the decision to risk cataclysmic war, the White House assistant was unwilling to make that assumption lightly. He reported that not a single member of the inner council really believed that the quarantine alone would accomplish Soviet withdrawal. The terror of total war was a living reality.

Success in Cuba clearly resulted as much from the flaws in Khrushchev's strategy as from Kennedy's counter strategy. Once the quarantine had been evoked, the only options left to the Soviet leader were to launch a thermonuclear attack against the U. S., or to back down. Evidently he had not even made plans for staging a diversionary aggression elsewhere in the event of being challenged in Cuba. Kennedy, on the other hand, guarded his options by preparing for a swift escalation of force if the Soviets failed to withdraw the missiles. But he left the terrible choice of nuclear retaliation entirely up to Khrushchev.

After more than two years in office, the President's Special Counsel, Theodore C. Sorensen, a long-time aide, gave two lectures at Columbia University soberly reassessing the business of decision-making in the White House; both his words and mood were a far cry from Kennedy's exuberant Press Club speech of 1960 which Sorensen had helped draft. Now the deputy chose to stress the perplexities of leadership: ". . . too often a President finds that events or the decisions of others have limited his freedom of maneuver—that, as he makes a choice, that door closes behind him. And he knows that, once that door is closed, it may never open again—and he may then find himself in a one-way tunnel, or in a baffling maze, or descending a slippery slope. He cannot count on turning back—yet he cannot see his way ahead. He knows that if he is to act, some eggs must be broken to make the omelet, as the old saying goes. But he also knows that an omelet cannot lay any more eggs." Sorensen also underlined five limitations that encumber a President. "He is free to choose only within the limits of permissibility, within the limits of available resources, within the limits of available time, within the limits of previous commitments, and within the limits of available information."

As President Johnson suddenly took over the reins, the totting up of success and failure made judgment difficult. Successful negotiation of a nuclear test ban had marked an easing of tension, even if momentary, with the Soviets. On the other hand, the Western Alliance, so carefully woven together since the war, had begun to show signs of unraveling. Despite the successful passage of the President's mutual trade bill in Congress, U. S. negotiations with the Common Market had reached a state of mutual recriminations. Domestically, the economic indicators were showing advancing prosperity while the political indicators continued to reveal deep pockets of poverty. On the racial front, the late President had been making a try with tardy haste to provide equal citizenship and opportunity for Negroes before pent-up frustrations boiled over. Yet the very effort was threatening to rouse bitter opposition from powerful sectors of the white community.

Amid such perplexities, it is hard to decide on a yardstick for measuring a President, much less on how to apply it. Even while pondering Neustadt's brilliant analysis of Presidential muscle structure, one instinctively comes to feel certain reservations. Like Machiavelli's earlier anatomy of power, it is susceptible to misreading. A President preoccupied with his personal stakes can make all the wrong choices—for the nation if not for himself. Taken too literally, preoccupation with power could result in a "what's-in-it-for-me?" attitude compounding caution with caution. Or, contrarily, preoccupation with power can produce a cynicism about its usage. Presidential leadership has other ingredients, including some as difficult to define as "intuition," "vision," "conviction," and—to borrow from Kennedy—"courage." In any diagnosis, these ingredients contribute much to the health or ills of the body politic. There is danger that by overly concentrating on the muscle the body culturist ignores what moves the muscle.

This is merely to conclude, contrary to Lord Bryce, that Presidents *ought* to be great men and that a prime characteristic of greatness is the ability to employ power consciously but never too self-consciously. History reveals that great Presidents must show a capacity not only to conserve power but to risk squandering it when the occasion demands. The nation has profited from such philanthropy.

THE LONELY JOB IN A CROWDED WHITE HOUSE

"A council to a magistrate, who is himself responsible for what he does, are generally nothing better than a clog upon his good intentions; are often the instruments and accomplices of his bad, and are almost always a cloak to his faults."

ALEXANDER HAMILTON
The Federalist,[1] Number Seventy

"A good White House staff can give a President that crucial margin of time, analysis, and judgment that makes an unmanageable problem more manageable."

THEODORE SORENSEN, 1963[2]

We tend to think of the Presidency as the lonely place where a single leader hangs his various hats. In fact, it is a bureaucracy on top of a bureaucracy. Yet only comparatively recently have the analysts come to comprehend that the way this bureaucracy is run has a great deal to do with a President's power. Disagreements over which is the best way have stirred lively disputes in Washington.

As late as the latter part of the 1930s, Presidential staffing was largely a makeshift arrangement—a couple of career clerks, assorted personnel borrowed from the old-line departments around town, and, of course, with the coming of the New Deal, the braintrusters who settled in the White House with or without official status. In 1939, Congress recognized an urgent appeal from the Brownlow Commission that the President needed help. Three secretaries and six administrative assistants—who were supposed to have a passion for anonymity—were provided for. The Budget Bureau was moved over from Treasury into the newly created Executive Office of the President.

Congress was hesitant about coming to the President's aid, not because of any clear-cut notions about his individual leadership but because of an ingrained reluctance to give him troops who might be used against Congress itself. When Roosevelt tacked the National Resources Planning Board onto his Executive Office, Congress simply cut off the funds: There was to be no long-range planning around the place. It was impossible to keep an accurate head count of Presidential personnel during the Roosevelt era because of the various dodges that had to be employed to get around congressional restrictions.

Roosevelt never seemed to mind the haphazard nature of his office. He was inclined to think of men rather than of titles or administrative charts. Secretary of War Henry Stimson, while a loyal deputy, confided to his diary: "[He] is the poorest administrator I have ever worked under in respect to the orderly procedure and routine of his performance." After Truman inherited this confusing organization, he decided rather ambitiously to set it up so "that it would work efficiently for the future no matter who was at the head of the government." [3]

The Executive Office began to grow in earnest. It reached an apogee of sorts under Eisenhower when the combined personnel of the White House and Executive Office climbed to 2,730. There were "*the*" assistant to the President, three deputy asistants, two secretaries, three special counsels, three administrative assistants, nine special assistants *to* the President, four special assistants *in* the White House Office, innumerable consultants, and a sizable collection of aides bearing such titles as Assistant to the Deputy Assistant to the President. Each of the special assistants had his own staff, numbering up to ten. Two Cabinets—the regular one and the National Security Council—were operating out of the President's office along with their staffs. An ever-changing cluster of agencies, advisory boards, committees, and commissions also were located in the Executive Office.

With the mounting congestion, Presidential employees spilled out of the East and West Wings of the White House and overflowed the spacious quarters next door that once had lodged the entire State, War, and Navy Departments. Partitions had to be erected in the dignified old building whose architectural vintage has been described as General Grant Gothic. It soon turned into a bureaucratic rabbit warren.

Finally, an Advisory Commission on Presidential Office Space came up with plans to raze the Executive Office Building and erect a splendid new one in its place. The President's own office would be moved from the lovely Oval Room opening onto the White House rose gardens to a place in closer proximity to his aides.

Numerous stories appeared during the Eisenhower era about the efficiency being brought to the Presidency. It was implied that the job had been automated to near pushbutton proportions. According to one magazine feature story, "Plans for emergency action are only part of the (National Security) Council's vast, new policymaking role in the U. S. Government. But that function could be crucial to the U. S. if war should come now to the Middle East. Then security officers in the Pentagon and the State Department would open up vaults, take out documents that already have been drawn up by the Council and approved by the President. It is these documents which would tell, in that case, whether U. S. forces would be ordered into battle again." [4]

There was abundant evidence that the Eisenhower White House put great stock in its institutional innovations. As adjunct to the NSC, a Planning Board was set up, composed of top representatives from each government department whose task it was to prepare policy papers for the Council's deliberation. A similar top level Operations Coordinating Board was created to implement decisions reached in the NSC. During one period, a Plans Coordinating Group maintained interlocking relations with the Operations Coordinating Board for the purpose of stimulating psychological initiatives in the Cold War.

Despite the wall of secrecy surrounding these bodies, it was evident that they occupied a high place among the priorities of the President. There were meticulous provisions for circulation of agenda and action papers, and elaborate negotiations over which officials would sit where at the meeting table. Similar formalities took place in the Cabinet. For the first time in history, a "Secretariat" was established to coordinate business under the supervision of a Cabinet Secretary together with special Cabinet assistants in all the Departments. Each item on the agenda required preparation of Cabinet papers, frequently running fifty pages or longer.

The Cabinet officer making a "presentation" was put through carefully rehearsed "previews" by the Secretariat, sometimes three or more times until he had honed his arguments to a fine edge. A system of flashing lights was installed in the Cabinet Room to keep him to a tight time schedule. (So far as can be discovered, the red light was never flashed.) Afterwards, progress reports were circulated to implement decisions taken in Cabinet meeting. Eisenhower was determined to make useful decision-making instruments of his two councils. He once warned his associates, "Any time somebody comes into my office and starts fishing in his coat pocket for a program to sell me, I'm going to tell him, 'Get out of here! Take it up in the Cabinet or the NSC!' " [5]

. . .

Eisenhower also went further than any of his predecessors in encouraging the rise of a deputy President. During the Second World War, Roosevelt had granted vast and unspecified authority to James S. Byrnes and Fred Vinson. At the time of the Korean conflict, Truman tried, with notable lack of success, to work out a similar arrangement with Charles E. Wilson, formerly of General Electric. But these were temporary and *ad hoc* deputations of power. The idea of having a chief Assistant in peacetime originated when Truman gave John R. Steelman the job. Though Steelman personally penciled "The" at the front of his title, he was never *the* Assistant. In addition to labor conciliation duties, he simply served as Johnny-on-the-spot for a wide variety of assignments until Truman could find others to take them.

The *"The"* remained in the title when Sherman Adams received it upon Eisenhower's arrival in the White House. Adams, tough and taciturn, set out to pump meaning into his job. Early in the Administration, an advisory group sent to the White House a suggested staff organization chart showing the lines of authority running directly up to the President. Adams promptly sent it back for redrafting: with Eisenhower's blessing, all the lines of authority were to run through Adams.

The relationship between these two men will absorb students of government for a long time to come. Adams showed no diffidence about blocking access to the President of important members of Congress—as when Senator John Sherman Cooper, Republican of Kentucky, was thwarted in his attempt to warn Eisenhower of brewing trouble in the Dixon-Yates enterprise. The Assistant even dissuaded Cabinet members from seeking private audiences, once telling two disputing department heads, "Either make up your minds, or else tell me and I will do it. We must not bother the President with this. He is trying to keep the world from war." [6]

Though Adams struggled manfully to meet his awesome responsibility, his downfall in 1958 suggested that there was a fatal flaw in his understanding of his job. His departure was precipitated by exposure of his slight involvement in the messy affairs of an old friend, Bernard Goldfine. More significant than the ethical aspects, the episode showed that though a President may delegate his authority, he cannot delegate his power. In the desperate battle for survival, Adams discovered that he had no defenders in Congress. He was hounded out of office as much for his legitimate acts on the President's behalf—acts which inevitably offended many congressmen—as for the specific sin of aiding Goldfine. His downfall provided a grim case study for anyone who might be tempted to become a President's alter ego.

But Eisenhower was not dissuaded. Even as he prepared to leave office, his final budget message recommended creation of a new super-cabinet post. "The First Secretary of the Government" would possess the status of a prime minister and be responsible for "coordinating all the international activities of the various departments." Writing to a friend, Eisenhower envisaged an idyllic existence for the new Secretary. This officer would be "relieved of the chore of meeting with Committees and long hours of detailed discussion and argument—he would be given time to think." The President failed to indicate how a man could coordinate so many activities and avoid attending committee meetings.

Many factors influenced Eisenhower's approach to running his office. He was conditioned by the Army staff system with its clearly delineated organization charts. He had a personal predisposition for the sort of administrative tidiness despised by Roosevelt and never achieved by Truman. More than his predecessors, he faced up to the fact that programs of any consequence invariably jump departmental boundaries and must be coordinated higher up. By building Presidential bureaucracy, Eisenhower was also showing an instinctive mistrust of the vast government bureaucracy beneath him which he had pledged to overhaul.

Yet, even while he was still in office, the criticisms commenced about what he had done to the Presidency. In 1959, Senator Henry Jackson, Democrat of Washington, headed a subcommittee of the Senate Committee on Government Operations which began an extensive review of the "National Policy Machinery." With Eisenhower's permission, the committee interrogated most of the officials involved with this machinery.

In a series of reports, the Jackson Committee expressed profound scepticism about the "institutionalized" Presidency that had grown up. It made caustic judgment of the National Security Council: "Despite the vigorous activity of the NSC system, it is not at all clear that the system now concerns itself with many of the most important questions determining our long-term national strategy or with many of the critical operational decisions which have fateful and enduring import on future policy." [7] The question was raised of whether the NSC really got involved with the key aspects of the national security budget, the make-up of the armed services, and the translation of policy goals into actual programs. NSC coordination, the Committee warned, was "essentially critical and cautionary, not creative . . . The net result has tended to be 'coordination' on the lowest common denominator of agreement, which is often tantamount to no coordination at all."

All this growth of machinery, the Committee argued, had not really helped the President. "The President has been left in an unenviable position. He has found it necessary to undertake an endless round of negotiations with his own department heads, or else he has been confronted at a very late date by crisis situations resulting from the lack of adequate coordination at an earlier stage. The burdens of the President have been increased correspondingly. . . ." [8]

The Committee's conclusions were equally glum in regard to various appendages to the NSC. About the Planning Board: ". . . interagency committees like the Planning Board can be helpful in criticizing and commenting. But if, in the interest of 'agreed solutions,' such committees blur the edges and destroy the coherence of these proposals, they do the President a disservice. There is strong reason to believe that this is now the case."

About the Operations Coordinating Board: "Actually, the OCB has little impact on the real coordination of policy execution. Yet, at the same time, the existence of this elaborate machinery creates a false sense of security by inviting the conclusion that the problem of teamwork in the execution of policy is well in hand . . . The case for abolishing the OCB is strong." [9]

The Jackson Committee saved its harshest criticism for the proposal to create a First Secretary of the Government. This officer, it argued, would be in an impossible position in relation to Congress, existing department heads, and the President himself. "Our governmental system has no place for a First Secretary," the committee study warned; ". . . only one official has the constitutional and political power required to assume that role and to maintain it. That official is the President of the United States. He cannot be relieved of his burdens by supplying him with a 'deputy' to do what only he can do." [10]

Not entirely by coincidence, these committee reports struck a responsive chord in President-elect Kennedy. During his campaign, he had kept in close touch with his Senate colleague who also served as Chairman of the Democratic National Committee. The findings suited the temperament of the young politician whose administrative experience had consisted of running a congressional office with a payroll of never more than thirty.

From the start, the new President and his staff brought a new style of operation to the White House. The Eisenhower way could be compared to a football team—elaborate planning, great attention to coordinating everybody, and interminable time spent in the huddles. The Kennedy team was more along the lines of basketball: everybody was on the move all the time. Nobody had a very clearly defined position. The President had a habit of throwing the ball in any direction and he expected it to be kept bouncing.

There was visible effort in the White House to achieve more flexible procedures. The morning staff conference, a rigid routine during the Eisenhower era, was dispensed with quickly. The spacious corner office once occupied so grandly by Sherman Adams remained vacant for some time. When an administrative assistant finally moved in, the clear understanding was that neither he nor anybody else was *"The"* Assistant. One Kennedy aide boasted that it would be impossible to draw up an organization chart for the White House since there was practically no hierarchy.

As a direct consequence of the Jackson Committee studies, the Operations Coordinating Board was abolished. In getting rid of the structure, however, Kennedy retained a senior career official from the OCB staff who had proved a highly effective operator. "That fellow knows how to spot the scatter rugs on the polished floor of government," Presidential Assistant McGeorge Bundy explained in a baroque metaphor. Other bureaucratic growth around the National Security Council and the Cabinet similarly was pared away. Kennedy tended to regard the formal NSC meeting primarily as a way of informing, not being informed by, his top officials. Meetings of the Cabinet were regarded as an avoidable nuisance. Partitions in the Executive Office Building were torn down and functions shifted to the departments. The President's own office, it was made known, would remain in the White House.

The new President sought to inform himself personally

and directly. He did not hesitate to cut across channels and down through echelons of the bureaucracy in getting what he needed or communicating his interest in a particular problem. No bureaucrat could feel safe from a Presidential phone call. Kennedy was remarkably cavalier in handing out assignments, frequently using the man who happened to be nearest at hand when a problem arose. It did not concern him that his aides might find themselves duplicating or even competing with each other. It was *their* job, not his, to recognize and reconcile conflicts.

This might have led to chaos except that the White House staff, despite its youth, was experienced in working together and working in the Washington milieu. At least a half-dozen of Kennedy's top assistants—Theodore Sorensen, Kenneth O'Donnell, Lawrence O'Brien, Ralph Dungan, Myer Feldman, and Pierre Salinger—had an understanding of their boss based on long and intimate association. By temperament, the aides were not noticeably given to jealous rivalry, and, unlike FDR who loved a good family feud, Kennedy was not disposed to foster it.

As part of the reform, there was serious effort to cut down on the number of interdepartmental committees. This proved more easily said than done. The committees, redesignated "task forces," continued to flourish. But Kennedy voiced a stubborn determination to make the regular departments, particularly the Department of State, carry their load as executors of the President's program. He was also determined, in line with the Jackson Committee recommendations, that his Secretary of State should perform the role of First Minister in the international field.

During his early months in office, a good many observers hopefully speculated that Kennedy was beginning to master the impossible task of running the modern Presidency. His monumental fiasco in authorizing the CIA-sponsored invasion in Cuba's Bay of Pigs rudely shattered many of these hopes. Almost immediately, the scholarly critics fastened not on him, but on his operating techniques to explain this humiliating defeat. In a Brookings Institution study, one critic diagnosed the Cuba situation as follows: "Kennedy had surrounded himself, as he preferred, with more than one set of advisers in a very fluid staff system, but apparently in the pinch he had not asked the probing questions himself or put together all of the pieces essential to a judgment and no one else had taken it on himself to do so." [11] Another, in *The New Leader*, argued: "[Kennedy's] concept of Presidential government has considerable merit compared to the committee system which it is intended to replace, but it is not likely to work in practice." [12]

The newspaper critics joined in. Arthur Krock, columnist for the *New York Times*, wrote disparagingly of the President's "disbelief" in a coordinated staff system. Krock argued that Kennedy had substituted "a scatteration of groups in which [there is] duplication of effort, divided authority and loose lines of organization. . . ." [13] Columnist Joseph Alsop sought to blame Presidential adviser Neustadt for what he called "The True Infirmity" in the White House. According to Alsop, Neustadt's book had wrongly depicted a style of leadership in which the President "retained all authority in his own hands by organizing his Administration the way a Swedish cook organizes a smorgasbord." The result, Alsop argued, was that Kennedy found himself the center of "an immense, confusing, distracting but continuous churning." Alsop voiced doubt "whether firm action will come out of infirm organization." [14]

Having publicly taken upon himself the responsibility for the ill-fated Cuban enterprise, the President was privately irritated by these criticisms. He remarked in one conversation that he *had* consulted all the members of the

NSC "except Ed Murrow and Frank Ellis." * His mistake, he felt, had been in relying on the assurances given him by the professionals in the Central Intelligence Agency. He characterized the advice given by the Joint Chiefs of Staff: "They advise you the way a man advises another one about whether he should marry a girl. He doesn't have to live with her." [15]

From Kennedy's perspective, the problem was not to organize his advisers differently but to get better advice. He voiced impatience with organizational tidiness in responding to a press conference question about the confusing chain of command for Inter-American affairs: "My experience in government is that when things are non-controversial, beautifully coordinated and all the rest, it may be that there isn't much going on . . . I do not hear any criticism of our organizational structure in several areas of the world which I know are rather inactive . . . So if you really want complete harmony and goodwill, . . . then the best way to do it is not to do anything." [16]

Adviser Neustadt, writing at first year's end from England where he was teaching, admiringly reiterated the objectives of the Kennedy way of organization: "To keep the White House staff flexible, generalist and tied to the President's personal business; to get department heads and their subordinates back into the act as responsible individuals; in the terms of Robert Lovett . . . to restore to policy-making the ingredient of human judgment by visible, responsible officials. What is impressive is that instead of giving up this philosophy of operations and moving to new philosophy and new structures to cure troubles, the President seems to reaffirm the ideas he began with in every public move he makes—and equally important, in the moves he does not make." [17]

.   .   .

---

* As Directors respectively of the United States Information Agency and the Civil Defense Administration, Murrow and Ellis were statutory members of NSC.

There were gradual modifications from the period at the beginning when the new Presidential assistants were almost boastfully indifferent to organization. Then more than a touch of arrogance showed itself among the youthful movers and shakers. Stewart Alsop, the magazine writer, once had remarked to Special Counsel Sorensen, "You people here in the White House might turn out to have more real power and influence than more conspicuous figures like members of the Cabinet." Sorensen replied, "If you mean that the President intends to run the Executive branch of the government with the help of his White House staff, you're right." The Cuban episode did bring more recognition of what running the government actually entails. For one thing, it demonstrated that staff assistants lose their value when they become advocates rather than eyes and ears for the President. It was commented at the time that there had been too much passion for power among those whose principal passion should have been for anonymity.

Almost surreptitiously, stricter system was imposed. McGeorge Bundy, as deputy for national security affairs, built up both new staff and procedures for coordinating the President's business. Informal groups began to take on some of the attributes of Eisenhower's old Planning Board and Operations Coordinating Board. But the resistance to "structure" at the White House still remained fierce. General Maxwell Taylor was brought in as Kennedy's military adviser, but at the first opportunity he was transferred to the Pentagon to become Chairman of the Joint Chiefs of Staff. A shakeup came in the State Department where three Kennedy aides were spun off from the White House and inserted in the conventional line of command. The President later remained determined, despite frustrations, to make the Department into an effective operations center.

Two successes of President Kennedy did provide some clues to how the system was supposed to work. The first, a fairly long-range Presidential initiative, was the concerted campaign to push Kennedy's trade bill through Congress.

A sizable staff was annexed to the Executive Office as a bolster to the State Department's weakness in dealing with Capitol Hill. But it was an *ad hoc* staff, quickly disbanded after the trade bill passed Congress. The President's office was not intended to become a lodging for permanent lobby groups.

The second success was the planning and coordination of the Cuban quarantine in 1962. Executed under conditions of great secrecy with operational details equivalent to a battle plan, the quarantine was run by a small group drawn from the National Security Council designated as the "Executive Committee." Underneath, a whole network of subcommittees tended to various details. The President was able to keep on top of the situation while, at appropriate times, retiring from the consultations to permit freer exchanges among his subordinates. Enthusiasts for Kennedy's way of running the Presidency were considerably heartened by the experience.

Criticism continued, the most frequent being that Kennedy's style of operation was more suited to trouble-shooting than to systematic and foresighted planning. The complaint was most often heard from those agencies of government whose business does not have crisis priority. The President's neglect of his Cabinet as a collective body of advisers, it was argued, contributed to this tendency to approach problems at random and in a hurry.

A certain tendency toward dogmatism is noticeable among the philosophers who speculate on the management of the President's office. So much depends upon the President. Eisenhower welcomed the businesslike arrangements for ordering his business. But Kennedy was equally sincerely committed to the more flexible techniques. Many of the Eisenhower innovations unquestionably were useful to a leader whose increasing concern was to develop better control over the braking mechanisms in government. Kennedy was seeking to prove that his innovations could help a

President who wished to take his foot off the brake and give a firm push on the gas pedal.

For either type of President, the growth of government presents difficulties of a dimension unknown to Franklin D. Roosevelt, who could create emergency agencies and shift titles and functions with cavalier abandon. The business of big government has acquired a momentum of its own. Especially those programs which affect strong group interests must sometimes make a President feel as though he is leading a heavy wagon down a steep hill—not so much pulling as hurrying to keep from being run over. The business of government has grown more intertwined so that few parts of it, at least from a President's perspective, fail to bear on the rest. The interdepartmental committee to deal with matters large and small has become a constant curse.

Finally, the business of government today requires the making of decisions not easily reversed. The intercontinental ballistic missile once launched cannot be called back; for a President, it has taken on symbolic meaning.

H

THE DILEMMAS OF
BEING HEARD

". . . In weakening each single authority in the govern-
ment by dividing powers and functions among each of
them, [the framers of the Constitution] were throwing
upon the nation at large, that is, upon unorganized public
opinion, more work than it had ever discharged in Eng-
land. . . ."

JAMES BRYCE [1]

Since persuasion is to be his principal power, the sobering
realization comes to each new President that he must ever
be speaking *to* as well as *for* a nation. Getting elected is
only the bare beginning of the communication process.
The President finds that he is only one bidder among many
seeking the favorable attention of the public to get his job
done. How well or badly he plays his role as the chief
publicist of government can make a marked difference in
Presidential power.

The burden is onerous. "Public opinion," President Kennedy's Special Counsel Theodore Sorensen declared somewhat waspishly, "is often erratic, inconsistent, arbitrary, and
unreasonable. . . . It rarely considers the needs of the next
generation or the history of the last. It is frequently ham-
pered by myths and misinformation, by stereotypes and
shibboleths, and by an innate resistance to innovation. It is

usually slow to form, promiscuous and perfidious in its affection, and always difficult to distinguish." [2]

A President soon learns, if he didn't know already, that public opinion in America is not a monolithic whole spreading out from Washington. There are publics and publics to which he must appeal. They group and regroup in varying combinations, coalescing on special occasions to sustain or frustrate his purpose. A President never can be entirely certain of the depth or duration of public opinion.

Polls provide a clue. In Franklin D. Roosevelt's time, when pollstering first became a discipline, the jargon about "image" and "trend analysis" invaded the White House. No President has neglected it since. But polls are crude indices at best, rarely revealing which publics want what and how intensely they want it. The President must have an instinct for these things. He must be sensitive, first of all, to Congress, his co-equal according to the Constitution and his most vociferous court of public opinion. He must be alert to the opinion of the vast Executive bureaucracy spread out beneath him which has its own pipelines to the public. He must make distinctions among the informed, the less informed, and the uninformed opinions of the public at large. He must take account of the organized publics which, since Lord Bryce wrote, have come to claim an ever more assertive role in the affairs of government.

Finally, a President today cannot neglect his new, nonvoting publics dwelling outside the territorial limits of the United States. He plays front and center on a world stage. What is thought and said among our ancient allies of Europe, the newly emerging countries of Asia and Africa and even within the closed communications system of the Soviet Union also has a great deal to do with his success or failure.

In *Presidential Power*, Neustadt distinguishes between two publics, each of which is important to the President. His professional reputation is built on what in spirit if not geography is labeled "the Washington Community"—all those politicians, members of the press, lobbyists, diplomats and the like who "are compelled to watch the President for reasons not of pleasure but vocation." His public prestige, on the other hand, is based on the less knowledgeable but no less important community-at-large.

The judgments of the two groups can be quite independent of one another. Truman often won grudging admiration in the Washington community even when he sank to low levels in public popularity. Eisenhower, on the other hand, was frequently criticized by the professionals; yet he left office still outstandingly popular with the general public. Neither is a desirable condition of Presidential life. Ideally, a President must earn the favor of both these publics if he is not to suffer an erosion of his powers.

How does a President communicate to the public in order to get support for the things he considers important? In the first glow of his election triumph it might seem that he has all the publicity advantages. "We will merchandise the hell out of the Eisenhower program," one White House aide boastfully asserted in 1953, relying on the undoubted fact that almost everything a President says or does is news.

But the man in office soon finds that there are severe limits set upon his capacity to communicate. Even President Franklin Roosevelt, surely one of the masters in this field, once wrote to an old associate: ". . . The public psychology and, for that matter, individual psychology, cannot, because of human weakness be attuned for long periods of time to a constant repetition of the highest note in the scale . . . Whereas in this country there is a free and sensational press, people tire of seeing the same name, day after day, in the important headlines of the papers, and the same voice, night after night, over the radio . . . If I had tried (in 1935) to keep up the pace of 1933 and 1934, the inevitable histrionics of the new actors, Long and Coughlin and Johnson, would have turned the eyes of the audience away from the main drama itself. . . ." [3]

A President today has to be even more conscious of the duty and the difficulty amid modern distractions. What he must try to explain is more complex and less intimately related to the life of the citizen than when Roosevelt could describe both depression and war as fairly straightforward issues. The balance of payments, fiscal policy, and the concept of military deterrence, for instance, raise problems for a President even in semantics.

The development of mass communications, paradoxically, has not made the task simpler. During Truman's first three postwar years in office there were eight occasions when he pre-empted all radio networks during an evening hour to take important policy issues to the country. Yet only once—when he removed price controls on meat— did his Hooper rating rise above 50 per cent of the potential listeners. His other pronouncements followed a generally descending scale of listenership, reaching the low rating of 30.7 per cent when he tried to explain why he had vetoed Taft-Hartley. More than uninterested, the public may not be amused to have its regular television and radio programs sacrificed to the President. Eisenhower took notice of this after a few years in office and chose to pre-empt only one major network each time for his reports to the nation, thus giving the viewer a choice between viewing his President or a situation comedy.

Though television offers a great potential for the President, it also has drawbacks. It demands entertainment for the eye as well as a quickened tempo for the ear. It puts a premium on spontaneity and change of pace. To suit its format, a President could be tempted to treat the affairs of state with the frivolity of a disc jockey.

During his final days in office, Mr. Truman escorted a television audience on a tour of the White House. It was

the first time a President had done such a thing, and it was
an awkward affair even when Truman took a brief turn at
the piano. Mr. Eisenhower carried matters further by holding a simulated Cabinet meeting before the cameras, as
well as one or two rather stiff "conferences" with Secretary
of State Dulles. It remained for Mr. Kennedy to seek to ex-
ploit television's full potential. Soon after entering the
White House, Kennedy allowed the cameras to come into
his office and watch the President unrehearsedly at work.

Less than a month after Kennedy's Inauguration, CBS
carried a program billed as "the first time television has
ever been permitted . . . during the actual conduct of official business." Because of a technical mishap, most of the
film made inside the White House proved to be out of
focus and had to be scrapped. But one rather brief and
fuzzy strip showed Mr. Kennedy receiving a telephone call
the day of a pro-Lumumba riot in a session of the U. N. Security Council. The transcript included the following dialogue:

CRONKITE (*in hushed tones*): The awaited call from
U. N. Ambassador Adlai Stevenson . . .

KENNEDY: Governor . . .

CRONKITE: . . . whom he—the President—customarily
addresses by his former title of Governor.

KENNEDY: Oh, yes, yes. How is that up there? Yes, that's
be fine. Oh, who is—who has withdrawn.

(*Cronkite interjects an explanation of the U. N. situation while Kennedy listens to Stevenson.*)

KENNEDY: Have they announced that they're going to
give the assistance or they're prepared to give it? I see.
That's ah . . . Right, fine. Look, now let me ask you, what
is the legitimacy of Gizenga?

(*Cronkite explains who Gizenga is.*)

KENNEDY: Right. Well, I'll get a hold of that. If there's
any further questions on this matter of the delegation—
I'll get on this business of getting it to the Senate, and ah,
I'll have Kenny O'Donnell talk to some member of your

staff if there are some questions further about it. O.K. Good. Thanks, Governor.

ABC carried intimacy even further with a program which took the viewer behind the closed doors while the President conferred with his assistants, attended a briefing by the Joint Chiefs of Staff, and talked with Disarmament Chief John McCloy about when to start negotiations with the Soviets.

MC CLOY: I think it probably would be pretty early fall, but from the way I can sense attitudes around town here, there's an awful lot of pessimism and an awful lot of studies that have to be resolved. We've got studies all over the place.

KENNEDY: As far as saying anything to them, that would look pretty late. I thought at least we ought to indicate our . . . otherwise, everybody's going to begin to assume that we're not as serious as . . . [*deletions by the producers*]

The ABC program boasted of showing a President's decision actually being made:

ANNOUNCER: The hour is late, the official day is ending, and now you will see the President in the more intimate moments of evening—moments that reveal his personal charm, the workings of an extraordinary mind, and the warmth with which he treats his close associates . . . Now Ted Sorensen is posing a question. For an insight into the workings of the Kennedy mind, watch how and when Sorensen finally gets his answer.

On the screen Sorensen could be seen thrusting a sheet of paper toward the President, apparently a list of names. Kennedy glanced at it, got up from his desk, walked into the next room, jiggled with the TV set, stood watching for a brief time, then walked back into his office and said to Sorensen, "That's O.K."

The intimate Presidency reached an ultimate when, during the crisis period surrounding integration of the University of Alabama in the summer of 1963, television cameramen wearing rubber sneakers were permitted to monitor proceedings at the White House and the Justice Department. Sponsors of the program, carried as an hour-long documentary, claimed that "A New Kind of Television Goes Backstage with History" and boasted that their cameras "captured the very essence of government in action."

Replying to NBC correspondent Ray Scherer about why he was "so available," Kennedy once explained that ". . . the responsibilities placed upon the President by the Constitution and by events are great. How we meet these responsibilities, how the people who are associated with me are meeting them, what our relationship is and how we function, it seems to me, goes to the heart of the Presidency, and the Presidency is an office which in a sense is shared by all the people." Mr. Kennedy seemed shrewdly aware of the fact of life expressed by C. P. Snow, that ". . . an overwhelming majority of men find a fascination in seeing power confidently used, and are hypnotised by it." [4]

The news conference, a fairly modern institution for Presidential communication, has also undergone change. It was first conducted on a regular basis by Woodrow Wilson as a cozy gathering at which the President conversed with Washington correspondents in great informality. Walter Lippmann, who attended Wilson conferences, recalls that reporters would crowd around the President's desk, the wire service members first asking the more urgent questions and hurrying off while others lingered to engage in free give and take with Wilson about the day's issues.

Though larger, the news conference was not much different when Franklin Roosevelt used it to great purpose. Under Truman it lost part of its informality by the move out of the President's office in the White House to a room in the old State Department building next door. Under

Eisenhower, the movie and TV cameras came into the conference.

Kennedy's decision to institute "live" televising of his news conference stripped away the last intimacy. Now the President stood directly before the public at large, able to communicate instantaneously to his constituents but also unprotected against any mishaps of word or expression. The Kennedy conference, grown too big for its previous quarters, took place in the modern auditorium of the new State Department building. Network representatives monitored the proceedings from glass-enclosed booths high above the crowd of regular reporters. Shotgun microphones roamed the room to pick up questions from far-off reporters; zoomar lenses brought the faces up close. The viewer sitting before his television set could see and hear much better than the participants.

Having been conditioned by the arduous television debates as a candidate, our late President did manage to exhibit mastery of this new type of news conference. Most of his answers were reasonably direct and syntactical. Gifted with a mind amazingly retentive of detail, he had a technique of overwhelming his interrogator with a flood of specifics, a practice which on occasion obscured the fact that he did not always provide a direct answer. For him, television seems to have served well the projection of his personal image.

Yet the observer cannot help questioning all these developments in the communication process. They appear to be better geared to selling a President than selling the things he stands for. Neither the televised news conference nor the "inside" looks at the President at work have been successful in this larger purpose of persuasion. Eavesdropping on a President as he "makes a decision" has a tendency to hoke up the real drama of decision-making. What the viewer is apt to see is a reality without substance. No matter how unrehearsed, it is shadow acting. When carried too far, it bastardizes the business of government and tempts the public to regard a President's job as less awesome than it really is.

To communicate in this age of mass communication is no easy matter. The politician has learned the fundamentals—how to be brief in delivery and abbreviated in gesture if he is to appear convincing. But he is still exploring what it takes to convince the faceless crowd watching him in the quiet privacy of the living room. There have been sad discoveries, as in the case of Kennedy's Madison Square Garden appeal for Medicare, that a speech rousingly received by the live audience may have almost no impact on the larger television audience.

The problem, of course, does not lie only in the media. Kennedy once commented almost nostalgically that politicians from John C. Calhoun to William Howard Taft "spent entire careers in grappling with a few dramatic issues on which the nation was sharply divided . . . The central domestic problems of our own time are more subtle and less simple. They relate, not to basic clashes of philosophy or ideology, but to ways and means of reaching common goals —to research for sophisticated solutions to complex and obstinate issues." [5]

It may be the ironic fact of life in modern Washington that communication, now that the technical facilities for communicating are so superb, stands in grave peril. How does a President give point and priority to the ideas with which he wishes to make a lasting imprint on the nation's memory? There are an old-fashioned few, of whom I count myself one, who are troubled by the declining sense of solemnity when a President talks to his publics. The preparation may require more drudgery, and the immediate response may not always seem worth the effort, but if the President offers good rhetoric, with disciplined ideas for content, it can have a percolative effect that lasts longer than the moment of delivery and goes further than the listening and viewing audiences. It extends the persuasive power of a President beyond his term of office, perhaps even beyond his lifetime. It makes the arguments of Lincoln as valid today as when they were first uttered.

Amid all the nagging concern around the White House over communication, there has been a marked decrease in this brand of Presidential rhetoric. It is a distressing neglect. For the White House, as Candidate Kennedy was so fond of quoting Teddy Roosevelt, is a "bully pulpit." Among the multitudinous roles a President must fill, his greatest challenge and greatest power must be a blending of those of poet and preacher.

III

The Congress

7

THE CONDITIONING OF CONGRESSMEN

". . . The locality deems no man a fit representative who has not by residence in its limits, and by making it his political home, the place where he exercises his civic rights, become soaked with its own local sentiment."

JAMES BRYCE, 1888 [1]

———

Fragmentation of power in Washington is nowhere more visible than in the breeding of congressmen. Compare, for example, the ambitious young American with his counterpart in England, both of whom by brains and temperament can lay claim to leadership.

In England, even in recent times, the boy aspiring to be Prime Minister does well to attend one of the more prominent public—which means, in fact, private—preparatory schools. He moves in natural course to a leading university. Quite early, he is apt to be marked as a politician of promise. Upon graduation, he often goes directly to London where, if he is particularly fortunate, he finds apprenticeship in or near his party headquarters. In time, he is assigned a constituency, usually a hopeless one at the beginning, to test his powers as a vote getter. With experience, he is promoted to a less marginal constituency where his talents and his party's strength may secure his election. He returns to London as a Member of Parliament. Despite fairly wretched conditions of pay and accommodation, he can confidently expect to make a lifetime career in the highest politics of his nation.

Of course the young Englishman's career may be shaped by historical circumstances. He may be unseated at the next general election and, if his party is in serious decline, he may fail to scramble back into office. Usually, however, the M. P. looks forward to a considerable stay in the House of Commons.

There the road to greatness lies along well-marked ways. The member must develop skill in the thrust and parry of parliamentary debate. The young member, particularly of the Opposition party, first attracts notice by his facility during the Question Period. Perhaps too much emphasis is placed on the cunning wit and the overpolished rhetoric; still, it is an art requiring agility and, at the same time, a sense of discretion. The hothead is not likely to go far.

There are other prerequisites to advancement. Lacking the rigid committee assignments of the U. S. congressman, the young Member of Parliament usually defines areas in which he strives to become proficient. But he does not limit himself to a specialty, domestic or foreign. As the years pass, he acquires stature through his prowess at parliamentary in-fighting and his wisdom in addressing himself to the troublesome problems of the times. Depending on talent and temperament, and the turn of events, he moves ahead. If his party is in opposition, he stands in line for a post in the Shadow Cabinet preparing for the takeover of power. In power, he may become a parliamentary undersecretary, a junior minister, a minister and ultimately, perhaps, Her Majesty's Prime Minister.

This is an escalator which has accommodated itself to change while changing very little. Entrance to universities today has become more democratically diversified. The son of the workingman stands a better chance of getting on the escalator, but he still must go through the conditioning process. He must prove his merit in the closed society of the House of Commons.

Consider, by way of contrast, how an aspiring young politician makes his way in the United States. The paths are more various yet curiously narrow. In the matter of schooling, the much publicized examples of Franklin D. Roosevelt, who attended Groton, and John F. Kennedy, Choate, tend to disguise the fact that the distinguished preparatory schools have been singularly barren of graduates who win elective office. (This has caused acute concern to the trustees of one of the oldest and best, the Phillips Exeter Academy.)

Similarly, while Harvard University has furnished goodly numbers—mostly of its faculty—to fill appointive posts in Washington, the young politician desiring to go to Congress would do well to attend his state university. For someone from the non-New England regions, the Ivy League counterparts of Oxford and Cambridge are not ideal places from which to commence a political career.

Political life for the migrant in America bears out Thomas Wolfe's discovery that "you can't go home again." Neither can the displaced young man go anywhere else with a reasonable certainty of breaking into politics in a big way. The entrance requirements, as in the past, are pretty well limited to the home-town boy who stayed close to home.

On completing his formal education, the worst possible apprenticeship for the young politician is to seek a job at national party headquarters. A job in the Washington bureaucracy is hardly more helpful, especially if it delays too long his return home. To be sure, handicaps have been overcome. Stuart Symington returned to his adopted state of Missouri after a decade of service in appointive positions in the government and managed to get himself elected Senator. Ken Hechler performed an even more prodigious feat. Having served as an assistant to President Truman, he shrewdly picked a constituency for himself in West Virginia, secured a teaching position in a small college there, and returned to Washington a short time later as Congressman. But these are the exceptions, noteworthy because they are rare.

Once the ambitious young politician has arrived in Congress, he finds the paths of advancement well defined. He hopes to get, by fortune or favor, a committee assignment where his interest lies. He does well to devote himself to the work of his committee and to avoid trespassing on others. Having acquired a bit of seniority he aspires to become chairman of a subcommittee. Using this as his platform, he may begin to attract attention to himself.

Attracting attention in Congress is by no means limited to activity in the cloakrooms and committee chambers, or to delivery of speeches in the Senate or House. It is seldom measured by the brilliance of debate. Rather, the aspiring young congressman has to find ways of communicating directly to the nation at large. He learns those techniques of news-making which will produce for him headline inches and television time. He devises ways of being heard outside Washington so that he will be listened to within the city. The cultivation of publicity becomes for him a necessary art. This dimension of politics has only recently begun to develop among the M. P.'s.

In Congress, as in Parliament, there is profit for the member who has mastered his subject. The difference lies in how each exercises that mastery. The young congressman has much more incentive to become an individual entrepreneur, to develop contacts among the press, cultivate a following among the pressure groups, and establish liaisons with key members of the Executive.

There is a quieter way to power in Congress, but it is limited to a comparative few. They are the safe ones who, by virtue of geographical fortune rather than party choice, represent the less closely contested constituencies. They are the favored ones who are escalated inexorably up the ladder of seniority. They need acquire no special competence nor spend much time cultivating the press and other outsiders. Any liaisons with the Executive are initiated by eager representatives of the Executive, not by them. They grow accustomed to dealing *à deux* with the President himself. They deal with one another charily, as feudal barons —which indeed they are.

For other members this way of life is remote. Those who must work the hardest to survive the political hurdles back home are least likely to surmount the barriers on the way to acquisition of power in Congress. In the Senate, the path to power is less circumscribed than in the House. After his freshman indoctrination, during which he is supposed to observe a vow of silence, the senator has more freedom for enterprise. He can achieve notoriety as well as a certain amount of influence if, like the maverick Senator Wayne Morse, he goes against the established order hard enough and noisily enough. But Morse is unique among senators. Others, like Hubert Humphrey, discover that they must show restraint in challenging the prerogatives of the hierarchs. Humphrey learned his lesson when, as a freshman, he raised questions about a sinecure chairmanship bestowed on the venerable Senator Harry Byrd of Virginia. It was a relevant matter, but Humphrey found himself the victim of a merciless boycott by his colleagues. An apt learner, Humphrey has gone on to become the Senate's Assistant Majority Leader.

Much has been written about admission to the so-called Inner Club of the two bodies. It takes credentials which have little to do with the ability to debate substantive issues. In fact, members of the Inner Club may differ widely on substantive issues. But they share a common attitude that differences should be negotiated, preferably in the quiet of the back rooms away from the public glare. During such negotiations, proper reverence must be shown toward

the rules and traditions of Congress even when they serve
to buttress a minority position. The ruling spirit is not too
different from Calhoun's ancient doctrine of concurrent
majority, which imposed the veto on government in the
absence of common consent from all the sectional power
groups. The aspirant for membership in the Inner Club
learns to heed the various voices in Congress precisely in
ratio to their vested power.

For those in the Senate and House who are officially designated "the leadership," the path to power is ordinarily
smooth and peaceful. During the past quarter-century,
there has been only one violent overthrow, when, in the
House of Representatives, Minority Leader Joseph Martin,
aged and ailing, was replaced against his will in 1959 by
younger and tougher Charles Halleck who differed very little on party doctrine. After Sam Rayburn died in 1961,
John McCormack, who had been behind him, moved one
rung up the ladder and became Speaker. In the Senate, the
contest for the posts of Majority and Minority Leader has
been at times more spirited, but it is seldom less predictable.

An important test for the leaders of the majority party is
their capacity to carry accommodation one step further to
include the occupant of the White House. (This situation
varies when, as during the latter six years of the Eisenhower Administration, the White House and Congress are
controlled by different parties, necessitating a mixed liai-
son.) The ambassadorial function of the leadership must
be two-way. Woe to the House or Senate leader who starts
to think of himself simply as the President's man!

The duty of the Minority Leaders, to paraphrase one of
the most famous of them, the late Senator Robert A. Taft,
is to oppose. Unlike Parliamentary opposition leaders, they
feel no great compulsion to offer a set of alternative policies.
Indeed, coalescing the strongest opposition in Congress usually means allowing the greatest possible latitude for each
member to be against the Administration, no matter how

contradictory the reasons. This develops qualities in the minority leadership which, as in the case of Taft after the GOP victory of 1952, are not readily transferable when the time comes to assume power and responsibility as the majority.

The succession of Kennedy and Johnson may mean that the Senate road to the Presidency is not so impassable, perhaps even reversing the old situation when the Governor's office with its greater political bargaining power provided the surer route. But no matter how powerful they may be within the hierarchy, most members of Congress have scant anticipation of ever moving into positions of Executive leadership. The reason for this is mostly of their own choosing; unlike members of Parliament, they would be obliged to forfeit their seats to make the move—an occasion usually reserved for retirement or defeat. During the past two decades, only one incumbent congressman—Stewart Udall, who became Kennedy's Secretary of the Interior—has quit to take a Cabinet post. On the other hand, two Cabinet members have resigned to run for the Senate: Eisenhower's Secretary of Interior, Douglas McKay, and Kennedy's Secretary of Health, Education and Welfare, Abraham Ribicoff. Even a top appointive position in the Executive was not so enticing as the independent power of freshman Senator.

Washington is ruled largely by congressmen without executive experience and by appointive bureaucrats who may rise to lofty positions without having pounded a precinct pavement or pushed a constituent's doorbell. This absence of common background adds fury to the continuing war between the branches. Within the Executive, there is too often disregard or disdain for the more earthy aspects of the political process. Within the Congress, attitudes toward the government's business are often shaped with a happy sense of not having to run that business. The congressman tends to become an accomplished second guesser. Even when he uses seignorial powers to intrude into policy formulation, he can be certain that no public board of review will ever ferret out his role or assign a share of the praise or blame to him.

Which is the better apprenticeship for power, the parliamentary system or ours? The British system, according to its critics, has definite limitations. It tends to be too stylized, too encouraging to the glib and cautious, too lacking in opportunity for the genuine entrepreneur. It works best, it is said, for the assimilated society, not one riven with ethnic, economic, and sectional stresses. Most pertinent of all, it could not be adopted in the United States without adopting the whole parliamentary structure of government —a remote and unappealing possibility.

Still, a comparison of the two systems is useful, if only to note the frustration for the talented young man in Washington who intends to pursue a career in his nation's politics. Anyone who spends much time among the congressmen and the bureaucrats can observe this frustration manifested in personal form. But the frustration goes deeper than the purely personal. In the far-flung activities of the American Executive, there can be assigned vast responsibility without adequate conditioning in the uses of power. Within the hierarchical enclaves of Congress, there can be great accumulation of power without the proper checks of responsibility.

8

CONGRESS: THE SEARCH
FOR ROLE

*"The first thing that a freshman Congressman must
learn is that he's pretty small potatoes in Washington, for
it is an unfortunate fact that as the federal government
continues to expand its functions, the Congressman finds
himself more and more a pleader of special problems and
a prisoner of the mailbox."*
WILLIAM W. BROOM, 1962 [1]

For the casual onlooker who visits the Capitol in Washington, perspective often depends on which portion of the
anatomy he happens to observe. He may watch the main
show for hours on end without benefit while its principal activity consists of scattered clusters of men and
women sustaining one another in barely audible mono-
tones amidst the vast emptiness of the Senate or House
chamber. Intermittently, a ringing of the bells brings relief
to the tedium, flushing other members from the Capitol's
hundred nooks and crannies and the more distant office
buildings. Once in a long while, a sudden word—a parliamentary inquiry or a motion—brings the leaders to their
feet and indicates that wit, too, can enter the proceedings.

The observer who spends much time on Capitol Hill
knows that the chamber drama is at best only a shadow
image of what goes on. He counts himself lucky to be pres-

ent during those celebrated moments when an impassioned oration may markedly affect the course of the legislative process or, more frequently, when a maladroit argument loses vital votes. But these are the rare spectacles. Most of the time the real drama is going on elsewhere—in the cloakrooms and corridors, in the inner sanctums of the leaders, in the member's own office.

There is paradox in this dispersal. Congress has staved off decline of its powers better than other parliamentary bodies of the western world. It retains a respectable capacity to consider and amend legislation, to revise revenue and appropriation bills, and to foreclose initiatives taken by the Executive. Neither of its two Houses has become subservient to the other in the manner of the British House of Lords. In the close division between majority and minority—closely divided by persuasion even when not by party line-up—the outcome of major legislative battles may turn on critically narrow margins. Modern Congress has played a cliffhanger drama, lending added role to each member.

Why then is there such lack of focus in the Legislative branch? In 1961, by a vote of 185 to 186, as Congressman Clem Miller of California wryly wrote to his constituents, ". . . the Administration's compromise upon a compromise of the original compromise on the Minimum Wage Bill . . . went down to defeat during this session." Sixty-four members had failed to record themselves. The easy explanation, Miller noted, was that the motion was brought up on a teller vote (*i.e.,* a head count) which did not allow time for absent members to hurry over from their offices. But there remained the question why the members were not present in the chamber.

Congressman Miller attempted an answer:

> So much of what occurs on the Floor is routine. There are only rare occasions when circumstances *demand* one's presence. Thus, what is of overriding significance gives way to what is immediate. The competing interests, the endless details of congressional routine, take hold. Members are

called to the Floor for a quorum call as the afternoon's debate begins. Soon, nearly everyone arrives to answer his name. Most stay for a while, listening and chatting. Then, inevitably, the drift begins. Pages hurry up and down the aisles with sheaves of messages, calling a congressman to argue with an executive department on behalf of a constituent, or to tell a garden club delegation why he favors the Shasta daisy for the national flower. Or the Member goes downstairs for lunch, or over to the Senate, or downtown to a conference. Gradually he is caught up in the inescapable workaday world of Congress. Almost without volition, he finds himself back in his office trying to keep up with the mail, interviewing and being interviewed by a stream of callers. Now, he is too far away to get back to the Floor for a teller vote. Once away from the Chamber, he is far away. The urgency, the insistence, is gone. A million words of testimony, the results of a thousand patient meetings may be going down the drain. But it is another world from the congressional office.[2]

Clem Miller had come to Washington from California as a result of the Democratic upsurge of 1958. In 1960, he got himself re-elected, and in 1962 was seeking a third term when his chartered plane crashed into a mountain during a campaign trek. He left a legacy of letters, written mostly to campaign associates and friends, which offer valuable insight into a junior congressman's search for role in Washington. These letters convey the loneliness of the sensitive congressman. Miller tried the frenetic social life of the Capital city—"a congressman can eat out five and six nights a week if he wishes to"—and decided to stay home in the evenings. "The feeling will not down that behind the tenderloin steak is the cold and indifferent practicality of the Washington lobby." [3] He found similar disappointment in dealing with the press. "I have talked to them in the Speaker's Lobby, but it is difficult for me to talk to newspapermen. I don't seem to have the hang of it. I don't like to talk in clichés and the headline phrase does not come easily . . . We have become a nation of headline readers. It is not at all surprising that the working press has come to require the same of politicians in its day-to-day reporting . . . It means that many capable legislators operate fairly silently, while others who might be of inferior competence are heard from quite frequently." [4]

Miller's most persistent unease was stirred by continuing uncertainty about the member's role in the House itself. He felt the restiveness described by Woodrow Wilson: ". . . No man, when chosen to the membership of a body possessing great powers and exalted prerogatives, likes to have his activity repressed, and himself suppressed, by imperative rules and precedents which seem to have been framed for the deliberate purpose of making usefulness unattainable by individual members. Yet such the new member finds the rules and precedents of the House to be." [5] The young California congressman concluded that, "The idea of the House as a forum for public expression is a huge fiction which should be recognized. Debate in the House is usually a shallow thing, difficult to follow, and it must be very difficult to report. Therefore, the press pays almost no attention to debate in the House. Reporters are where power is. They won't waste their valuable time in the House press gallery unless an important vote is to be taken. They are to be found in the Speaker's Lobby where the powerful are." [6]

Miller observed that others frequenting the Speaker's Lobby have power besides the Speaker. He felt keen disappointment over the Speaker's impotence before the committee oligarchs. He described an experience as member of a deputation calling on Speaker Rayburn to try to get action on the Depressed Areas Bill which was bottled up in the Rules Committee. During the interview, the Speaker repeatedly pointed toward the Rules Committee chambers directly overhead and displayed no eagerness to challenge the power residing there. Finally, pressed hard, Rayburn wished to know whether Miller and his colleagues could produce the needed votes on a floor test. They assured him they could—by a wide margin. Miller commented ruefully, "And right here is raised the dilemma of the Leadership. Yes, they lead, but they lead only because they win. If they cannot be certain of winning, they don't want to go. Latent power, negative power, is so much better than power committed that lacks victory as a capstone. Hence, the legislative timidity of the Congress, both House and Senate." [7]

Miller's ponderings led him inevitably to question the distribution of power in Congress. He recognized that the individual member could build or destroy a certain amount of legislative influence among fellow members who are keen judges of his "strengths and weaknesses, foibles and tricks." But he saw, too, that the more potent power is "hierarchical" in its nature. "Power adheres to committee chairmen and filters slowly down to the lower ranks," he wrote.

For the ordinary member competing with the massive power of hierarchy, Miller offered no simple solutions. He himself joined the Democratic Study Group, a cluster of northern liberals seeking to use their combined power more effectively. But he had no illusions about the group. Was the DSG, he asked himself, "a spearhead for liberal legislation? Or would closer description say that it constitutes a counterweight for the use of the Leadership? Propulsive or kinetic? It is difficult to say."

Miller had not resolved these dilemmas at the time of his death. He talked with this writer a short time before his fatal campaign trip, sitting in the Speaker's Lobby late one evening during the debate over foreign aid appropriations. The atmosphere was heavy with pending trouble for the program, particularly from southern Democrats whose region gradually has shifted away from its former attachment to internationalism. Miller was troubled about shifts in his own power base. His campaign probings back home had revealed widespread apathy toward foreign aid and other important issues of foreign policy. The young congressman wondered how long he could survive while sticking to his own set of legislative priorities against constituency pressures to become more parochial.

Possibly Miller was unduly pessimistic that evening. The fact is that even after his death—too close to the election for his name to be removed from the ballot—the voters gave him a handsome majority.

The Senate once had a justified reputation as forum for debate. Today, that reputation is mostly a memory. One of the last of the sustained discussions of foreign policy was stimulated in 1951 by Senator Taft's dissent over dispatching troops to Western Europe. Major shifts of strategy have taken place under Eisenhower and Kennedy without provoking great debate. When Senate Majority Leader Mike Mansfield proposed, during a lull in the Berlin crisis, that the body discuss possible alternatives to administration policy, he found no takers. The opening of the debate on the Trade Expansion Act, surely an auspicious occasion, required seven quorum calls. As one disgruntled correspondent reported, "Even when the Senate does attempt debate, on most subjects this consists merely of the monotonous reading, often unrelated in time, of prepared manuscripts. Zealous readers of the *Congressional Record* for September, 1962, will find, for example, carefully researched speeches about Katanga. One day Connecticut's Senator Dodd complained bitterly that U. S. policy in Katanga was foolish. Two days later Senator Church of Idaho replied and three days after that Senator Humphrey delivered a second response." [8]

The same reporter compared the nature of senatorial duty, present and past. "The pre-Civil War Senators of memory—Calhoun, Webster, Clay, Benton—devoted years of study to the big issues. Now the pace is frantic and the time for reflection minimal. Today's Senators must run errands for growing numbers of constituents, greet visitors, be seen at social functions, tend to commitee work, berate bureaucrats, investigate, approve reports, placate friends, and, alas, a number must accept far-off speaking engagements for pay to balance the family budget. The typical Senator also must dig hard into the pork barrel on behalf of constituents for contracts, projects, loans. His prospects for reelection may depend far more on what he can deliver than on the quality of his debating style. As the pace quickens, senatorial bureaucracy flourishes. More and more, speeches bear the cold touch of the ghost writer. The frantic schedule inevitably cuts deeply into the time available for attendance on the Senate floor. Except when bells clamor for a vote, it is unusual to find more than one-tenth of the membership in the Senate chamber. Debaters require listeners, and empty chairs do not provoke the best in a man." [9]

Both Houses of Congress have a goodly quota of able members soberly concerned about problems that go beyond their narrow constituencies and troubled about the role they are called on to play. Some try to speak as the conscience of Congress. From time to time individual members have stood up to voice deep anxieties about their common condition, and little knots of colleagues invariably gather about to congratulate the speaker for his wisdom, shake his hand and then go their separate ways.

The dilemmas lie deep. The quest for effective power has become tied up inextricably with the search for knowledge. It expresses itself in terms of bitter competition with the expert forces of the Executive. Congress is constantly torn between the temptation to build its own bureaucracy of experts and the fear that this could lead to further dispersal of its powers.

Against the vaunted expertise of the Executive, Congress displays a sense of inferiority which manifests itself in various ways. Cursed be the official who tries to cut off its sources of information! Lewis Strauss, the first Cabinet appointee to be rejected since 1925, annoyed the Senators for many reasons, but the central complaint about his prior service as Chairman of the Atomic Energy Commission was that he "wouldn't tell us the things we need to know."

Asserting the Constitutional provision that the President "shall from time to time give . . . information of the State of the Union," Congress has exacted from the Executive a constant stream of reports. Most of them are of limited utility. A former member of Congress has commented bitingly on the "life cycle" of the government report: "In the final stage . . . the entire text of the report reads as follows: 'To the Honorable————: I have the high honor to transmit herewith our annual report for the past year. Respectfully Submitted.' Then there follows from two to two hundred pages of indigestible statistical tables. The tragedy is that the Chief Executive and the legislators will both tolerate such as a mockery of the reporting function." [10]

Yet the effort to track down and corral the necessary knowledge engages innumerable posses in Congress. In recent years, this investigative function has increased by leaps and bounds. Hundreds of sleuths are employed by congressional committees. It provides a time-consuming occupation for those in the Executive who must satisfy this voracious appetite for information. An enterprising member compiled statistics to prove that top Defense Department military and civil personnel spent the equivalent of 1,200 days in testifying and preparing testimony during a recent session of Congress.

Hard-pressed committee staff directors vie to produce the higher ups in government as well as experts who can be lured away from universities and laboratories to serve as witnesses. The more high-brow hearings take on the attributes of the university seminar. A probe by the Joint Economic Committee into employment and growth may be divided into a dozen subcategories, each continuing over an extended period. Published hearings run to tens of dozens of the thick volumes with green or tan covers that Congress dispenses freely to all who express an interest.

One comparatively new departure for Congress as a research institution has been the practice of farming out study projects to outsiders. The Senate Foreign Relations Committee set the pace when it decided that the time had come for "an exploration in depth of U. S. foreign policies throughout the world." A project assigned to the Center for International Affairs at Harvard was entitled "The Principal Ideological Conflicts, Variations Thereon, Their Manifestations and Their Present and Potential Impact on Foreign Policy of the United States."

There is more than a touch of pathos in this latter-day rush to the house of intellect. The results give evidence that members are in danger of falling victim to the special jargon of the academics. A Senate Foreign Relations Committee project, "Possible Nonmilitary Scientific Developments and Their Potential Impact on Foreign Policy Problems of the United States," reached the conclusion in ninety-seven pages of weighty words and line graphs that scientific developments will indeed have an enormous impact on foreign policy problems. The report recommended a further study of "specific foreign policy problems on which research and development would appear to offer good prospect of beneficial results. . . ."

The trouble is that Congress lacks the capacity to assimilate this outpouring of the experts. The published volumes multiply and gather dust. The member grows fretful or, worse, becomes cynical, hemmed in by his expanding library of unread paperback tomes. One subcommittee chairman, an asiduous promoter of study projects, conceded that his reports would never be read by his colleagues but argued that the congressional imprimatur still serves to stimulate public interest—which, he felt, serves to stimulate Congress. By his description, Congress is thus engaged in a multicycle agitation resembling the modern washing machine.

It is a noteworthy fact that many of the great probes conducted by congressional committees wind up inconclusively. Some, like the lengthy House investigation of the regulatory commissions, are content to expose a few malfunctions and avoid the larger legislative challenges. Others make zealous findings which are just as zealously ignored by their parent bodies. Now and again, a publicity break can produce legislative results that a thousand days of testimony would not ensure. In 1962, the news resulting from the tragic effects of the drug, Thalidomide, revived Senator Kefauver's near-dormant probe of the drug industry and sent a bill for stiffer federal controls through both Houses without a dissenting vote.

Entrepreneurs in Congress learn to be resourceful in taking advantage of news developments and, indeed, in creating their own. The newcomer to the congressional hearing is constantly shocked to discover just how far this manipulation can be carried. One disgruntled witness at the Kefauver hearings remarked, ". . . the industries called to testify have the mistaken idea that something legal is going on. But there's nothing legal about it; it's a publicity battle and industry should respond in kind." [11]

To such complaints of sensationalism, the congressman makes counter complaints. A House committee chairman wrote this reporter a lengthy letter lamenting the lack of attention being paid to his "orderly" probe of the government's stockpiling program. "If we had emphasized only the more 'newsworthy' aspects of the case and capsuled some of the more glaring faults committed, a lot of splashy headlines might have resulted," he protested. "But they wouldn't have told the complete story, nor would our hearings really have detailed completely the ugly ramifications . . . nor served as a possible guide to 'how not to spend the taxpayers' money.' " [12] What the congressman was really saying was that Congress, lacking the prod of public attention, fails to pay attention to itself.

To borrow the late Senator Vandenberg's metaphor which has become a favorite cliché, Congress demands of the Executive policy-makers that it be part of the take-offs as well as the crash landings. This presents obvious problems as a way of directing a ship of state that now is space-bound. How to inject Congress into policy-making at the critical stages? The major issues bearing on the nation's defense provide the best example of the problem. After holding hundreds of interviews on Capitol Hill, one political scientist has reported, "Most Congressmen (and it is worth noting that most of these men were on relevant committees) assert that Congress has very little to say about military policy and allege that the military matters it is concerned with are the peripheral matters of production, waste, living conditions, etc. No one with whom I talked ever maintained that Congress has any significant role in the formulation of military policy. . . ." [13]

This is a terrible admission of failure in a period when advances in military policy have been so swift that the books on strategy, like the weapons, are often outdated before they are beyond the draft stage. The broad terms of the dialogue have shifted over a decade and a half from the Louis Johnson doctrine of meat-axe economy in our defenses, to the Dullesian doctrine of "massive retaliation" based on a comfortable capacity to obliterate the enemy, and hence to the McNamara doctrine of "counterforce" which assumes that each protagonist will be able to deliver deadly retaliation if the other protagonist strikes first.

Before these revolutionary developments, Congress has tried hard to adjust its review procedures. But even for committee members, defense is a confusing business. The hearings, often simultaneously conducted by the eight groups claiming some manner of jursidiction, not only create problems of scheduling but also cause a witness

K

to walk a tricky tightrope of consistency lest he appear to give a different shading of emphasis in his various appearances. The publicity mechanisms add to the confusion, part of the testimony being taken publicly, part in closed session. Part is rushed to the press in the statements of self-serving witnesses and committee members; other parts leak out gradually in the form of rumor. Substantial information is only released after the Pentagon censor has made his deletions and most of the news correspondents have lost interest. The member, trying to deal responsibly with data that is often highly classified, finds himself confronted with mental hazards.

The military vocabulary itself has become almost unintelligible to the non-expert. The member can no longer count on the old system of nomenclature that differentiated a bomber from a battleship. The names may be colloquial—Hound Dog or Sky Bolt; of historic literary significance—Davy Crockett, Little John, and an improved model, Honest John; derived from ancient mythology—Jupiter and Titan; or just plain bastardizations—Goer and Dynasoar. Minuteman belongs to the same species as Atlas, though of an advanced order, but Nike-Zeus is an altogether different weapon system from Nike-Ajax or Nike-Hercules.

The congressman finds himself bewildered when he examines the problem of the B-70 which was suddenly renamed the RS-70 for political rather than strategic reasons—Air Force logic deciding that a reconnaisance plane stood a better chance than did a bomber of getting appropriations. This manned aircraft was envisaged to fly at three times the speed of sound and to break the heat barrier. On airborne alert over the North Pole, it could be dispatched to Moscow ahead of a missile fired from the United States proper, its human crew providing a means of recall in the event the blip on the radar screen turned out to be something other than an enemy attack. But is the

RS-70 worth the billions of dollars needed to make it operational in the age of the missile? Both Eisenhower and Kennedy decided in the negative. Yet, leading committee members in Congress then decided otherwise. With remarkably little discussion, huge funds for the plane were voted by Congress year after year and duly impounded by the Executive.

Who was right? The President's critics argued that his decision had been dictated by an arbitrary budget ceiling. Critics of Congress argued that it was simply responding to constituency pressures induced by the airplane industry. Even as the debate went on, experts pointed out that the RS-70 was already obsolete, though still years before the plane could be operational. Thus, a major issue of military strategy as well as of Constitutional power reached a state of impasse.

Despite their clamor, the more realistic members of Congress accept the fact that there is no point in ultimate showdowns with the Executive. Once, during a controversy over Eisenhower's defense economies, a staff aide suggested to Chairman Richard Russell of the Senate Armed Services Committee that the only way to clear up the confusion was to demand a look at the Pentagon's war plans. To which Russell replied, "I can't help remembering that President Lincoln would have won his war a lot sooner if there hadn't been a congressional committee trying to run it for him."

The shrewd official in the Executive comes to know pretty expertly which bases on Capitol Hill have to be touched on which kinds of business. Some of these informal clearances have obvious value. A congressional patriarch like Carl Vinson, Chairman of House Armed Services, develops a sense of continuity during an advisory career that has spanned three wars and witnessed the growth of U. S. military might all the way from the cavalry and the one-ocean navy. A Secretary of Defense, whose average career has been two years in duration, does well to keep in touch with Mr. Vinson.

A great deal of this consultative business, however, has an unreal quality. The harassed official finds it the least troublesome, even if time-consuming, way of keeping Congress quiet. The members, particularly those not privy to this process, grow restive.

The zest for effective "oversight"—a term in increasing usage in Executive-Legislative relations—has led to a device of doubtful constitutionality known as the legislative veto. Initiated in the Executive Reorganization Act of 1939, it had all the appearances of a fair swap: The President was to be permitted to devise plans for better management of the growing bureaucracy; Congress, in turn, could reject a particular reorganization plan simply by adopting a concurrent resolution within a sixty-day period. Since 1939, more than twenty acts of Congress have provided for such a legislative veto. Several specified that the veto could be exercised by one House or the other. Still others bestowed the veto privilege on a single committee, and, in one instance, on a committee chairman.

As a result, this device has become a highly controversial way of sharing power. One senior congressman—advocating adoption of a legislative veto over Defense Department decisions to shut down military installations—stated the potential quite clearly: "Let us send this [veto authority] to our committee and the gentleman from Georgia and I will take care of the country as we have been doing. I know [Administration officials] are quite intrigued about getting the government out of business, but we do not want to destroy Joe Martin's Navy Yard, we do not want to destroy Jim Van Zandt's Navy Yard, we do not want to destroy Porter Hardy's Navy Yard . . ." [14] This particular veto provoked a lively squabble when the committee "disallowed" a number of base closings while President Eisenhower claimed that the veto authority was "invalid."

The dispute was still unresolved when Congress, because of committee rivalry over jurisdiction, allowed the provision to lapse. More recently, President Kennedy, confronted with a similar veto provision for the foreign aid program, declared that it was unconstitutional both as a violation of the separation of powers as well as an improper delegation of power to committee. Like his predecessors, however, Kennedy sought to avoid a direct Constitutional clash with Congress by heartily endorsing "the desirability of consultation between officials of the Executive branch and the committees."

So far, it should be noted, the advocates of the legislative veto have been curiously random in their efforts. They have not attempted to enter the area where the veto would be most logical—that is, over the issuance of regulations by the various Executive agencies.[15] This kind of review, long in practice in the British Parliament, does not appear to whet much appetite in Congress.

Much has changed since the era of congressional supremacy of the late nineteenth century described by Woodrow Wilson. But the change has only aggravated the ailment Wilson labeled "our disintegrate methods of legislation." Power in Congress is still parceled out among the standing committee chairmen. As government has grown infinitely bigger, these "petty barons," in Wilson's phrase, have found ever wider opportunities to display their strength.

In this feudal order, the great committees on appropriation—or rather their various subcommittees—hold marked advantages over the "authorizing" committees. Their techniques are simple and straightforward. Their members, concentrating on the item-by-item statistics of the budget sheet, are relieved of the abstractions that so bedevil their colleagues. Because they work behind closed doors, the outsider gets only inklings from the published hearings of a system that makes men like Otto E. Passman and John

J. Rooney and George Mahon, comparatively unknown elsewhere, into awesome figures in Washington. They work at great speed and with very little staff assistance to make decisions of staggering importance. And yet, before so great a task, they exert their power to the hilt. Senator William Fulbright, Chairman of Foreign Relations, has time and again raised objections to legislative riders affecting foreign policy which are tucked away in appropriation bills in violation of Congress's own rules.

Eugene McCarthy, one of the more thoughtful Senators who has weighed the dilemmas of Congress, has concluded there ought to be institutional change. He has declared, "The need in very general terms runs in two directions. One is in the direction of giving either more authority or more discretion in the use of authority to the President in such fields as public finance, expenditures, taxation, and foreign trade, and in extending existing programs or new programs over a longer period of time. The other is in the direction of involving Congress more directly and intimately in current policy decisions through possible extension of the idea of Joint Committee on Atomic Energy into such fields as foreign affairs, intelligence activities, space exploration, and decisions relating to the domestic economy." [16]

While yielding more to the President than most of his colleagues would, Senator McCarthy has suggested a way for Congress to play a more vital role that has long intrigued members. This is to combine forces, House and Senate, with the expectation of performing more effectively by acting jointly. The most ambitious effort in this direction arose out of the Legislative Reorganization Act of 1946 which provided for a "Joint Budget Committee," comprising all of the members of the House and Senate appropriation and revenue committees. Over a hundred men strong, the Committee was to meet each January and draw up an overall budget for the government during the coming year. When outlay was expected to exceed income, the

Committee would propose specific ways of restoring the balance; when revenue exceeded expenditure, it would suggest what to do with the surplus. In theory, Congress, by joint endeavor, would re-establish its rightful control over the government's purse strings.

In practice, the Joint Budget Committee on the Legislative was a bust. During its first year, anticipating a budget surplus, the Committee members fell to fighting over whether to cut taxes or reduce the national debt; they never reached a conclusion. In succeeding years, there was similar lack of results. Though this Committee remains a statutory obligation, it no longer even bothers to meet.

The experience of the Joint Economic Committee, also created by the Reorganization Act of 1946, has been more heartening. In recent years, it has managed to establish an important role in the annual review of the state of the economy. Directly following the issuance of the President's Economic Report, it summons not only the President's own advisers, but also independent experts from the universities and the business community, and by careful probing puts the Administration on guard against slipshod argument and poorly conceived policies. A number of the Committee members have acquired considerable skill in focusing the issues and helping set the terms of the nation's economic debate. The Joint Economic Committee also performs an educative role for Congress. Its deliberations on national growth rate, anticyclical policy and other problems are more in tune with the times than the nineteenth-century economic arguments debated in some of the committees.

A quite different example has been set by the Joint Committee on Atomic Energy. Created simultaneously with the Atomic Energy Commission by the McMahon Act of 1946, it soon managed to achieve a relationship to that agency which came close to serving as co-executor. The Joint Committee has helped determine the size and shape of the nation's nuclear stockpile, the nature of the weapons, the decision to produce the hydrogen bomb, the ill-fated billion-dollar investment in the nuclear airplane, as well as countless other atomic matters large and small. One prominent Committee member was prompted to declare that ". . . in the case of certain vital policy decisions, the urging from the Joint Committee has played so powerful a role that it can be said the Committee made the decisions, with the advice and consent of the executive branch." [17]

The intrusion of the Joint Atomic Energy Committee into the Executive realm has provoked bitter fighting in Washington. It has refused, usually with success, to accept the usual plea of Executive privilege by which certain inside information on decision making is withheld from Congress. It has regularly disregarded the procedures and budgetary controls laid down by the President. In invading the domain of the Atomic Energy Commission, it has used the same divide-and-conquer technique against the five Commissioners so often employed by the Executive against Congress. Partly for this reason, there has been a movement within the AEC to establish a single boss.

The Joint Committee on Atomic Energy can claim success for its energetic role. Without the Committee's prodding, a recent study concluded, "Almost certainly, the national investment in atomic energy would have been substantially less, and our present level of technology considerably less advanced." [18] Still, it was an achievement made outside the regular legislative process—indeed, without the broader involvement of Congress. This comparatively small group—nine members from each House—has served as "a legislative-administrative hybrid, whose operation has taken away from the Executive far more than it has given to Congress." [19]

A few years ago, Senator Albert Gore inaugurated a series of evening meetings to which he invited colleagues. They dined in the old Supreme Court Chamber in the

Capitol and joined in round-table discussions with invited guests. In attempting to explain the popularity of these occasions, Gore remarked, "Nowadays, we don't ever seem to have a chance to get together and talk things over."

This was a strange admission from a member of an institution supposedly dedicated to the proposition of getting together and talking things over. Gore hinted at a concern felt by many at the failure of Congress to come to grips with its business, at the way it sublets its powers and then has to devise frantic strategies to try to recoup them. These lonely members sense at times that too much of their job is being farmed out—to the experts, who bring it back more complicated than ever, and to the committee barons, who have the means of exercising power and the itch to do so.

Perhaps the inevitable trend in Congress is toward ever greater delegation to its subgroups, which in turn seek their hybrid relationships with the Executive. But before such a development is accepted as the logical role for Congress in an age of big government, there is need to examine more closely the baronial power of the committees.

THE NATURE OF
BARONIAL POWER

"Power is nowhere concentrated; it is rather deliberately and of set policy scattered amongst many small chiefs. These petty barons, some of them not a little powerful, but none of them within reach of the full powers of rule, may at will exercise an almost despotic sway within their own shires . . ."

WOODROW WILSON, 1884 [1]

"The committees with their chairmen are like a string of forts . . . the attackers . . . are spread out, with poor communications and hence poor coordination. They have no base of power from which to menace the chairmen . . ."

CONGRESSMAN CLEM MILLER, 1962 [2]

Nothing illustrates better the power structure of Congress than the latter-day celebrity of Congressman Wilbur Mills. For many years a comparatively obscure member, Mills burst suddenly into national prominence. In the opening week of one recent session, he was the subject of cover-story treatment in the leading news magazines. During adjournment, his modest headquarters in the Post Office of Kensett, Arkansas, is regularly besieged with calls from press and President's men alike.

The explanation for such celebrity is simple. Through

seniority, Mills had achieved the Chairmanship of the House Committee on Ways and Means which was entrusted with initial review of a large amount of the major legislation considered vital by the Kennedy Administration: reciprocal trade, tax reform and reduction, old age medical assistance, unemployment compensation, and regulation of the national debt ceiling. The fortunes of the late President depended to no small degree on his capacity to work with the Chairman.

The contrast between the two men's rise to power could not be more striking. Congress had served merely as a way station for John Kennedy, never fully absorbing his energies as he sought and attained national leadership. The Chairman, on the other hand, had never been tempted by leadership beyond the confines of the House of Representatives. Mills came to Washington when still a very young man, representing a rural district which was then the second least populous in the nation. Over the years he has been contested only twice by a Democratic opponent, never by a Republican. Mills has reciprocated this devotion. Year after year, he has driven home the day after Congress adjourns and remained there till the opening of the next session. He has never been abroad.

Mills got his Ways and Means Committee assignment reportedly because Speaker Rayburn admired his legal acumen. Removed from the more dramatic spectacles of Congress, he has labored at legislation that few of his colleagues even pretend to understand. Because of an early start up the committee ladder, he was able to reach the top at the comparatively youthful age of forty-eight. He heads one of the oldest and most eminent fiefdoms in Congress.

Established in 1789, the Ways and Means Committee was, until the Civil War, a sort of House within the House, having charge of both revenue and appropriation measures. Today, despite the later proliferation of committees, Ways and Means still retains all its original jurisdiction over the revenue side of the ledger and now includes the various welfare programs containing built-in tax features. As stipulated by the Constitution, revenue measures must originate on the House side—a fact which allows Mills' group to claim precedence over its counterpart in the other body, the Senate Finance Committee. The Committee also enjoys precedence in the House itself where, by tradition, revenue measures are brought up under a rule prohibiting amendments offered from the floor. This means that ordinary members have no opportunity to tinker. A complicated tax bill is usually allotted two days of debate, then voted up or down.

With such power there have developed extraordinary efforts to ensure stability in the Ways and Means Committee. No matter how widely the party ratio in the House shifts, the Committee keeps a fixed ratio—three to two— of majority and minority members. It meets mostly in plenary session, all twenty-five members usually faithful in attendance. Assignments to the Committee regularly go to the senior and the safe. Most recently, ten of the fifteen Democratic members have represented either southern one-party constituencies or big city ones tightly controlled by the party machine. Six of the ten minority members are from solidly Republican, rural districts.

As he presides over his domain, Chairman Mills must reckon with various forces. Committee members tend toward specialization. One has been an ardent defender of the nation's thrift institutions, working to preserve the low tax status of the mutual savings and loan companies. Another, from Kentucky, has kept a close watch over tax proposals affecting liquor, tobacco, and race tracks. Still another, representing a port city, has been keenly interested in revenues derived from foreign commerce and overseas investment.

Tax reform provides a good case study of the testing of the Chairman's power. The U. S. tax code, once a thin document, now numbers over a thousand pages, incorporating ninety-two chapters and thousands of sections. Almost everything after Chapter One's "Normal Taxes and Surtaxes" is for the purpose of specifying the exceptions to the normal. Vast sectors of the nation's economy have been nurtured in the interstices of the code. As Mills and his Committee colleagues attempt to revise this fantastic document, they discover that each comma and codicil affects somebody's vital interests; each loophole in the law is buttressed by powerful pressure groups.

The Chairman sets the tempo for the deliberations, both visible and invisible. After the public hearings on Treasury proposals, there are lengthy Executive sessions, marked at intervals by the issuance of mimeographed releases entitled "Discussion Draft" or "Tentative Decisions for the Purpose of Drafting Language." Each release provokes renewed activity, both from the Treasury Department and the lobbyists, carried on behind the closed doors of the individual Committee members. It is a period of urgent persuasions. During 1961 revisions, a senior Committee member expelled from his office a hotel magnate who grew arrogant in claiming the right to tax-exempt status for his membership in five country clubs. On the other hand, Mills and others were favorably impressed by a magazine publisher's plea that his yacht had served as his major means of promotional advertising.

Though the language of proposed amendments passes back and forth between the Committee and the staff of the Joint Committee on Internal Revenue Taxation for technical draftsmanship, Mills retains a firm control over the schedule. Many drafts go through five or six rewrites. Nobody else can be entirely sure when the process is at an end. During the 1961 revisions, Mills engineered a series of delicate compromises between Treasury demands for tightening the code and the entreaties of those who were being squeezed. Savings and loan assiociations, which formerly paid a pittance in federal income taxes, suddenly

found their exemptions almost eliminated. Then the powerful U. S. Savings and Loan League made its presence felt
on Capitol Hill and the Committee came up with a second
draft, reducing the estimated tax yield by about half. (More
than one-fourth of the congressmen, it has been estimated,
have affiliations with savings and loan institutions.) Co-
operatives, previously exempted, were taxed, but the Rural
Electrification Administration Co-ops, having a formidable
lobby group, managed to remain untouched.

Mills pays close heed to pressures from all sides. The
Administration's proposal to tax overseas earnings of U. S.
corporations was watered down drastically despite Treasury
protests. But when the director of the AFL-CIO Department of Legislation announced that this would make the
whole bill obnoxious to organized labor, Mills immediately
inserted an amendment that restored much of what both
Treasury and the AFL-CIO wanted.

The Chairman offers no apologies for all this weighing
and balancing, but considers that it is an indispensable
part of the legislative process. He argues that his primary
concern must be to coalesce majority support for a bill in
Committee and in the full House. The Ways and Means
Chairman, he believes firmly, must guard a reputation for
invincibility if his handicraft is not to be torn apart by the
competing pressures.

The critic can argue in turn that this is hardly a very
rational way to arrive at a tax code. It has the same smell
of special interest that characterized tariff legislation until
the reciprocal trade program transferred rate fixing authority to the Executive. Now that taxation is regarded as a
major instrument of government's economic policy, there
is need for speed and flexibility in combatting the cyclical
swings which Mills and his colleagues cannot supply.

Yet as long as Congress involves itself in the specifics of
taxation, it would be difficult to devise an alternative system to the one administered by Chairman Mills. Tax reform could never be handled in plenary session. It is a job

that must be delegated to a small group and firmly directed by a skillful leader. Though a product of the seniority system, Mills displays uncommon capacity for his job, dealing with the technicians on their own terms and treating representatives from the Executive as consultants rather than antagonists. Perhaps because of his provincial origins, he appears comparatively unencumbered by constituency pressure that might impose a conflict of interest on important tax matters. From a President's point of view, Mr. Mills is one of the hierarchs who helps to make congressional relations tolerable.

By way of contrast, consider the role of Congressman Otto Passman, Chairman of the House Appropriations Subcommittee on Foreign Operations. Passman, a self-styled "country boy" from the rural delta country of Louisiana, is a professed enemy of the foreign aid program which he oversees. He has voted against every aid authorization bill since the Greek-Turkish program, which he supported shortly after he arrived in Congress in 1947. A high-strung, erratic man, he dresses in dapper silk suits and delivers impassioned speeches accompanied by weird gyrations of hip and shoulder known to his colleagues as the "Passman dance." Both Presidents Eisenhower and Kennedy first attempted to deal with the Chairman on a man-to-man basis, and both soon gave up in disgust.

Though he affects folksy friendliness in his dealings with the Executive, Chairman Passman breathes hostility toward every attempt at persuasion. His suspicion-ridden description of the efforts made by the Kennedy Administration to sell the AID program gives a clue to his state of mind:

First, the Administration requested an excessive amount for foreign aid. They pulled Douglas Dillon out of the Treasury to testify for the program with his usual smile and personality, overstating the case, as usual. Second, the

Democratic party was brought in with [National Chairman John M.] Bailey sending wires to Democratic officials all over the country trying to get them to exert pressure on Congress in behalf of the program. Third, an epistle from Doug and Dean [Secretary of the Treasury Dillon and Secretary of State Rusk], blowing up the reasons for the program, was sent to all Members of Congress. Fourth, the program was talked up at State Department briefings for editors. Fifth, the President of Pakistan [Ayub Khan] was invited here by [Vice-President Lyndon B.] Johnson to give a pep talk for foreign aid. Sixth, the Citizens' Committee for International Development was organized to exert further pressure. Seventh, I was interviewed on 'Meet the Press' by hostile questioners who I think tried to make me look silly. Eighth, [House Majority Leader John W.] McCormack was elected to write 2,400 mayors across the U. S. A.—including some in my own district—on behalf of the program. Ninth, [Peace Corps Director] Sargent Shriver made a personal visit to every office on the Hill. He was coming in behalf of the Peace Corps, but foreign aid was mixed in. Tenth, when we were ready to mark up the bill in Subcommittee I jotted down some figures to show my thinking. A Republican Subcommittee member leaked the figures to the President a few hours before Subcommittee action. But despite terrific pressure from downtown, the Subcommittee backed me up. Eleventh, the White House kept contacting business groups all over the country until 2 a.m. in the morning of full Committee action [Sept. 1] asking businessmen to pressure Committee Members into reversing the Subcommittee cuts. While I was presenting the Subcommittee report in the full Committee meeting, Administration agents continued to place telephone calls to Committee members in the room. During the same meeting, letters from an Assistant Secretary of State to Committee members, all calling for more funds, were actually slipped under the door.[3]

"Am I just supposed to take what they tell me they need every year for foreign aid, and just go ahead and vote it, or should I earn my money and sweat the facts out of these people?" Passman asked one reporter.[4] There is a difference between Passman's "facts" and those of the foreign aid administrators. He is glib in reciting the book-keeping statistics of the program, regularly playing tricks with the unexpended balances in order to prove that the program is overfunded. AID administrators begin to despair of ever setting the record straight. This inclination to play tricks can go further. Once, Passman telephoned the Secretary of Treasury during committee meeting and, while the other members listened to his side of the conversation, appeared to evoke consent to a deep slash in the Latin American aid fund. Afterward, when a suspicious member double-checked, it was discovered that the Secretary had done no such thing.

The Chairman can be callous with lesser officials of the Executive, suddenly scheduling hearings on Saturdays or extending them late into the evenings. The record of these closed-door affairs, published in several fat volumes as evidence of Passman's diligence, are regularly censored of his more unbridled views. Still, it is possible to get the smell of these proceedings. At the outset of the hearings in 1962, while the Secretary of State waited, the Chairman read aloud a news story which claimed derisively that he, Passman, was softening his hostility toward the program. The year before he had labelled it "idiotic," earlier that same year "asinine" but recently only "preposterous."

The hearings resemble an inquisition more than a sober, intelligent effort to get at the troublesome problems of foreign aid. Passman shows himself obsessed with minutiae but little concerned with trying to grasp the fundamental facts and fallacies of economic development. He monopolizes the questioning, and always appears convinced that he is talking to a pack of congenital liars. In 1962, one AID official, the assistant administrator for the Africa-Europe Bureau, was kept on the witness stand for seventeen days

L

and one night over a five-week period. Four days were consumed by the Cameroons alone. The poor man, who had only joined the agency a few months earlier, found himself spending more time defending the program than in trying to manage it.

Yet Passman manages to get away with his behavior. Regularly he and his little subcommittee cut deeply into the sums already authorized by Congress. Just as regularly, the full Appropriations Committee, whose chairman shares Passman's hostility toward foreign aid, leaves the cuts untouched. The full House has made restorations only twice, both in the military-assistance categories. During the annual ritual, the President turns desperately to the Senate for more substantial help only to watch the effects be whittled away again by Passman's influence on the Senate-House Conference.

The fact is that Passman holds a great many advantages in this power struggle with a President. He deals with a program unbuttressed by either constituent or strong interest group support. Beset with a thousand and one demands, congressmen have little time or inclination to master the details of foreign aid. They freely delegate the decision-making, even to such an eccentric expert as Passman. His discretion is enormous. If he had chosen to play a constructive role in the manner of Chairman Mills, he could do much to coalesce and nurture support for this basically unpopular program. Having chosen instead to be destructive, he has sufficient power to thwart any such coalition.

Logic can be claimed for the committee system. It justifies the distinction made long ago by John Stuart Mill "between the function of making laws, for which a numerous popular assembly is radically unfit, and that of getting good laws made, which is its proper duty . . ." Mill stressed the need for a "legislative commission" to per-

form the former task which should consist of "a small
number of highly trained political minds." [5]

That the committees of Congress do not always meet
Mill's specifications is not a new discovery. Controlled by
"the elders of the assembly," according to Woodrow Wilson,
and leading a "peculiar, corporate life," according to Dean
Acheson, many of them are impervious to the higher politics of the nation. They can remain singularly unaffected
by ties to the President or political party. Of their negative
power Wilson wrote sorrowfully that when a bill "goes
from the clerk's desk to a committee room it crosses a
bridge of sighs to dim dungeons of silence whence it will
never return." [6] Acheson modified Wilson's analysis in the
case of major administration measures which "can be, and
are, produced before the bar of Congress—often haggard
and transformed by their imprisonment—by a presidential
habeas corpus; if the demand is made often enough and
vigorously enough." [7] It is surprising how little attention
has been paid to the mechanics of the committees. For
the reporters in Washington, their internal workings have
remained largely unexplored, too complex and too lacking
in drama to be considered good story material. Until
lately, the political scientists also have ignored this important area of study and analysis.

One recent inquiry into the House Appropriations Committee by Richard Fenno, Jr., shows what there is to learn.
By committee standards, the House Appropriations Committee is an uncommonly self-contained group. Its fifty
members exhibit a strong spirit of unity which crosses party
lines and pits them against the Executive, the Senate
Appropriations Committee across the Capitol, and the
House of Representatives itself. They voice grave fear
about the consequence of any differences among them. As
one senior member has explained, "If we don't have a bill
that we can all agree on and support, we ought not to
report it out. To do that is like throwing a piece of meat

to a bunch of hungry animals." The statistics show that
House Appropriations rarely throws such a piece of meat.
Over an eleven-year period, ninety-five per cent of all
appropriation bills were reported out of the House Committee without a dissent. This remarkable display of cohesion
had its effect on the parent body. Of 443 case studies, the
House accepted the Committee's recommendations in 387,
or 87.4 per cent of them.[8]

How is such committee comity attained when dealing
regularly with issues that divide the nation sharply? Probably the greatest conditioning influence for the members is
their unswerving deference to seniority. The Chairman and
the ranking minority member, until the latter's recent retirement, had served a combined total of sixty-eight years
in Congress, and for the last nineteen years had alternated
in the Committee chairmanship.

The newcomer joins the Committee having already acquired a sense of reverence for its role. "Where the money
is, that's where the power is," is how he expresses it. His
apprenticeship impresses on him the fact that greater
power is to be attained by accommodating to Appropriations' tight oligarchic rule. The Chairman determines to a
large extent how power will be distributed among the lesser
members. In 1956, Chairman Cannon, himself an arch
foe of foreign aid, displaced the subcommittee chairman
on Foreign Operations, J. Vaughan Gary, to promote Passman to this post.

The junior member finds the pressures for accommodation equally relentless within the subcommittee. Until he
has served his apprenticeship, he is expected to keep silent
except when matters arise affecting his immediate constituency interests. Neither he nor any other member, always excepting the omnipotent Chairman and ranking
minority member, is privileged to visit a subcommittee to
which he is not assigned. And he soon learns that it is
"frowned upon" for him to try to offer in full committee

an amendment that intrudes on some other subcommittee's business.

By tradition and by daily practice, the Committee imposes a discipline that is rarely broken. The member works hard and often acquires a reputation for special competence in one area. But he neither meddles in nor questions the tight ordering of the oligarchy.

The habit of farming out work to committees can be traced to the beginnings of Congress, but the notion of granting these groups so much autonomy developed only later. During the earliest decades, the House of Representatives employed select committees to perfect details of legislation after the general principle had been formulated by the members acting as a Committee of the Whole. Jefferson's *Manual of Parliamentary Practice* stated emphatically that a bill should be committed to a committee friendly to its chief features, for "the child is not to be put to a nurse that cares not for it." Between 1790 and 1910, according to an authoritative history of the House, the Speaker generally exercised appointive power over members and chairmen of the committees.[9] But custom began to dictate that the membership on the standing committees was continued from one Congress to the next. Before long, the automatic promotion to chairmanship of the most senior committee member of the majority party, though never written into the rules, became a regular practice.

Quite early, the problem of the arrogant committee chairman raised its head. During the Ninth Congress, a resolution was introduced by a member to compel weekly reports from the committees, with the explanation that he desired "to prevent in future the most important business of the nation from being retarded by a Chairman of the Committee of Ways and Means, or any other committee, by going to Baltimore or elsewhere, without leave of absence . . . to prevent in future the Chairman of the Committee of Ways and Means from keeping for months the estimates for the appropriations necessary for the ensuing year in his pocket, or locked up in his desk . . . and, finally, to prevent hereafter bills of importance being brought forward, and forced through the House, near the close of a session, when many members are gone home . . ." [10] The member's complaint is a familiar one.

Despite occasional revolts, the power of the committee chairman continued to accrete until, in 1884, Woodrow Wilson reached the conclusion, "I know not how better to describe our form of government in a single phrase than by calling it a government by the chairmen of the Standing Committees of Congress . . ." [11]

Ironically, the two major legislative reforms of the twentieth century—the revolt against Speaker Joe Cannon in 1910 and the Legislative Reorganization Act of 1946— both served to reinforce the oligarchy of the chairmen. Cannon's overthrow ended the Speaker's dominance over the Rules Committee which regulates the flow of committee business in the House. The Speaker's power to appoint majority party members to the standing committees was also taken away and given to a Committee on Committees. By diluting the strength of the elected leader, the House added to the strength of the hierarchy.

The reform of 1946 was intended, among other things, to bring order to the increasingly disintegrate committee system. The number of committees was drastically reduced—from forty-eight to nineteen in the House, thirty-three to fifteen in the Senate—and their jurisdictions carefully specified. To formalize committee procedures, requirements were set governing meeting days, quorums for transacting business, and maintenance of written records.

In theory, the arbitrary power of the chairman was being circumscribed. In practice, his capacity to frustrate the elected leadership of the House or Senate was measurably increased. Since each committee's mandate was laid down in the law, the leadership of Congress was no longer free to create *ad hoc* committees to avoid assignment of a bill to "a nurse that cares not for it."

The Reorganization Act also mandated each standing committee to "exercise continuous watchfulness of the execution by the administrative agencies concerned of any laws, the subject matter of which is within the jurisdiction of such committee. . . ." This "watchdog" function effectively bestowed on a chairman an arsenal of independent power to investigate, hold hearings, and require systematic reporting by the Executive. He could regularly challenge the Executive's right to withhold privileged information and even assert a demand for prior committee clearance of Executive agency decisions. In these negotiations between the chairman and the Executive, the elected leadership of Congress was to have little voice.

A description of the committee chairman's power at mid-century would probably come as a shock to Woodrow Wilson:

> Just as the standing committees control legislative action, so the chairmen are masters of their committees. Selected on the basis of seniority, locally elected and locally responsible, these 'lord-proprietors' hold key positions in the power structure of Congress. They arrange the agenda of the committees, appoint the subcommittees, and refer bills to them. They decide what pending measures shall be considered and when, call committee meetings, and decide whether or not to hold hearings and when. They approve lists of scheduled witnesses, select their staffs, and authorize staff studies and preside at committee hearings. They handle reported bills on the floor and participate as principal managers in conference committees. They are in a position to expedite measures they favor and to retard or pigeonhole those they dislike. Strong chairmen can often induce in executive sessions the kind of committee actions that they desire. In the House of Representatives, where debate is limited, the chairman in charge of a bill allots time to whomever he pleases during debate on the floor;

he also has the right to open and close the debate on bills reported by his committee; and he may move the previous question whenever he thinks best. In short, committee chairmen exercise crucial powers over the legislative process.[12]

The Reorganization Act's attempt to reduce the fragmentation of the committee system has had quite a contrary effect. For it has not prevented the spawning of subcommittees. Numbering one hundred and eighty before the 1946 reform, they now total, by latest count, more than two hundred and fifty. They constitute a locus of legislative action still further removed from the surveillance and the control of Congress and its elected leadership. For the committee member, they present demands on his time and attention that can be dizzying. Senator Everett Dirksen, a member of fifteen subcommittees, has described his predicament frankly: "I would not dare say to the people of Illinois that I knew all about all things that go on . . . To do so I would really need roller skates to get from one subcommittee to another . . ." [13]

These "miniature legislatures" play a substantial part in the legislative process. One congressional staff member observed, "Given an active subcommittee chairman working in a specialized field with a staff of his own, the parent committee can do no more than change the grammar of a subcommittee report." [14] More than mere specialization, the subcommittee system permits development of tight little cadres of special interest legislators and gives them great leverage. As a conspicuous example, the House Agriculture Committee rarely contains more than a member or two representing the urban consumer. It concentrates primarily on reconciling the various agricultural interests. Democratic members are more disposed toward cotton, tobacco, peanuts, and rice; Republicans lean toward corn and wheat. A notable effect of a switch in party control in Congress, according to one scholarly analysis, has been to change priorities in the federal support program.[15]

House Agriculture members are distributed among ten commodity subcommittees so that, with rare exceptions, each serves on the one of his constituency's dominant crop. This leads to each subcommittee's lobbying vigorously for its own commodity. The business of constructing agricultural legislation in full committee often resolves itself into combining the various subcommittees' reports to make an "omnibus" farm bill, thus frustrating the best efforts of an Administration, Republican or Democratic, to promote a farm program that makes sense in overall terms.

The mushrooming of subcommittees has not necessarily meant a weakening of the full committee chairman's reign. He plays a decisive role in fixing their number and size, outlining their jurisdiction, setting the party ratio, picking the majority members and, finally, dispensing funds to be spent for staff and investigations. This amounts to quite a package of patronage at his disposal. Some subcommittees have acquired clearly defined titles and functions; others may be identified only by number, having their work assigned to them at the committee chairman's discretion. In designating heads of these subcommittees, the chairman is not bound by the same inexorable rule of seniority that governed his own selection. A willful committee chairman can and frequently has bypassed a ranking member, or else handed him a moribund subcommittee.

The chairman's arbitrary use of power within the committee must be used circumspectly. From time to time, there have been insurrections and, on occasion, a committee has successfully crippled its chairman. But the objective of these revolts has usually been to win greater autonomy for the subcommittees. When succcessful, this has often meant further disintegration of the power structure in Congress.

With the exception of the 1960 fight to enlarge the House Rules Committee, the leaders of both Houses have remained chary of attempting to intervene in committee procedures.* Only with greatest reluctance do they act to bypass a committee or discharge a bill from its custody. They tend to regard any effort to remake a committee as a herculean labor. Only after six years of carefully planned appointments did the Democratic leadership in the House manage to build a majority within the Education and Labor Committee that did not share the anti-labor and anti-education bias of its then chairman.

The absolute rule of seniority for choosing the chairmen is sturdily defended. After returning to the Senate following his term as Vice-President, Alben Barkley spoke out strongly against those who sought to prevent the Dixiecrat Senator Eastland, of Mississippi, from becoming Chairman of the Judiciary Committee. "Jealousies, ambitions, and all the frailties of human nature would crop out in the electioneering methods of men who wanted to be chairmen . . ." he argued.[16] As a result the committee continues to serve as the citadel of the oligarchs. The chairman cracks the whip over his members but remains bitterly defiant of any attempt by the elected leadership to crack the whip over him. When it suits his views or his ambitions, he can be a powerful ally for a President. Or, if it suits, he can defy the President and challenge him with persistent rearguard actions. With any canniness, he can hold areas of the Executive in a form of thralldom.

What a chairman does and how he does it is—to a surprising degree in a government of checks and balances —up to him. Only three senators in this century have been denied the automatic seniority claim to chairmanship, and the last instance was in 1925. Only one in recent memory has voluntarily abdicated once he attained this baronial power—and he was over ninety years of age.

---

* The struggle over the Rules Committee represents a special problem of leadership which will be discussed in the next chapter.

LEADERSHIP AND REFORM

"The Senate establishment, as I see it . . . is almost the antithesis of democracy. It is not selected by any democratic process. It appears to be quite unresponsive to the caucuses of the two parties, be they Reublican or Democratic. It is what might be called a self-perpetuating oligarchy with mild, but only mild, overtones of plutocracy."

SENATOR JOSEPH CLARK,
February 19, 1963[1]

"What I believe those who complain of an 'establishment' are, in the final analysis, complaining against is the ever-present fact of frustration, the frustration of working in this body, the frustration of half a loaf, the frustration of compromise that of necessity is always with us. Who among us does not feel this heavy cloak of dissatisfaction? Less than absolute power to achieve one's will is the essence of frustration. Yet less than absolute power to achieve one's will is also an essential of democracy. The practice of democracy is therefore frustrating, and let us be sure that when it ceases to be so for any group or faction, at that same time there will also have ceased to be a democracy."

SENATE MAJORITY LEADER MIKE MANSFIELD,
February 25, 1963[2]

———

A basic fact about the Senate of the United States, which helps to explain its predicament as a legislative body, is that quite literally it cannot operate under its own parliamentary rules of procedure. Work proceeds mainly through a parliamentary device known as "unanimous consent to suspend the rules." A single senator can bring business to a grinding halt by refusing to make consent unanimous.

This creates awesome difficulty for the Senate leadership to keep the Senate moving—much less to achieve majority support for a program. The malcontent senator can stall proceedings daily simply by objecting to the unanimous consent request to dispense with the reading of the preceding day's Journal. By custom, he is free to invoke his objections as it suits him, sometimes blocking a pressing business as a means of showing pique about entirely unrelated business. The Senate Majority Leader, on the other hand, is bound by a more rigid code of conduct. If he should take advantage of a member's absence to sneak through a unanimous consent agreement, he risks provoking a grudge fight that could be costly to him.

In the constant struggle against anarchy in the Senate, the Majority Leader has limited weapons. His powers are nowhere written into the rules. By fairly recent practice, he has acquired the right to be recognized first among those competing for the Presiding Officer's attention—and even this prerogative is regularly challenged by other senators with claims of having been a split second faster on their feet. He sets the agenda and working hours of the Senate, but he has only the most indirect influence over its tempo.

The leadership does have certain powers of persuasion. The Democratic Majority Leader serves as Chairman of the party Conference as well as the Policy and Steering Committees. This puts him in a strategic position in the flow of committee assignments and other patronage deemed important by his colleagues. It also permits the building of a modest bureaucracy to assist him.

With such makeshift powers, it is a phenomenon of more than passing notice in Washington when the leadership of the Senate does in fact lead. That is why Lyndon Johnson rapidly acquired such reputation when he took over the Majority Leader's post after the Democrats captured Congress in 1954, midway in Eisenhower's first term. During Johnson's six-year reign, the Senate survived its bitter bout with McCarthyism and began to make a record for hard work, reasonable efficiency, and a capacity to pass legislative measures of greater sweep and daring than either the House of Representatives or President Eisenhower found acceptable. In 1957, after a debate of 121 hours and 31 minutes—which nobody considered a filibuster—the Senate adopted its first civil rights bill in eighty-two years. Johnson's reputation reached new heights when the Democrats won further congressional victories in the 1958 elections. Some prophets in Washington who hadn't read the Constitution circulated wild notions that the Majority Leader ought to lay down a stern ultimatum to the President and direct the affairs of state from his ornate office just off the Senate Chamber.

The future President never entertained such notions, but he was zealously committed to the proposition of making the Senate viable. He displayed little interest in institutional reforms. His most significant departure from tradition was to inaugurate the practice of assigning every freshman senator in his party a major committee post before letting the more senior ones accumulate two or three. This opened a crack in the seniority system which has had continuing repercussions.

For the edification of visitors to his inner sanctum, Johnson used to turn on a gadget attached to his telephone which permitted them to monitor the messages of exhortation and entreaty that beat upon a Majority Leader as he attempted to deal, *primus inter pares*, with his ninety-nine colleagues. Johnson's leadership was nine-tenths psychological. He played a continual game of one-upmanship on the senators, and much of the time he got away with it. A consummate public relations man, he used to disappear from the view of the press for weeks on end while working on a legislative gambit; then he would reappear to carry it out, triumphantly providing reporters with a running narration.

As Majority Leader, Johnson maintained the posture of Big Daddy. The psychological warfare he waged depended upon a communication system bordering on the psychic. If Johnson was ever caught off guard, no one survived to tell about it. During critical periods, such as that of the civil rights fight, he was all over the place, cornering colleagues and talking incessantly. One long arm draped over a fellow-senator's shoulder, his head alternately thrown back and then thrust up close to his victim's as he rammed home his points, he appeared to work a kind of hypnosis. His persistent theme was that he cared less about the legislative substance than that the Senate should do its job in a calm and orderly fashion.

Many senators, both liberal and conservative, rankled under the intensely driving technique of leadership Johnson displayed. He was certainly not the body's most popular member. He could hardly be said to stand for a clearly defined philosophy. But for a time he did demonstrate that an operator, shrewd, tough, and creative, could assert a degree of leadership in the Senate.

His successor, Mike Mansfield of Montana, who took over at the beginning of the Kennedy Administration, quickly found that Johnson's power had not remained with the office. A gaunt man whose face bears the telltale signs of suffering, Mansfield has not pretended to have Johnson's talents or his antennae. He is among the first to argue that Johnson was "the best Majority Leader the Senate ever had" —and that he is not.

Mansfield has tried to lead through kindliness and painstaking attention to each senator's needs. Faced with growing unruliness, he has lacked Johnson's capacity for getting tough. He has been publicly depicted by northern liberal colleagues as a pawn of an "Establishment," southern-conservative oriented, which rules the Senate. Despite Mansfield's efforts, there have been symptoms of a deepening malaise in the Senate which is leading to a revival of former disorders.

It is possible to concentrate too much on the personality of the Senate's leadership. For all his talents, Lyndon Johnson was peculiarly favored by time and circumstance. He headed an opposition-party majority whose principal task was to maintain a negotiated entente with a fairly quiescent President. Mansfield, on the other hand, has faced a more trying test of leadership. He must attempt to march to the relentless pace provided by highly urgent Presidential programs of an activist President without getting too far ahead of the lagging oligarchs of his party in Congress. The ordeal of this diligent and able man raises serious questions about the way the Senate treats its elected leaders.

The situation of the leadership is even more complicated in the House of Representatives. There has been a latter-day reversal of roles between the two bodies. Once it was the Senate, composed of the ambassadors of the semi-sovereign states, that was considered to be the more "deliberative." The House, a product of direct democracy, was to be the place where public urgencies and popular passions could be expressed. As George Washington is alleged to have explained to Thomas Jefferson, "We pour House legislation into the Senatorial saucer to cool it."

During recent years, however, a number of major measures adopted by the Senate have been given the cooling treatment in the House of Representatives—or, as often as not, put into deep freeze. Power mechanisms in the House are less visible than those in the Senate. The observer, attracted by the highly personal drama among the senators, comes to accept a certain amount of mystery about how congressmen work their will. He observes the impediments placed in the way of majority rule and the cumbersome procedures for circumventing those impediments. Even more than in the Senate, raw power is vested in the oligarchy of the House. The string of committee fortresses is reinforced by a secondary barricade against majority rule which is the formidable Committee on Rules. Most legislation surviving ordinary committee review must receive its additional blessing before being considered by the full membership of the House.

The Rules Committee does not function merely as a traffic cop. It sets the basic terms of the legislative process: how long a bill shall be debated, whether amendments are to be permitted, and whether differences with the Senate version may be negotiated in conference. The Rules Committee constitutes an influence that shapes the very substance of legislation from the hearing stage onward.

In so populous a body as the House of Representatives, there had to exist a steering group to maintain a degree of order amid the competing demands. But with so much power, there was bound to be a struggle over who should rule the Rules Committee. It has, in fact, been the dominant power struggle in the House for most of this century. Congressman Richard Bolling, both a member and a serious student of the Rules Committee, dates House pre-eminence over the Senate as obstructor of legislation from the late 1930s, when a conservative coalition of southern Democrats and rural Republicans managed to attain a majority on the Committee.

But the origins of this power play can be traced back even earlier—to 1910 when the revolt against Speaker Cannon forced his retirement from membership on the Committee. Viewed as a reform at the time, it set the conditions which permitted the leadership of the oligarchs to assert a continuing challenge to the elected leadership of the House. It established a gap between responsibility and power in the House that was destined to lead to trouble.

The recent history of the House partially obscured this situation because of the long reign of Sam Rayburn, who became Speaker in 1940 soon after the "coalition" took over the Rules Committee. This stern, ascetic Texan, who wore habitually a frown of rectitude, was held in consid-erable awe by his colleagues. Venerable personages in Congress were seen to quaver in his presence. Restless younger members would plot against him privately like school boys, but would subside into bashful acquiescence in his presence. Rayburn had rather rigid notions about "responsibility," and these helped keep the House on a steady course not only during wartime, but also during the six years of divided party government under President Eisenhower.

In retrospect it can be seen that Rayburn's personal strength still could not overcome the fundamental weakness of the modern Speakership. Though the Speaker has certain influence over committee assignments, this was reduced when the Legislative Reorganization Act of 1946 reinforced the jurisdiction of the great standing committees. The Speaker's power as presiding officer has been attenuated in an era when the individual congressman rarely brings important business before the full House. The Speaker has patronage powers in dispensing rooms, clerkships, and the like, but while this can impel the respect of the more junior members, it is not likely to cut any ice with an obstinate oligarchy.

Rayburn was always extremely chary about challenging the oligarchs. He never used his prerogative of appointing conferees with the Senate to bypass an intractable committee chairman who was sabotaging a piece of legislation. Until the last years of his reign, he refused to tangle frontally with the Rules Committee coalition headed by ultra-conservative Chairman Howard W. Smith.

There was always much speculation about Rayburn's private conversations with Smith. The Speaker tried to nourish the myth of ultimate invincibility about these secret dealings. At one session's close, he told a reporter that Chairman Smith had reported out everything he had been asked to report. The reporter named a major measure that had remained bottled up in Smith's committee. "I didn't ask for it," replied Rayburn with an air of triumph.

M

Over the years it became increasingly clear that the Speaker lacked the means to get Rules Committee action even when he asked for it.

Despite his strength, Rayburn had little stomach for attempting to change the system. When the showdown no longer could be avoided, he chose the least radical course of reform: rather than attempting a purge of the Rules Committee—one member, a Mississippi Democrat, had actively opposed his own party in the 1960 elections—the Speaker sought instead to expand the Committee's size. The battle was hard-fought and won by only five votes in the House. The addition of two Democrats and a Republican has provided only a slim margin over the conservative coalition—so slim, in fact, that it has been overturned on a number of crucial votes.

Rayburn's death brought the problems of leadership in the House more clearly into the open. His successor, former Majority Leader John McCormack, has sadly lacked the personal force that provided partial compensation for the handicaps of the Speakership. A courtly but sometimes crass politician, McCormack has resorted to feverish wheeling and dealing in an effort to compensate for his weaknesses. Typically, in the effort to consolidate the enlargement of the Rules Committee, he bargained away a valuable vacancy on the Ways and Means Committee to a southern conservative—only to be overruled in caucus by disaffected Democrats, both liberal and conservative. In prospect are an increasing number of confused and purposeless clashes.

Regularly, members of Congress rise to bemoan the prevailing order of things, to condemn "horse and buggy" procedures, and to implore their colleagues to make Congress a more fitting institution for its time. Though their partisan commitments may vary, they share a common concern that the disintegrate nature of Congress has contributed to a diminution of the proper role of Congress.

They echo the accusation made by a leading newspaper columnist: "Today Congress is not even the second most influential branch of the Government. It is third." [3] And regularly they present proposals for reform to their colleagues. One proposal to create a commission to study reform has been endorsed by the party whips on both sides of the aisle.

Analysis turns up more deep-seated reasons for resistance to reform than simply obstinacy. These lie, first of all, in the crushing work load which Congress must handle somehow: a peacetime federal budget that has grown from $35 billion in 1946 to nearly $100 billion in 1963; twenty thousand bills, albeit many of them trivial or duplicatory, thrown into the legislature hopper each two years; four thousand committee reports incorporating millions of words of testimony; three thousand hours of floor debate filling sixty-five thousand pages of *The Congressional Record*.

The statistics give only the barest indication of the size and the diversity of the burden. There is a desperate urge not only to distribute that burden among the committees and subcommittees, but to make the distribution as swift and automatic as possible. The seniority system on which the oligarchy bases its power is reinforced by this feeling of need for automated procedures in Congress. Any alternative to seniority would involve the congressmen in decision-making that could be both personal and painful. They fear that internal struggles for power would make Congress even more vulnerable to outside manipulation—by the massively organized pressure groups in Washington, by the experts in the Executive, and by the President himself.

In the House of Representatives particularly, this sense of vulnerability is heightened by the way many members find themselves manipulated back home. They are constantly aware that their political bases can be carved and recarved by state legislatures—themselves the products of even more grotesque districting. The reapportionment battles after the 1960 census revealed how unrepresentative

the House of Representatives has become. The old requirement that congressional districts be compact, contig-
uous, and approximately equal in population was abandoned
during the prolonged fight following the census of 1920.
By 1960, districting had developed into fantastic feats of
geographic and population configuration, ranging from the
1,014,460 constituents represented by a member from California to the 177,431 of a member from Michigan.

Power in the House can rest on a shaky foundation.
Speaker Rayburn, representing the sixth smallest district
in the nation, was repeatedly threatened by hostile forces
in Texas who sought to enlarge his constituency to include
a large number of conservative Republicans in suburban
Dallas. Chairman Howard Smith, on the other hand, was
obligingly provided with a new "safe" district in rural
Virginia by the Byrd machine when his old one grew too
urbanized for comfort.

Gerrymandering and faulty apportionment have given
excessive representation in the House to both rural and declining metropolitan areas. They have also contributed, in
the estimate of political scientist James MacGregor Burns,
to a situation in which only about 125 out of the 435
districts can be considered "reasonably competitive." But it
would be impossible to measure the more subtle effect of
this tampering with the foundations on which the House
is built. It has tended to breed a cynicism among members
about the House claim to its Constitutional birthright as
the *popular* body of Congress. The checks against majority
rule inside the House are scarcely more undemocratic than
the external checks.

The Supreme Court's momentous decision in 1962,
Baker *vs.* Carr, which for the first time subjected the in-
equities of state legislative apportionment to judicial review, will undoubtedly have an eventual effect on the
House of Representatives. Already, a subsequent Court
decree upsetting Georgia's county unit system has led to

the defeat of one old oligarch from Atlanta. The day may come when the division of congressional constituencies will no longer be the toy of state party politics.

Substantial resistance to reform in Congress arises from the haphazard results that have sprung from past reforms. As described earlier, the overthrow of Speaker Cannon helped set the Rules Committee on the autonomous course that causes much of the present trouble. The Reorganization Act of 1946 helped consolidate the dominion of the standing committee chairmen. In 1949, the House voted to establish a twenty-one day rule by which standing committees could bypass the blockage of the Rules Committee. Revoked two years later, the rule had served only to place greater power in the hands of the chairmen, not the leadership.

Contemporary reformers are by no means clear about which way they wish to shift power in Congress. They complain feelingly about the seniority system; yet, as in the rebellious opening sessions of the Eighty-Eighth Congress, they also complain when one of them fails to get his due rights under seniority. They berate the leadership for its various weaknesses, but have made no attempt to strengthen the leadership's power to deal with the oligarchs. In the Senate, reforming members have fought hard against the filibuster but willingly resorted to filibuster themselves when, as in the fight over the communication satellite bill, it seemed expedient.

But the greatest weakness of the reformers is their lack of strategy for accomplishing reform. During their latest discussions in the Senate, there were solemn proposals to elect all committee chairmen by secret ballot in committee and retire them at the age of seventy; to strip the Senate Finance Committee of vast areas of its jurisdiction; and to limit floor speeches to three hours length. Much good might ensue from each of these reforms. In tandem, however, they can be expected to produce bitter-end defiance from every one who enjoys or anticipates the present prerogatives of oligarchic power.

Any assessment of reform in Congress inevitably returns to the question of role. The underlying premise of a great many reformers, dating from the young Woodrow Wilson, has been that Congress ought to be reshaped more in the image of the British Parliament. Such an ambition runs directly against the separatism built into our system by the founding fathers. But assuming the system could be so drastically altered, it would be a dubious gain for American government. The existing tension between the two branches of government, kept properly in bounds, contributes to the vigor of policy-making. Despite the bulk and urgency of government's business, congressional review plays a valuable role. Nothing guarantees that the President has sufficiently considered each item in the vast portfolio that he transmits to Capitol Hill. Working with discretion, Congress and its committees provide an essential deliberative process.

What is needed, in this writer's judgment, is to ensure *better* deliberation. The aim of reform should not be to make Congress more automatically responsive to the Executive, but to make Congress more responsive to *itself*. Unavoidably, this involves delicate adjustments to the power mechanism.

The primary adjustment would be to shift the balance of power, even if only by degrees, in favor of the elected leadership in Congress over the oligarchic leadership.* This need not mean bestowing unlimited power in the hands of a Speaker or a Majority Leader. But the leadership in both House and Senate, duly chosen by the majority, must be granted at least as much authority in its dealings with the committee chairmen as these latter have within their own committees. Though seniority might well remain the

---

* Congressman Bolling has been engaged in trying to devise the minimal changes in procedure which could achieve such a shift.

least troublesome standard for selecting most chairmen, it ought not to be the absolute standard. An occasional demotion of a chairman, coolly administered by the leadership whose recognized prerogative is to review these assignments at the start of each new Congress, would work wonders in breaking deadlocks and ensuring a genuinely deliberative process. In the House of Representatives, the autonomous reign of the Rules Committee should be ended.

With the leadership possessing more authority to lead, not merely to conciliate, its chief purpose should be to insure that the really important decisions are made by Congress as a whole. This means counteracting the drift which lures members like the late Congressman Clem Miller away from the floor. In both Houses, the leaders must have greater control in scheduling debate and voting in order to prevent the hopeless parliamentary ensnarlments that benefit only the obstructionists. In the Senate, there ought to be a rule of relevancy during active discussion of a bill so that the senators can no longer bore each other to distraction. Possibly Senator John Sherman Cooper's proposal to impose a curb on written speeches would have a magnetic effect in attracting senators back to the Senate. "We would find out who are the good speakers and who are the bad speakers, and we might learn who really had studied the bill," Senator Cooper has observed wryly.

Contrary to many reformers, this writer has serious doubt about whether that peculiar animal of senatorial passion, the filibuster, should be completely throttled. Unlike the secret obstructionism in the committee rooms, the filibuster is carried on in full public view. It serves as a measuring device for recording intensity of feeling about an issue, not merely numerical support and opposition. Of course the filibuster takes on an ugly image when resorted to by a minority of southern senators who themselves deny the rights of a minority in their region. But it can also serve as a valid check on the hasty emotions that sweep

Congress from time to time. To impose too tight strictures would nullify the valid purposes of the marathon contest.

The more desirable reform would permit a simple majority of senators to call up and make perfecting amendments to legislation, leaving the threat of filibuster only for its final passage. In that way the issue would at least be brought in focus before the Senate. At present, the opponents of a bill can so thoroughly confuse the proceedings during preliminary stages that the fundamental issue may never get considered.

To those who are frightened by the prospect of vesting more power in the leadership, the answer must be made that power has to be vested somewhere. It can be shifted upward or downward in Congress. There are abundant pressures to fragment further the power now residing with the oligarchs. Conceivably, the need for specialization will require more and more subcommittees, joint committees, and composite committees. But unless Congress is to become a three-ring circus where the performances go on separately without much regard for the whole, there is urgent need to achieve greater cohesion. Someone has to stimulate the centripetal forces.

Otherwise, there is an increasing prospect of frivolity in the legislative process. The way is inviting for ambitious wheelers and dealers in Congress who set up their own ententes with the Executive and, on occasion, even venture into negotiations with foreign principalities. Such behavior victimizes Congress and discredits its legitimate role.

Congress does not guard its deliberative character by excessive reliance on internal roadblocks. Instead, these often lead to improper allocation of time and energy, diverting the members from their important work by provoking phony arguments and futile maneuvers. Anyone who has followed the debate on foreign aid, for example, is aware of very real questions never adequately probed, of deep concerns never explored. The proponents of the aid program have been too busy conniving to overcome its enemies' advantages to give it the searching review it should have.

It is important not to overstate the case for reform, for well-conceived measures do get enacted. During the decades since the Second World War, Congress has responded repeatedly to the Presidential challenges—and similarly has blocked Presidential proposals that were ill-timed or ill-considered. Not all the fragmentation in government can be blamed on the Legislative branch.

But there have been important areas in which the absence of coherent legislative policy-making has contributed to confusion in government. For example, direct federal aid to education has been stalled in Congress, by one device or another, since 1948. Yet Congress now appropriates nearly two billion dollars annually on education from kindergarten through graduate school. The mounting program —or rather, hodgepodge of programs—has been, as one observer put it, not "injected" but "insinuated" into the educational system, and is having a massive effect in shaping educational priorities in this country.

Because of the way it has backed into this field, at no time has Congress adequately deliberated education policy or imposed restraints against the dangers of unplanned federal involvement. The loudest opponents of federal interference in the schools have lobbied for special-interest programs that impose criteria on subjects to be taught, research programs to be sponsored, and that otherwise constitute direct interference. Most members do not even realize the extent of this involvement. According to one tally, congressional surveillance of the education programs is divided among eighteen committees of the House and Senate—not to mention, of course, the countless subcommittees.[4]

Order needs to be made out of this chaos. One instance of slipshod intrusion into a sensitive area was the Loyalty Oath, concocted on the spur of the moment by a Senate

committee aide and attached without debate to the National Defense Education Act of 1958. Its requirement that
private institutions participate as security agents in screen-
ing student applicants for federal loans was flatly rejected
by more than a hundred of the nation's leading colleges
and universities which refused to join the program. Presidents Eisenhower and Kennedy and Vice-Presidents Nixon
and Johnson stoutly demanded repeal of the Oath, as did a
number of congressional leaders. Yet so cumbersome are the
procedures of Congress that it took four years to erase this
particular provision from the statute books.

Perhaps critics become overly engaged in citing instances
of congressional behavior which they consider unwise. Not
all the wisdom lies at the opposite end of Pennsylvania
Avenue in Washington. But the more serious criticism is
that Congress, by failures of corporate wisdom, plays a less
worthy role than it rightfully should. The great hope is that
by better organization of its powers the critic might be
able to say, as Walter Bagehot once said of the British
House of Commons, that Congress has more brains than
everyone in it.

IV

The Parties

THE LOSS OF ROLE

"Of all these [previous commitments of the President], party platforms and campaign promises are often the least confining. . . ."

THEODORE SORENSEN, 1963 [1]

A veteran British observer in the United States has remarked that if he were suddenly set down in one of our partisan gatherings he could tell instantly, without benefit of signs or slogans, whether it was Democratic or Republican. His boast implies that there is a difference between the two great American parties that goes beyond doctrine—a difference that can be seen or heard or felt wherever Democrats or Republicans gather. It presupposes that America's party system represents a dichotomy going deeper than mere politics.

Certainly the political reporter who attends many national conventions notes marked differences. It is not simply a matter of the style of the clothes or, as in Great Britain, the accents of speech. Both Democrats and Republicans are a happy mix. Both have lady politicians who range from chic to chintz, orators who run the grammatical gamut. Today, the style of the parties has very little to do with the superficialities.

But certain superficial generalizations are possible. With the Democrats everything is generally bigger, noisier, more

fratricidal. The party lives in a lusty confusion. People
have to shout to be heard. The party pros are more conspicuous; the amateurs carry on more unrestrainedly. There
is more zest, more sheer love of the game of politics.

Republicans are usually quieter, and their gatherings
are smoother, more efficient, often better run. Republicans
keep closer to their pre-arranged time schedules. They view
with horror the unexpected occurrence. One senses that
for them party politics is an accepted adjunct to the busi-
nes of good government; it is to be endured but not necessarily enjoyed.

At no time are the differences so apparent as when each
party girds itself for intramural warfare. Democrats approach their fights raucously, almost gleefully. Each national convention goes through a crisis of confidence
which, it is freely predicted, will prove fateful for the party.
Republicans, though they do not always avoid unnecessary
battle, are more grim about it, more concerned that above
all else party harmony be preserved.

Any study of the role of parties in America must take
account of the many ways in which the two parties are
alike. Viewed from the perspective of, say, a Soviet citizen,
these similarities loom so large as to obscure the differences. Both are committed to the existing form of government, the predominantly private enterprise economy, and
the two-party system. Except as a stratagem during campaigns, each views with suspicion the third party movements in America. Each, in effect, is committed to the
preservation of the other as its chief competitor.

Organizationally the party is a fairly loose confederation
of state and local groupings whose main claim to national
identity comes at the quadrennial conventions. Both Democrats and Republicans wrestle constantly with the problem of maintaining a semblance of centralized direction
without benefit of strong ties of discipline.

Both parties are tormented by issues that unite members

of opposing parties within a state or region against out-siders of both parties. Each party has influential members who find closer identity with the opposition than they do with their own. For political companionship Senator Byrd, Democrat of Virginia, certainly prefers Senator Goldwater, Republican of Arizona, to Senator Douglas, Democrat of Illinois—who, in turn, prefers Senator Javits, Republican of New York.

So much for likenesses. It is true nonetheless that each party has ties that bind member to member, if not in love, at least in a continuing relationship of convenience. During a lecture at Princeton, Sidney Hyman made a half-jesting attempt at defining these ties: "The Democrats are a large group of second-class roughnecks led nationally by a small group of first-class aristrocrats, while the Republicans are a small group of second-class aristocrats led nationally by a large group of first-class roughnecks."

Depending on how one defines aristocrat and roughneck, Hyman's thesis is not without historical support. The Democratic Party traces its origin to 1792 when Thomas Jefferson and James Madison ventured on a "botanizing ex-pedition" into New York and New England. Besides pick-ing flowers, the two men managed to establish an alliance between the planters of Virginia and the professional poli-ticians of New York, including the progenitors of Tam-many Hall. As scholars have since pointed out, this entente set the permanent pattern of the party.

Two noteworthy characteristics resulted. First, the Dem-cratic Party traditionally brings together North and South, rural farmer and urban factory worker. The party grew up embracing diversity. The cacophony of dissension within its ranks is a familiar sound. Except for the rude break of the Civil War period, the uneasy alliance established by Jefferson and Madison has survived all strains till the pres-ent day.

Secondly, this alliance, deriving its mass support pri-marily from the have-nots, mostly turns to the haves for its leadership. From Jefferson's time to Lyndon B. Johnson's, the party of the common man has been commanded with remarkable regularity by men of wealth and/or cultural heritage. Harry Truman was the most recent exception, but he had not been intended for first place on the ticket. Kennedy, while belonging to an ethnic and religious minority, was a member of an emergent Irish upper-class in America. With the exception of Humphrey, the other chief Democratic possibilities in the 1960 contest—Symington and Stevenson—also were millionaires.

By an amalgam of farm and factory workers, of northern minority groups and southern Bourbons, the Democratic Party—unlike the Republican—has elected local, state, and federal officials in every part of the union. At the next Presidential election, it will have occupied the White House during twenty-four out of thirty-two years. It will have held the majority in both Houses of Congress during all but four of those years. For three-quarters of President Eisenhower's time of office, the Democrats constituted that strange anomaly possible only in American government—a majority opposition party in Congress.

In Democratic strength also lies recurrent weakness. Because the party tries to unite within itself so many factions, it always has had difficulty selecting *the* men and *the* platform to stand for the whole. Despite its widespread electoral successes, the party has trouble rallying grass-roots support behind its Presidential nominees. Since the Civil War, Roosevelt has been the only Democratic President to enter office with a majority of the popular vote. Kennedy went to the White House with fewer votes than the combined total for Democratic congressmen that year.

The Grand Old Party has different problems. For Republicans, who make no attempt to trace their ancestry beyond Abraham Lincoln, the Civil War erected a great China Wall preventing a successful conquest of the South. Despite recent successes in gathering a large Presidential vote and in capturing a few House seats, Republicanism still lacks organizational structure and effective party cadres throughout much of the region.

The Civil War also left lingering strongholds *for* as well as *against* the Grand Old Party, but these too have been subject to erosion. The more durable party strength developed during the period of the Industrial Revolution in the late nineteenth century when Republicanism, by voicing the rising expectations of the emerging middle class, brought together capitalist, manager, white-collar worker, and, in good times, the farmer. Though a minority in terms of voting strength, these groups achieved majority power for long periods of time by the skillful advertisement of men and issues to capture the popular imagination.

This is not to say that the Republican Party has lacked internal stresses. These arise mainly in the tension between what might be called the conservatives of tradition and the conservatives of the status quo. The conservatives of tradition, for example, regard America's postwar call to internationalism as a new challenge to which they can apply old principles. Those who seek simply to conserve the status quo look on internationalism as a radical departure to be stubbornly resisted. The division between these two attitudes goes wide and deep within the GOP.

One other characteristic of Republicanism deserves notice. This more conservative of America's two parties has been the more reticent in thrusting to the fore leaders who can be readily identified with great wealth and privilege. Republican top-drawer leadership has been more often drawn from the Horatio Algers of the nation—men who made good the hard way. It was this quest for self-made heroes, rather than any abnormal love of militarism, that has prompted the party to seek out so many generals. Of the twelve Republicans elected to the Presidency since the party's birth, five (Grant, Hayes, Garfield, Harrison, Eisenhower) had previously enjoyed illustrious careers in the army, not counting Rough Rider Teddy Roosevelt. Of the

Democrats, only Andrew Jackson ever figured prominently in the military.

Republicans, more than Democrats, are acutely conscious of the need for "the man who can win." This can create real dilemmas at convention time. The party faithful thrice sorrowfully rejected candidate Robert Taft, whom they loved, for candidates Willkie, Dewey, and Eisenhower whom they considered better vote-getters. The struggle between heart and head in the party will undoubtedly figure in the coming choice.

In contrasting Republicans and Democrats, one must be extremely cautious about making judgments that apply only to the present. History has a way of upsetting such applecarts. It is useless to try to define too precisely the differences between conservatism *vs.* liberalism, fiscal rectitude *vs.* free spending, the business interest *vs.* the public interest. Republicans and Democrats exhibit in varying degree one or another of these propensities.

Party differences have varied widely in point of time. For example, consider the bedrock Constitutional argument which has figured so often in partisan argument, of states' rights as opposed to centralized government. Viewed over the long run, the Democratic Party of the nineteenth century was more inclined toward states' rights, whereas the Democratic Party of the twentieth century has been less inclined. Even those lusty states'-righters, the southern Democrats, subdued conviction when they helped bring about much of the New and Fair Deal economic legislation. Conversely, the Republicans of Lincoln's time were adamant nation-firsters, while today even Republicans of Nelson Rockefeller's stripe pay lip service to states' rights. The future undoubtedly will hold further shifts of dogma.

Much depends on which party occupies the White House and thereby is chiefly responsible for the nation's destiny. In the past the Democratic Party has been more conspicuously the party of innovation; the Republican Party, with the notable exceptions of the Lincoln and Theodore Roosevelt eras, has been the party of consolidation. Democrats have been swept into power in response to popular unrest and desire for change. Republicans have tended to benefit from popular desire for stability and order. Third party movements, like the Populists, have served to pioneer new ideas that fall outside tradional party conflict or, like the Dixiecrats, to fight rear-guard actions for the old and outmoded.

By such broad analysis, it is possible to develop a comfortable theory about the role of the political parties in American government. Though they were never envisaged by the Constitution-makers and were, in fact, viewed with active hostility by the nation's first President, they grew to serve a useful purpose in finding a common denominator of agreement among the factions and in offering a common banner, if not a common ideology, around which disputatious politicians and citizenry could rally. The parties have provided essential machinery for selecting candidates and staging elections. In the nation's capital, they have made it easier to organize Congress and the Presidency and to seek a common purpose between the two.

By the sheer good fortune of American politics, the party verdict at election time usually has been decisive. Only twice in history have the mechanics of the electoral system made it necessary to throw the Presidential contest into the House of Representatives where cabals could try to rule. So far, third party movements have not managed to acquire the pivotal power necessary to affect the organization of government.

Over the years, however, there has been increasing discontent with the parties or, more specifically, with the limitations of their role in national affairs. The most common complaint is that the parties have not kept pace with the growth of big government. They are ruled by certain laws that frustrate effective politics. The first of these is the law of inevitable anarchy that seizes a party when it loses control of the White House. Contrary to Lord Acton's axiom, power may corrupt but being out of power tends to corrupt the American political party more absolutely. Overnight, along with its campaign furniture, the party apparatus goes into storage. The rejected nominee, while bearing the nondescript title of "titular leader," lacks the authority or wherewithal to exercise leadership over the party, especially over its members in Congress. Even the attempt to do so arouses antagonism.

Being out of office creates enormous problems for the party's "image," not to mention its operating efficiency. Until its quadrennial rebirth during a Presidential election year, the words and deeds of the party contingent in Congress dominate the news and capture the public's attention. The faces of those who prevail in the legislative arena, usually faces upon which time and toil have worked certain ravages, become the familiar ones.

The National Committee of the party out of power, impoverished and engaged in factional disputes, strives valiantly to keep the issues and itself alive. While the Republicans held the White House, the Democrats gave birth to an Advisory Council as an adjunct to the National Committee whose purpose was to provide policy-planning on a national party level. The Council, which ultimately included all of the potential Presidential candidates except then Senate Majority Leader Johnson, had a valuable part in stimulating party debate on the large issues and building a case against the Republican Administration. It also prodded the party leaders in Congress to be more ambitious than if left to their own judgments.

Some observers predicted that the Advisory Council would become a permanent part of the party structure. Unfortunately, this ignored a second law that comes into effect once a party wins. Direction of national party policy must be handed over totally to the White House, which leads to atrophy of any existing policy organs. The Democratic Advisory Council simply went out of business soon after Kennedy's election; it was argued that the new President could not afford a competing brain trust. No one recalled that the original urging of a Council had come during the later years of the Truman Administration when the President desperately needed party advisers who could compete with those in Congress.

A third law of American party politics is that the party members in Congress may often vote with greater unity when they don't have a leader in the White House than when they do. The President has limited means of imposing party discipline *for* rather than *against* programs. Patronage can be a clumsy instrument. For the senior members in Congress, it provokes more hostility when withheld than gratitude when bestowed. Campaign support, too, is often a matter of indifference to the hierarchs, especially when a President volunteers it in the forlorn hope of favors. For a President to consider intervening in the party primaries to defeat a particularly recalcitrant congressman or senator recalls memories of FDR's "purge" effort in 1938 directed against three Democratic incumbents in the Senate. All three were returned by handsome margins.

The vagary of party organization is nowhere more visible than in the way each party collects and disburses its funds. The National Committee's effort is primarily expended in paying off past Presidential campaign costs and sustaining its own permanent staff. As use of television has caused the cost of politics to skyrocket, there have been frenetic "galas," employing stage and screen celebrities. This is mainly a way to tap the lobbyists. The occasions have little interest for the rank-and-file party members, and rarely provide enough extra money to be of substantial help in the lesser contests. For both Democrats and Republicans, separate campaign committees in the House and Senate have always collected their own funds and distributed them without regard for National Committee preferences. By their standards, seniority often rates above party loyalty, and members from the safe districts are likely to be allotted more money than some who may be facing stiff competition. The new candidate for Congress counts very little on assistance from his national party organization; at best, he may get handouts of a few thousand dollars. But to run for the House in marginal urban districts may cost upward of a hundred thousand dollars and to run for the Senate in the larger states seldom costs less than a million. It provides a fertile field for the pressure groups.

The postwar history of the parties has shown few signs of a renaissance. Despite President Eisenhower's firm intent to revitalize the GOP, it had not much more visible evidence of permanent structure and strength at the end of his two terms of office than at the beginning. The Republicans have even been unwilling to risk the potential stress of an Advisory Council attached to party headquarters. President Kennedy entered office with an explicit commitment to party role. "Legislative leadership is not possible without party leadership," he declared in 1960. "No President, it seems to me, can escape politics. He has not only been chosen by the nation—he has been chosen by his party. And if he insists that he is 'President of all the people' and should therefore offend none of them—if he blurs the issues and differences between the two parties—if he neglects the party machinery and avoids his party's leadership—then he has not only weakened the political party as an instrument of the democratic process—he has dealt a blow to the democratic process itself." [2]

These were strong words. However, the President's acts did not always carry out this commitment. In making his chief appointments, Kennedy showed little partiality for the party label; his Secretary of Treasury was a Republican, his Secretary of Defense an independent, and his Secretary of State a purely nominal Democrat. Brother Robert who, as Attorney General, was expected to serve as his principal agent in party matters, likewise staffed the Justice Department with non-partisan deputies.

Attention to party affairs during Kennedy's three years

was very sporadic at best. The President made a brave start at an intensive campaign drive during the mid-term elections, but when the Cuban crisis arose he cancelled all future appearances for himself and his Cabinet officers. The Attorney General was much too preoccupied with trouble-shooting for his brother in matters of governmental urgency to pay continuing attention to the party. A brother-in-law, Stephen Smith, was delegated the task of smoothing out frictions in various state organizations. National Democratic Chairman John Bailey, boss of Democratic politics in Connecticut, seemed to be content to operate on a low key in his Washington post.

One area of party activity gave promise of breaking from the traditional pattern when Kennedy chose to put a veteran campaign aide rather than the traditional man of wealth in charge of party finances. There were to be significant efforts to step up fund-raising and to promote direct membership in the national party for annual dues-payers. There was also talk of better "co-ordination" in dealing out the money. Some of the President's assistants argued strongly that party reform could be brought about through a bigger and better controlled campaign chest.

Theoreticians and politicians alike have agreed that there is need for reform of the parties. At least two Presidents in recent times have toyed with the idea of shaping a new two-party system to replace the old one. During his third term, President Franklin D. Roosevelt privately communicated several times through an intermediary with Wendell Willkie about the prospects of coalescing liberal Democrats and Republicans in a new party. Willkie died before any concrete steps had been taken. During his first years in office, President Eisenhower also talked frustratedly to intimates about the prospect of creating a new party and even tried to devise a name for it.[3] But he, too, never aired the idea in public.

Scholarly critics successively have endorsed the necessity of drastic change in the party system. According to the latest of them, Professor James MacGregor Burns of Williams College, most of the blame for what he describes as "the deadlock of democracy" can be attributed to the failure of the parties. Burns examines the model of government elaborated by James Madison, based on countervailing powers and weak party leadership and requiring government by "coalition, compromise and consensus," and compares this with the model of government established by Thomas Jefferson which "by organizing power more centrally and hierarchically through a national party led by the chief executive, permits leaders to govern more freely and vigorously and expeditiously, subject to majoritarian control in competitive elections." [4]

Professor Burns envisages a party realignment somewhat different from the banding together of liberals contemplated by FDR and Willkie or Eisenhower's party of "progressive moderates." By his analysis, there exists in America a four-party system, both Democrats and Republicans being presently divided into Presidential and congressional parties. Burns' goal is to consolidate the bifurcated party organizations into two genuinely national parties with grass-roots membership. The consolidated party would establish dominancy of the Presidential over the congressional wing. It would also require a greater degree of conformity to party principles among its candidates. "Such a party system would permit flexibility to meet local conditions, but with a limit," Burns admonishes. "It would not allow a local candidate or officeholder using the party label to follow so dissident a line that the image, the solidarity, and the integrity of the national party became tarnished." [5]

To help accomplish this purpose, Burns proposes to abolish the seniority system in Congress, to consolidate Presidential and congressional candidates on a single national party ticket, to fix four-year terms in the House of Representatives coinciding with the President's term, to repeal the two-term limitation on the Presidency, and to re-form the electoral college system. But the central impetus for party reform, he argues, must come from the President. "The presidential leader must, in short, be more than a skil-ful manipulator or brilliant interpreter. He must be a con-structive innovator, who can re-shape to some degree the constellation of political forces in which he operates." Bor-rowing rhetoric from the late President Kennedy, Burns pre-dicts that such a Presidential leader "would have written for himself an imperishable new profile in courage." Burns promises that ". . . the presidential party that first gains control of its congressional party will dominate the politics of the center left or the center right for decades to come." [6]

Professor Burns offers a stirring challenge, but the chal-lenge also poses a number of dilemmas. During his long fight to attain high office, the President of recent times has had frequent cause to wonder about the efficacy of party. Unlike his predecessors of an earlier era, he owes his nomination far less to the meticulous wooing of party lead-ers than to a highly personalized form of campaigning. Even after his nomination, he has felt obliged to maintain a certain distance between his own and the party's cumber-some organization. He comes into office comparatively un-committed to the party potentates. One recent observer has concluded that only the mechanics of the electoral col-lege system makes it necessary for today's Presidential can-didate to align himself with a major party at all, and that ". . . if we adopted a system in which the President was elected merely by a plurality of the popular vote, there might come a time when a candidate could capture the office solely through his glamour, his personal organization, and his shrewd use of the mass media." [7]

Once in office, a President is apt to regard his problems from a somewhat different perspective than from Burns'. Looking at the organization of power in Washington, he cannot recognize anything so distinct as a four-party system.

Congress could as well be described as a no-party system
which distributes much of its power without regard for party
contest. A President, Democrat or Republican, finds himself
measuring Congress in terms of the coalitions for him or
against him on specific issues. His task of building a winning
coalition provides a constant temptation to devise
means of persuasion other than appeals to party loyalty.
He often feels the urge to pick up support where he can
find it—even when it means fuzzing the party issues by
wooing opposition members who have shrewdly calculated
their own political stakes in being wooed. Even on a potentially
hot party issue, as when Kennedy clashed with the
steel barons, it is usually the opposition leaders who have
the option of whether to stage a major fight. A President
often finds it more convenient to gloss things over after
he has achieved his purpose.

A President is tempted to rise above his party in other
ways. His seemingly vast power of appointment, contract
allocation, and the rest is really quite circumscribed. His
primary job is to keep government operating on an even
keel. He must weigh the patronage claims of his party
against his own need for competent assistance. More often
than not, the party organization is quite inadequate for
this kind of recruitment.

Washington is crowded with power groupings which
have propaganda systems and ties with the grass roots effective
to their specialized needs. They make it a point to
be conspicuously bipartisan in their pressure activities, frequently
maintaining separate specialists for Republican
and Democratic operations. A President must question at
times whether the parties any longer are accommodating
the pressure groups or whether the pressure groups are accommodating
the parties.

Finally, a President looks at the issues and finds that the
ones giving him greatest concern have outgrown party
definition. In foreign policy, in defense and, more recently,
in the delicate management of economic policy, he finds

himself striving for unpartisan answers and unpartisan support. He seeks to establish a technocracy of policy-making in these fields. He enlists his principal advisers not from the ranks of party zealots, but from an incipient Establishment in America which more or less disregards the party label. His team hardly corresponds to what Burns would call a Presidential party.

These are some of the reasons why a President hesitates to sound the clarion call for party reform. Any effort to rejuvenate the system must require increased involvement by him. How does he begin the work of rejuvenation? As he surveys the fragile network of state and local organizations he has good cause to doubt whether he can forge an army capable of winning supremacy over the party warlords in Congress. For a Democratic President, the prospect of building direct party ties in the South strong enough to withstand the divisive tugs appears to require labor far too great for his brief span in office. He can perceive only dimly the far-off prospects, but he sees with stark realism the immediate consequences.

If a President is subject to such schizophrenia, is there any hope that the party may play a greater role in the functioning of government? To predict this with any degree of certainty is exceedingly difficult. Undoubtedly, the occurrence of a domestic crisis in the form of a severe depression would restore vigor to party ideology; a foreign catastrophe in the form of a major war would dissipate it further. Assuming that the problems confronting government continue to be sticky but not catastrophic, the role of the party is less clear.

Six years of divided party rule under Eisenhower offered stark proof that the voters are quite willing to measure Presidents and congressmen by different standards. No one gave much credence to President Eisenhower's campaign warnings that election of an opposition Congress would result in a condition of "cold war" between the two branches of government. In fact, a sizable body of public opinion appeared to believe that a President of one party and a Congress of the other could do a better job of keeping tabs on each other. Why not add one further check to the numerous ones already written into the Constitution?

Though business did proceed during this period, it was possible to discern symptoms of disorder. Divided party government tended to breed a sense of non-responsibility in both the Executive and Congress, each blaming the other for mutual sins and shortcomings. Without the goad of party loyalty, however gentle that goad may be, there was greater temptation for behind-the-scenes connivance rather than across-the-table collaboration. Always the possibility lurked that at a critical juncture a dreadful stalemate might occur. The capacity of Mr. Eisenhower to get along with Messrs. Johnson and Rayburn was not indicative of what might have happened under Mr. Nixon, whose capacity to get along with Democrats was, to say the least, unproven.

Protracted bipartisanship can lead to a minimal kind of politics with everything played in low key. It reduces the incentive for initiatives from the Administration in power. At the same time it lessens the healthy clash that occurs when a government is vigorously challenged by the party in opposition. Finally, despite all the talk about unity at the water's edge, one may question whether this kind of "bipartisanship" really presents a very convincing image abroad. Hopefully, the time is past when the world needs to be reassured that America is united. But allies and enemies do have cause to wonder at times about who speaks for America in an effective way.

Close examination of the historic role of parties in America prevents one from writing confidently about what they may become. Their historical record is one of constant flux. The Jeffersonian model was not an enduring one, even during Jefferson's own administration. A fatal flaw in reformer Burns' argument is that historian Burns has found so little evidence that the Presidential party ever achieved the sustained dominance he advocates so earnestly. It is doubtful that any act of Presidential initiative could create, as he suggests, a condition permanent enough to "dominate the politics of the center left or the center right for decades to come." Party politics in America has never been quite so predictable. The emergence of Senator Barry Goldwater as champion for genuinely conservative Republicanism is hardly cause for cheer about dividing parties along stark ideological lines.

To be sceptical about the prospects of party reform, however, does not mean to denigrate the need. A President, as well as others who desire orderly and effective government, ought to give constant thought to ways of vitalizing the party system. Particularly in matters of campaign finance, there is prospect of building a cohesive national party structure. Today the constituent demands on President and Congress—now that they must count the whole free world as a non-voting constituency—are more varied and more difficult to reconcile than ever in the past. The two branches of government, intended by the founding fathers to be separate and coordinate, are beset with pressures that would widen the gulf existing between them. The parties have a necessary role as one tried—if not always true—means of bridging that gulf.

V

Outsiders
on the Inside

THE SUBTLE ART OF PRESSURE

"If a faction consists of less than a majority, relief is supplied by the republican principle, which enables the majority to defeat its sinister views by regular vote: It may clog the administration, it may convulse the society; but it will be unable to execute and mask its violence under the forms of the Constitution."

JAMES MADISON,
The Federalist, Number Ten[1]

"The old-time lobbyist has gone, but the new brand, though more respectable, has perhaps a more damaging effect by working on the timidity of lawmakers rather than on their cupidity."

CONGRESSMAN ROBERT LUCE [2]

For a tightly ordered subgovernment, as in the case of sugar discussed in Chapter One, the factions are frequently able to work out their differences within the power arrangement. But times come when the clash of factional interest necessitates an appeal to higher powers and larger publics.

This was the case during the mid-fifties when domestic beet and cane interests began a concerted effort to revise the sugar act in order to boost their own quotas and cut the very large quota allocated to pre-communist Cuba. Forty-nine senators had gone on record in support of such

o

a change. A drastic revision passed the House of Representatives where the delegations of twenty-three states were pledged to the domestic sugar cause. At this juncture the Cuban interests, seeking desperately to rally support for their cause, hired an array of Washington talent, including the services of Samuel E. Stavisky who lists himself as "Management Consultant in Public Relations and Government Relations."

A man with long experience in the nation's capital as reporter for the *Washington Post*, Stavisky has described what ensued in a fascinating document, accompanied by photostatic evidence, entitled "The Sweetest Story Ever Sold." In brief, it claims that he and his associates played a significant role in thwarting congressional action against Cuba during the 1955 session and in obtaining the next year a new and highly favorable quota for Cuban sugar which persisted until Castro's takeover. By Stavisky's estimate, "Effective public relations helped the Cuban sugar industry gain an extra million tons of sugar quota in the American market."

Stavisky's document provides a valuable case study in modern techniques of political persuasion. Commencing not with the politicians but with the press, Stavisky reasoned that he had a complex story to get across on a subject about which most reporters couldn't care less. He invited small groups of his former colleagues for sumptuous meals at Washington's Colony Restaurant where he discussed the subject with a former newsman's feel for the "facts" and the "angle." Assisted by a liberal expense account, he "encouraged" reporters to visit Cuba and see the problems for themselves. A few were provided with direct travel subsidies when they couldn't get their publications to finance them. One correspondent even charged off his gambling losses in Havana, Stavisky recollects.

These efforts began to pay off in a sudden spate of stories about Cuba and its sugar problems. A number bore the notation, gratifying to a reporter's ego, that they had been based on "a personal conference with President Batista." But the recurrent theme was one emphasized by Stavisky: in the words of one news column, "Whether Cubans eat or go hungry depends on the absorption in the United States market of a large portion of their sugar." A second Stavisky theme—the threat of communist takeover in Cuba —usually followed.

Equally important to his campaign, Stavisky soon worked out a news angle that made the fate of Cuban sugar of important local interest all over the United States. By a meticulous IBM punch-card breakdown of shipping invoices, he was able to trace the origin of more than $400 million in U. S. exports to Cuba according to state, city, congressional district, product, industry, and company. A steady flow of stories began to appear in small papers across the country with such edifying facts as "Cuba is the most important market for [Columbia] basin red beans . . ." (*Wenatchee* [Washington] *World*); "The Cuban imports are important to the industrial prosperity of Texas" (*Littlefield* [Texas] *Leader*); "Cuban Sugar Makes Possible Exports of Rice" (*Yellsville* [Arkansas] *Mountain Echo*); "Much Ohio Lard Goes to Cubans" (*Tiffin* [Ohio] *Advertiser-Tribune*). In the western tier of the North Central states, whose congressmen were considered hostile to sugar imports, the information that 708 manufacturers had sold Cuba more than $22 million of goods in a single year was treated as news by dozens of papers. Stavisky also sorted out his statistics to appeal to industry, farm, and labor publications. With an especial solicitude for the American consumer, there soon appeared a number of magazine feature stories critical of the domestic sugar growers under such eye-catching titles as "Flies in the Sugar Bowl" and " 'Sugar' for U. S. Sugar Producers at the Expense of Many." When the Department of Agriculture issued a routine report with a section on "Cuba as a Market for United States Agricultural Products," Stavisky made certain that it did not suffer the ignominious fate of many such government publications.

The initial stages of this pressure campaign involved little direct contact with the policy-makers. Stavisky measured his impact in column-inches. His scrapbook for that campaign is crammed with newspaper clippings from all over the country; many are identical word-for-word to his press releases—except that usually there is omission of any reference to their source of origin.

The work of this Washington insider was not limited to cultivating the grass roots of public opinion. He was very much "interested" when a congressional friend, member of the House Foreign Affairs Committee, decided to head a legislative study mission to Cuba for the purpose of finding out the facts. By Stavisky's arrangement, the representatives and their assistants were welcomed warmly and entertained graciously during their brief visit in Havana. Afterward, the burden on the overworked staff members of the Foreign Affairs Committee was eased by draft material for the report submitted by Stavisky for their consideration. The published report prompted the newspaper headline: "U. S. Warned Against Cut in Cuban Sugar." A few days later, when President Eisenhower issued a denial that he had made any commitments to domestic sugar producers and that he would sponsor his own study of the sugar legislation, Stavisky concluded happily that the mad rush to change the quotas had been stymied.

Administration policy was coaxed a bit further when Vice-President Nixon departed on one of his celebrated tours of Latin America, with Havana as his first stop. Having long maintained friendly relations with the Vice-President and his associates, Stavisky was able to give them a pre-trip briefing on the Cuban situation, naturally emphasizing the questions likely to be asked about sugar. Also naturally, he supplied reporters who were to accompany the Vice-President with those same questions. After the group arrived in Havana, an AP dispatch reported, "Vice-President Richard M. Nixon said . . . he does not believe the United States will cut sugar purchases from Cuba for at least two years. He said there is no certainty of a cut even then." This fairly firm commitment, an example of policy-making by press conference, caused consternation among officials back in Washington.

Throughout the 1955 session of Congress, Stavisky stressed the themes that a quota revision would constitute a "breach of faith" and amounted to "changing the rules in the middle of the game." He helped arrange a "goodwill mission" to the U. S. sponsored by the American Chamber of Commerce in Havana, and accompanied the group as it toured the country to sell Cuba's case at men's luncheon-club meetings. In obeisance to chauvinism, only U. S. citizens living in Cuba were included in the mission. Stavisky kept them on a relentless course, maximizing publicity by moving his troops onward after each luncheon meeting in order to make the afternoon editions of the newspapers in the next community. The tour concentrated in particular on Virginia, whose senior senator, Harry Byrd, as Chairman of the Senate committee dealing with sugar legislation was a crucial target for conversion.

Stavisky's office likewise stimulated a steady flow to various newspapers of letters-to-the-editor, aware that this is usually the most widely read feature outside the comic pages. A special campaign was directed at labor unions using arguments about "economic self-interest, American security, and friendship for Cuba's strong anti-communist labor movement." Despite the self-interest opposition of the AFL beet workers and the CIO packing-house workers, their parent unions strongly endorsed Cuba's cause.

Amid all this favorable publicity, there were signs of mounting opposition to a quota cut in Congress. Senator William Fulbright of Arkansas announced that he would fight any attempt to change the sugar act. Aside from his interest as a senior member of the Senate Foreign Relations Committee, Fulbright claimed that the curbs on Cuban sugar were hurting the sales of rice, which his home state produces in large quantity. Belatedly, the domestic beet and sugar growers recognized, according to one reporter's dispatch, that they were "falling dangerously behind in the intense competition for public approval," and launched a counteroffensive. Two southern California congressmen charged that Cuba had organized "one of the largest lobbying groups ever assembled . . . to come here and attempt to confuse and mislead the Congress." When the 1955 session ended without a change in the Sugar Act, Nebraska Congressman A. L. Miller claimed, according to a headline in the Omaha *World-Herald*, that the " 'Cuban Lobby' Killed Sugar Bill."

Stavisky was not slow in responding to this attack. During the final days of the 1955 session, Senator Allen Ellender of Louisiana, an advocate for the domestic cane interests, had attended closed hearings of the Senate Finance Committee and had taken along beet and cane lobbyists as expert advisers. This was a violation of Senate custom, not infrequently breeched, which escaped notice amid the flood of congressional happenings at session's end. Demonstrating that news need not always be fresh, Stavisky supplied the details several weeks later to syndicated columnist Drew Pearson, who promptly headlined his column: "Apologies to Senator Ellender for underestimating his work for domestic sugar interests."

Early in 1956, the Senate passed a measure highly favorable to Cuba which, after compromises in conference with the House, still assured Cuba of its position as major supplier. But before this final outcome, the President of the American Chamber of Commerce of Cuba had written Stavisky, ". . . your help and that of your organization was basic and impossible to exaggerate. Without it, we would have found ourselves orphans in the storm . . ."

Undoubtedly there is much exaggeration in the tales about exploits of the insider in Washington. Still, this Cuban sugar story provides a useful narrative, for it illuminates certain techniques of the modern lobbyist. The story should not be regarded as an exposé. Stavisky did not bribe anyone nor otherwise engage in secret or unscrupulous activities. Though others—the reporters, the Congressional Committee aides, and Vice-President Nixon—might be embarrassed to have their roles revealed, they could hardly be arraigned in either a court of law or of their peers.

Moreover, it cannot be demonstrated that public policy was done a disservice by Stavisky's activities. His cause had considerable merit. He was confronted with competing pressure groups, equally organized and sophisticated. Had it been possible for government to conduct its business in a vacuum, the outcome might have been the same. But given the existing system of pressures, it is extremely doubtful that the outcome would have been the same if Stavisky had not acted as he did. He managed to focus the attention of distracted policy-makers on his problem, to trigger actions by some, and to thwart actions by others. Probably none of the policy-makers did anything that he did not wish to do, but a good many might have been too preoccupied or too timid to do what they did if they had not been egged on.

The founding fathers accepted the inevitable presence of what Madison called "the disease of faction" in the body politic, but it was their devout expectation that government in America, being both federal and republican, would minimize the ills. Their dilemma was how to limit the role of the interest groups while ensuring citizens the right to petition for "redress of grievances." A century and a half later, a House Committee still pondered this dilemma: "One of the central purposes of government is that people should be able to reach it; the central purpose of what we call 'lobbying' is that they should reach it with maximum impact and possibility of success." [3] Organized interest groups have become an accepted phenomenon of the Washington power structure.

The way of lobbying, too, has gone through considerable evolution. The first use of the word, according to H. L. Mencken, was in 1829 when it was applied to seekers after special privilege, known as "lobby-agents," in the New York Capitol in Albany. Soon the word, along with the agents, migrated to Washington. During the mammoth battles over tariff, railroad rights, patent privileges, and anti-monopoly legislation, lobbying became an expression of derogation. Walt Whitman linked "lobbiers" along with "kept editors" and assorted other villains as "the lousy combings and born freedom-sellers of the earth." James Buchanan wrote President-elect Franklin Pierce in 1852: "The host of contractors, speculators, stockjobbers, and lobby members which haunt the halls of Congress, all desirous *per fas aut nefas* and on any and every pretext to get their arms into the public treasury are sufficient to alarm every friend of his country." [4]

During this period, there was an attempt to impose restraints when the House of Representatives adopted a rule barring the customary privilege of seats on the floor to those newspapermen employed to prosecute claims pending before Congress. Just how far lobbying extended into the legislative process was documented by a congressional committee report in 1855 which indicated that Samuel Colt, inventor of the famous pistol, had paid a "contingent fee" of $10,000 to a congressman for services to be performed in obtaining a patent extension. Colt's chief lobbyist, Alexander Hay, maintained headquarters in various hotels and dispensed food and liquor to congressmen—along with the services of three charming ladies known as Spiritualists who were reportedly adept at "moving with the Members."

During the latter part of the nineteenth century, venality was considered a commonplace way of influencing the policy-makers in Washington. "Even as late as 1923, when

I entered Congress," wrote Representative Emanuel Celler, "the halls were still resounding with the scandals brought to light ten years earlier concerning lobbying activities of the National Association of Manufacturers which opposed the Underwood Tariff bill." [5] The NAM had employed the chief page of the House to eavesdrop on the cloakroom activities, and an NAM lobbyist had his own private office in the Capitol for the purpose of collecting advance reports by both majority and minority members on pending legislation.

After four months of probing and sixty volumes of testimony, a House Committee reached the awed conclusion that the NAM was "an organization having purposes and aspirations . . . so vast and far-reaching as to excite at once admiration and fear—admiration for the genius that conceived them and fear for the ultimate effects which the successful accomplishment of all these ambitions might have in a Government such as ours." [6]

Except for the censure of one offending congressman, nothing much came of these exposures in terms of concrete reform. But they did help to set in motion a metamorphosis from the "old" to the "new" brand of lobbying. The "old" NAM bribed congressmen and employed legislative spies; the "new" prefers to work in public, openly offering advice and assistance to politicians. The "old" NAM sent paid intermediaries to "influence" the drafting of the Republican Convention Platform; the "new" prepares a "Platform of American Industry" and offers to testify at both party conventions. In 1906 and 1908, election agents of the NAM entered congressional districts to organize "protective associations" on behalf of favored candidates; the "white list" of the AFL-supported congressmen automatically served as the "black list" for the NAM. Today the NAM distributes a selected voting record on all congressmen and lets constituents draw their own conclusions.

Formerly there was an arrogant disregard for public opinion; an NAM witness defiantly told a congressional

investigator, "I consider this exposé—if it is called an exposé
—a sunlight ray from heaven." Today the NAM refers
to its "bank account" theory of public relations, which
"necessitates making regular and frequent deposits in the
Bank of Public Good-Will so that valid checks can be
drawn on this account when desirable . . ." [7] Public relations and informational activities now consume the greater
part of the NAM's budget; it reports that only a small fraction of the budget is spent for "lobbying" purposes.

But the NAM has not grown more modest in its ambitions. This organization, which in peak years enrolls only
about six per cent of the nation's manufacturing enterprises and is largely directed by a few gigantic corporations,
regularly purports to speak as the representative voice of
American industry. According to an analysis, 125 firms held
63 per cent of all directorships in the NAM, with only a
dozen or so of them having assets of less than $10 million. [8]

In Washington there are quite a number of these institutionalized interest groups which, though duly registered as
lobbyists, firmly deny that this label describes the range and
scope of their activities. Many of them have grown large
and scarcely less bureaucratic than the government. The
labor unions whose marble temples are scattered about the
city, the farm organizations, and the others may vary in
their pursuits within the cloakrooms of Congress, but they
all maintain year-round surveillance of the Executive bureaus, the regulatory agencies, and each other.

Old-style lobbying has by no means disappeared from
Washington. Any reporter who has nosed around has his
own catalogue of unsavory deals, though he may not always
be able to prove how much money changed hands. Pressure
boys with bluff and bully methods still move on Capitol
Hill; witness the Teamsters' effort to save their skins during
the labor reform fight. There is no lack of emoluments for
the congressman, ranging from legal fees for his law firm

back home to handsome "honoraria" when he delivers a speech at interest-group gatherings.

But the smart lobbyist shies away from the crude approach. He knows that a single misadventure can queer the whole deal, as when Senator Francis Case exposed a bribe offered by an oil lobbyist during the fight over natural gas regulation. In that particular case, President Eisenhower felt obliged to veto a bill he favored strongly because it had been "tainted" by pressure tactics.

The smart lobbyist like Stavisky prefers to devote great energy to what he describes as "building a climate of public opinion." By skillful intrusions into the communication system, he strives not only to awaken general public sympathy for his cause but also to coagulate support among other interest groups. Thus sustained, he turns his attention to the policy-making process. He knows he can be most effective by being helpful, by being timely, and, not least, by being accurate. According to the testimony of lobbyists themselves, the cardinal sin is to supply faulty information which puts a trusting policy-maker in an exposed position.[9]

"While the methods of the 'old' lobby have not been completely abandoned," one veteran government servant has written, "the 'new' lobby is everywhere respected, accepted, and causes few editorial writers to thunder. It is not difficult to discover the reasons—active citizens are themselves caught up in the system while the passive citizen, if he pays any attention to it at all, sees nothing unusual in it."[10]

There has not been quite the same sophistication—or complacency—about latter-day revelations concerning the role of foreign lobbyists in Washington. Protests of outrage were heard in Congress during the fight over the Sugar Act when it was revealed that a number of influential Washington lawyers were receiving fees based on how many quota tons would be allocated to their foreign clients. Recently, an effort was launched in the Senate to prevent payment to a Washington lobbyist, a former member of the Philippine War Damage Commission, who had subsequently gone to work for Philippine claimants. The Senate Foreign Relations Committee has accumulated other damaging evidence relating to foreign agents who lobby rather than spy.

There is much to be gleaned. The recent history of the Trujillo dictatorship in the Dominican Republic provided horrendous examples of efforts to buy influence in Washington. According to charges filed in federal court by Attorney General Robert Kennedy, the Generalissimo hired New York society columnist Igor Cassini for the reason suggested in a report sent Trujillo by the Dominican consul general in New York: "He (Cassini) entertains the idea of arranging a meeting for you with Mr. Joseph Kennedy, father of the President, or with the President himself, both of whom, according to Cassini, are his intimate friends and with whom he maintains close and frequent relations." [11] Though the rendezvous between the two heads of state never came off, Cassini did manage to get himself sent, along with Ambassador Robert Murphy, on a secret Presidential mission to the Dominican Republic. Afterward, another report from the consul general in New York related that Cassini felt assured "from confidential talks with the elder Kennedy that the President had already decided favorably in the Dominican case, even going over the heads of adverse opinion in the Department of State." [12]

It is unlikely that the course of American foreign policy was much affected by this pathetic effort to merchandise a Presidential friendship. Similarly, Trujillo was also more dupe than beneficiary when, in 1959, he entered into a secret contract with the President of the Mutual Broadcasting System, Alexander L. Guterma. For the consideration of $750,000 paid in advance, Guterma agreed that during an eighteen-month period Mutual would broadcast a "monthly minimum of 425 minutes of news and commentary regarding the Dominican Republic." According to the written contract, the U. S. radio network would refrain from broadcasting any news inconsistent with the best interests of the Dominican Republic in [Trujillo's] sole and exclusive judgment." The primary purpose of the broadcasts would be "to exemplify the stability and tranquility of the Dominican Republic and its unequivocal position and stand against Communism."

No one knows whether Guterma could have fulfilled his part of this scandalous bargain. Despite Trujillo's largesse, he shortly went bankrupt, was ousted from Mutual, and later ended up in prison convicted of stock fraud and failure to register as a foreign agent. There had been only a few efforts to show how well the American radio network could perform. Before the contract was signed, Guterma's lawyer had telephoned a story from Ciudad Trujillo about political opinion in the Dominican Republic, and this was broadcast twice from Washington. During the negotiations, according to later testimony of Trujillo's deputy, Mutual's head had volunteered, "Give me an idea, some piece of news you would like to broadcast." They had agreed on a trumped-up story about producing a Dominican movie which next day was duly carried on Walter Winchell's program from New York.

Other Mutual officials later swore that they were totally ignorant of the deal, but evidently they were at least aware of Guterma's interest in the Dominican Republic. Guterma once placed a call from Ciudad Trujillo to Mutual's Washington office. Robert Hurleigh, then Vice-President of the network, testified that his superior "said he had a congressman there who had . . . made a speech before the Legislature, or whatever the name is, and he thought this would be a good broadcast, so we took the congressman in on a beeper. . . ." Portions of the transcription were used on newscasts during the day. On another occasion, Hurleigh sent Guterma a note calling attention to an interview with

Senator Allen Ellender relating to the Caribbean. Tapes of both these broadcasts were forwarded to Trujillo. Hurleigh testified that he learned about the contract only after he succeeded Guterma as President of Mutual and happened to be visiting the Dominican Republic on a press junket.

Foreign agentry has been a fast growing business in the U. S. during recent years. Several hundred representatives of foreign governments have now registered at the Justice Department (as both Cassini and Guterma failed to do). They reflect the awareness of other nations that diplomatic representation is not necessarily the best way of getting things done in Washington. A memorandum prepared for the government of Ghana by one leading U. S. public relations firm argued that "public advocacy" by a foreign country's diplomats is generally regarded as "improper interference in the internal affairs of the United States" and "a highly ineffective method to convert or persuade the American public. . . ." The memorandum advised that, "One of the cardinal rules of effective public relations, particularly in the political sphere, is to remove the source of the idea (in this case the Government of Ghana or its representatives) as far as possible from the advocates (whether they be private individuals, organizations, or media)."

Many registered foreign agents are simply promoters of tourism and trade, while others carry on the strictly legal work necessary to back-stop embassy negotiations. But a growing number, like Samuel Stavisky, are specialists in public and governmental relations, experts at stimulating "opinion" and triggering action on behalf of their clients.

The Trujillo deals are not the only ones to deserve critical scrutiny. In 1954, the government of Guatemala, headed by Carlos Castillo Armas, hired John A. Clements Associates at a fee of $8,000 a month for a U. S. public relations campaign to be managed, according to the Justice Department registration, by Clements and Patrick Mc-

Mahon. These two men were simultaneously serving as editors of the magazine *American Mercury*. Not entirely by coincidence, the magazine published a number of articles about Guatemala during this period, including three of a political nature. While still on the Guatemala payroll, Mc-Mahon also worked as consultant to a House committee investigating communism in Guatemala and, according to his own statement, "prepared [its] report and helped edit the hearings. . . ."

Other examples of impropriety have arisen from the long campaign waged in the United States by the Nationalist Chinese to gain support for their return to the mainland.

Item: Early in 1959, the North American Newspaper Alliance distributed a series of stories written from Formosa by Don Frifield. The reader was not informed that NANA's correspondent was also employed by Hamilton Wright, the U. S. public relations firm handling the Nationalist China account. Hamilton Wright paid Frifield $19,700 for "editorial services."

Item: In June, 1958, during one of the crises over the off-shore islands of Quemoy and Matsu, Radio City Music Hall in New York offered as a supplemental feature a documentary film entitled "Fortress Formosa." Screen credits indicated it had been "produced" by Twentieth Century-Fox and "arranged by Hamilton Wright." Subsequently distributed to movie theaters all over the country, the movie gave the viewer no hint that it had been filmed, in Technicolor and CinemaScope, by Nationalist China's registered agent and turned over without cost to Twentieth Century-Fox.

Item: On October 14, 1960, the day after the third "Great Debate" in which the Presidential candidates scrapped over Quemoy and Matsu, NBC's "Today" carried on its news roundup a report of Chiang Kai-shek's angry denunciation of Kennedy's position. While the television viewers heard Chiang being quoted as voicing firm determination to resist the surrender of the islands, they watched a film sequence of Nationalist Chinese troops and tanks parading in full battle array. This film was another production of Hamilton Wright supplied *gratis* to the NBC film library and used without credit.

Item: In a catalogue of free programs offered to independent television stations, Radiant Films of New York City has listed the half-hour documentaries, "Miracle in Free China" (". . . where Madame and Generalissimo Chiang Kai-shek and their ten million followers are marking time for the return to the mainland!"), and "Face of Free China" ("How American defense in the Pacific is tied into the general defense of the free world through the U. S. Alliance with the Republic of China.") The only mention of who produced and paid for these documentaries is the cryptic notice in the catalogue that they were "Filmed by the world-renowned Hamilton Wright Organization."

Employment of private public relations firms in the U. S. on behalf of foreign governments dates largely from the end of the Second World War. Sometimes this was a matter of special necessity. The Roy Bernard Company of New York, which works for West Germany, took the account when the Bonn government was still not entitled to send an official mission to this country. A number of firms moved quickly into what was proving to be a highly profitable field of enterprise. Hamilton Wright, in addition to Nationalist China, handled Italy and Mexico; Hill and Knowlton, Inc., Japan; Harold L. Oran, Inc., South Vietnam; Curtis J. Hoxter, Inc., Austria, Guatemala, and Brazil; Max Rogel, Inc., Nicaragua.[13] The size of a foreign government's pressure operation in the United States has often appeared to be in inverse ratio to the country's size and relative importance to U. S. foreign policy.

The practice has been conditioned by the way a foreign government behaves back home. General Batista of Cuba approached one New York public relations firm to inquire how much it would cost to get favorable stories in the *New York Times*. But it is also true that foreign clients have been given false expectations by overzealous publicists. A prospectus prepared by Max Rogel, Inc., soliciting the Nicaragua account, claimed that, "We now have a comprehensive news service that makes it possible to flash a story or a photograph to every major daily newspaper in the United States. This story will come across the wire into the offices of these newspapers. It will be treated as a news story and received as such . . . This is an operation that is very similar to the workings of the two major news services in the United States. It is, in actuality, a service extended to us by one of these two news services on an exclusive basis." What the prospectus apparently referred to was the PR Newswire in New York, which transmits publicity releases around the city and has no official connection with either the Associated Press or United Press International.

Those whose business it is to sell influence are not apt to underestimate their accomplishments. Many of the feats of this new breed of foreign agents prove upon investigation to be pretty trivial stuff—a conspicuous waste of a foreign government's money or, in some cases, of U. S. aid funds given to the foreign government. But it would be a mistake to disregard this activity, for it reveals how vulnerable the American system of government can be to the manipulation of the accomplished insider.

Our communication system poses special problems. A leading public relations man handling foreign accounts has estimated that his firm "places" between a hundred and two hundred stories a week in the newspapers and claims that it is easy to do the newsman's job for him. "From my point of view as a p.r. man, this is good," he has said, "but from journalism's point of view it is not good. The number of reporters with time to dig beneath the surface facts seems to be getting smaller and smaller. We fill a vacuum in the flow of news."

This condition is due in part to the economics of U. S.

P

news coverage. Despite the hordes of reporters who congregate in Washington or accompany high officials on foreign tours, the ranks of American journalists regularly covering most of the world are thin. By estimate, nine-tenths of the news from the small and faraway countries is handled by part-time employees known as stringers, who piece out their income with other jobs. Until events reach the crisis point in many places, news coverage is a hit-or-miss proposition. This has led to the practice of travel subsidies with which the agents of a distant country try to lure a Washington correspondent. One reporter, who made an expenses-paid junket to Nicaragua, claimed that for such "marginal" stories the foreign government must pay the freight or nobody will go. "After all," he protested, "who gives a damn about Nicaragua?"

Economics plays an even larger role in the video business. It permits a commercial firm like Hamilton Wright, which maintains excellent camera crews, to operate with absolute confidence of placing its client's product. A typical contract, drawn up with Chile, has specified that newsreels and commentary would be prepared and delivered free of charge to Fox-Movietone, MGM Newsreel, Paramount, Warner-Pathé, and Universal-International. And there is the addendum: "This organization guarantees that five or more of the above newsreels shall be accepted and shown by one of the above-mentioned companies throughout its entire chain of theaters in the United States."

Among public relations firms, it is generally agreed that the theater newsreel is a declining news form and is pretty well forced to live on such handouts. Television networks are more alert to attempts at infiltration by influence peddlers. One editor for NBC News has made the distinction that he will accept film footage but not the accompanying scripts from the public relations outfits. "They try to use us, but we use them," he commented. A more fertile field for planting film has been the independent television stations. These have such consuming needs that a number of middleman outfits, like Radiant Films, specialize in distributing free films prepared by others. The distributors are paid not by the television station but by the supplier of film. Sterling Movies U. S. A., Inc., one of the biggest, puts out a fat catalogue of offerings that have been prepared to fill half- and quarter-hour time slots in a TV station's schedule. Among the foreign listings in a recent issue were eight films on Algeria ("The background story on this critical area in world affairs . . ."), four on the Sahara, two on Morocco, and three on Tunisia. Investigation turned up the fact that the Algerian films had been financed by the French government which hired New York producers to edit them, dub in English voices, and arrange the distribution. This was hardly the way to guarantee objectivity in treating highly controversial areas of foreign policy.

The notion that foreign agents are infiltrating our communication system and influencing our policy-makers has a sinister ring. Yet taken as a whole, their work is probably no more mysterious or unscrupulous than the work done for domestic clients. This varies, of course, from client to client and lobbyist to lobbyist; in this unlicensed profession the practitioners have been able to devise their own rules as they go along. The foreign client, especially if it happens to be the government of a little country off the beaten path of American tourism, stands a better chance of concealing shoddy wares. But the problem posed by pressure groups, domestic and foreign, is largely the same: how to reconcile the "special interest" with the "public interest" remains a formidable question now that interest groups have grown infinitely more sophisticated and subtle in pursuing their objectives.

Congressman Celler, having defined lobbying as "the total of all communicated influences upon legislators . . . ," distinguishes between the "good" and "bad" as "not whether the objectives of persuasion are selfish or altruistic, liberal or conservative, prolabor or probusiness, but solely and simply whether the message conveyed is intelligible, accurate, and informative, or cryptic, deceptive, and obscure." [14] He provides a distinction which has been the touchstone for governmental regulation in this field. By law, lobbyists are required to register with Congress and to offer a financial accounting of their activities. Agents of foreign governments are obliged to make full disclosure to the U. S. Department of Justice. "Resting on the fundamental Constitutional principle," according to an interpretation by Supreme Court Justice Hugo Black, "that our people adequately informed may be trusted to distinguish between the true and the false, the [Foreign Agents Registration Act of 1938] is intended to label information of foreign origin so the hearers and readers may not be deceived by the belief that the information comes from a disinterested source."

But the spotlight of publicity by which Congress intended to illumine these activities has been somewhat less than pitiless. Under the rather vague definitions of the Lobby Act, there is room for a great deal of latitude on the part of the lobbyist in listing his activities and expenditures. His larger role of influencing others to influence the policy-makers falls outside the purview of the act. The sums of money reported to Congress each year, it is commonly recognized, are only the top of the iceberg.

The law is more rigorous in regard to foreign lobbyists. Over the past quarter-century, there have been several prosecutions and convictions for failure to register under the foreign-agent act. Beside demanding full disclosure, the act also requires the labelling of all communications intended to influence "any section of the public . . . with reference to the political or public interests, policies, or relations of a government of a foreign country. . . ." But few people come to inspect the Justice Department's files and many of the filings give no more than the barest details. The labelling provision has proved totally inadequate to cope with the manner in which propaganda finds its way to the public nowadays: foreign agent to producer to distributor to middleman to media representative.

One other method of regulation has been the Federal Communications Commission's requirement that a radio or TV station disclose to its audience "exactly who is paying for or furnishing the broadcast material . . . [on] political matters or controversial issues of public importance." In 1958, Westinghouse Broadcasting was censured for failing to label film used on one of its news programs that had been supplied by the National Association of Manufacturers. The FCC maintained that there should be "the highest degree of diligence on the part of the licensee . . . in ascertaining . . . the actual source . . . and identifying this source plainly to the viewing public." But the Commissioners also have boggled at the awesome task of monitoring communications sufficiently to determine the origin of everything that goes over the air waves.

Some who are deeply concerned about the freewheeling ways of special interest groups in Washington have proposed that a more effective restraint would be to compel disclosure by the officials on whom pressure is being brought. A bill filed repeatedly in Congress by Senators Clifford Case, Republican of New Jersey, and Maurine Neuberger, Democrat of Oregon, would require all top officials in the Legislative and Executive branches to report annually their sources of income, including gifts worth $100 or more, and to list further their financial assets and liabilities, together with dealings in securities, commodities, and real property. Such records, to be kept on file with the Comptroller General for inspection by the public and press, would undoubtedly serve to expose or inhibit conflicts of interest that now go unnoticed. So far congressmen have displayed precious little enthusiasm for thus monitoring themselves.

During the heyday of the scandals over the lobbyists, scholars became convinced that the real rulers in America were unseen and unknown to the multitude, but that "always they are there and always they are few." Government could only be understood, so the theory went, when it was realized how group pressures functioned within the framework of our governmental system. According to some interpreters, a legislative act was inevitably "the calculable resultant of a struggle between pressure groups, never a decision between opposing conceptions of the national welfare." [15]

Time has modified and refined this thesis. Pressure-group activity has moved beyond the legislative process to affect all agencies of policy-making. It has even pervaded the realm of the courts where, as civil rights organizations have amply demonstrated, the strategy of bringing test cases can be a fruitful field of pressure-group endeavor.[16]

The definition of what constitutes a pressure group has broadened considerably. On vital national issues not engendering automatic public support, the executive agencies of the government have learned how to collaborate in pressure operations with private groups. Volunteer organizations, ranging from the League of Women Voters to the atomic scientists, have proved themselves on occasion as adept as the professional lobbyists in promoting a particular cause. Now and again, the struggles among the pressure groups do make it possible to discern what can be described as "opposing conceptions of the national welfare."

Still, only a congenital optimist would argue that amid all this competition an "invisible hand," *à la* Adam Smith, is serving as an automatic self-regulator to provide the maximum public "good." The pressure necessary to effectuate a policy or sustain a program usually gives strong bargaining advantage to those with immediate and obvious interests. To promote larger and long-range interests of the nation requires vast expenditures of energy and skill by many people, not least by the President.

There is no guarantee that the various factions pursuing a particular interest will combine to achieve creative results. Witness, as a case study in frustration, the way the education lobby in Washington has managed to checkmate itself for more than a decade because of disputes over federal aid to higher *vs.* lower schools, public *vs.* parochial, and even scholarships *vs.* loans. In this case and others, professional lobbyists who reside too long in the nation's capital sometimes acquire careerist ambitions that make them arrogant and ineffectual agents of those they are supposed to serve.

Amid all the clamor of the interest groups one often suspects that there are voices not being heard. Congressman Clem Miller described the plight of two farm groups —the walnut growers and the independent poultrymen— who were driven to Washington by dire needs. Both were suffering the same problem: economic crisis because of overabundance. The walnut growers, well organized, were able to carry out a shrewd campaign of agitation on Capitol Hill, to stage an industry "presentation" at the Department of Agriculture and, within two weeks, to get the government help they wanted. The poultrymen had no organization, and Congressman Miller, upon inquiring, discovered that "Of the seven thousand bills in Congress, there was not one on poultry or eggs." He also learned that no hearings had been scheduled. "The prevailing view was that since there was no agreement on policy, hearings would serve no purpose." After considerable prodding, hearings were finally held at which the poultrymen described their pitiable condition. But Miller reported sadly, "All of the men were active poultrymen who had to get back to their flocks. They were leaving that night. Who was to carry the ball for them here in Washington during the next critical weeks? Who was going to do the telephoning? Who was going to co-ordinate policy between New Jersey, California, Alabama, Wisconsin, Georgia and Kansas? The answer from them was 'No one.' We had been given a problem. It was ours now. The result to date: a resolution of the Agriculture Committee urging the Secretary [of Agriculture] to 'implement such programs of purchase, diversion, and export of poultry products as will lead toward improvement of the present critical situation.' Results for the poultrymen: Nothing." [17]

Too much reliance on pressure groups to take the initiative can result in failure of urgent problems to get adequate governmental attention. In the case of many programs launched with great fanfare, lack of sustained pressure can lead to subsequent neglect by the policy-makers. The thoughtful observer has reason to wonder whether the nation's present economic situation, predominantly affluent but with widespread pockets of deep distress, may not be hardening into a permanent condition because the politicians are not getting the message.

Congressmen, harassed and faction-ridden though they be, are aware of this failure. A recent poll of 175 Senators and Representatives raised the question whether there is "some field of interest which is not represented by an organized lobby . . . but which, in your opinion, should be." The yeas outran the nays, 62.1 per cent to 37.9. A Senator added a pessimistic conclusion undoubtedly shared by many: "One group which will never be adequately represented—-the ordinary citizen and taxpayer." [18]

13

THE NEWS MANAGERS

There is one legitimate place where news can be managed—at the desks of our newspaper city editors and at the desks of our radio and television station news directors. . . .

Pierre Salinger,
PRESIDENTIAL PRESS SECRETARY[1]

News generated by actions of the government as to content and timing are part of the arsenal of weaponry that a President has in application of military force and related forces to the solution of political problems, or to the application of international political pressure.

Arthur Sylvester,
ASSISTANT SECRETARY OF DEFENSE (PUBLIC AFFAIRS)[2]

No cry resounds more regularly in Washington than that someone in high office is attempting to "manage the news." To judge from the outraged protests one might suppose that the information about government ought somehow to flow by natural processes until its confluence with the great sea of public opinion. Actually, news is a commodity involving anxious managerial concern all along the way.

News is a fundamental force in the struggle to govern. Each day, hundreds of thousands of words are spoken, tens of dozens of events occur. The press and other media perform the arduous task of sorting out and assigning priorities to these words and events. This capacity to choose, with speed and brevity, which stories command widespread attention and which go unnoticed, constitutes a power far more formidable than the purely editorial preferences of the press.

Communication, of course, is essential to every government, even that of a closed totalitarian system. But there are important differences. In the Soviet Union, news is treated as a pre-packaged product to be distributed or withheld, blown up or minimized, according to the specification of the political leaders. By frank definition of the communists, news is an instrument of government and the party for the education of the people.

In the British parliamentary system, the press does not play as large a daily role as in America. The Prime Minister and his cabinet colleagues are obliged to report initially to the House of Commons which is, by ancient understanding, the "embodiment" of the nation. Reporters are accustomed to serve as bystanders, recording and commenting on the two-way discourse within the official government.

In Washington, reporters are accustomed to a more intimate role. Unofficial communication between the executive and legislative branches of government—and within each branch—goes on regularly through the press, well in advance of official communication. Few policies of consequence are launched without prior briefing of the press. More than in any other major capital, the reporter accepts and even asserts the right to keep government informed about itself. He expects access to policy-making at every stage of the process.

The reasons for this intimacy lie in the Constitutional ordering of power. Because ours is a government of "separated institutions sharing powers," there is need for constant communication if the wheels of policy are to mesh at all. Yet none of the contentious rivals designated by the Constitution would be satisfied to rely solely on a reporting system beholden to any other. The press, having its independence buttressed by private ownership as well as by Constitutional mandate, must help serve this intelligence function.

But the press functions do not stop there. Since power is fragmented in the American system, public opinion is called on more regularly than elsewhere to act as arbiter among the competing policies and politicians. Programs can live or die depending on whether they attract enough attention to build a favorable consensus among interested publics. Indeed, amid the onward rush of events, politicians often measure the news as substitute for a more difficult assessment of the popular attitudes.

These functions—which have become increasingly urgent as government has grown big and its powers more variegated —have thrust the reporter into a role for which he is not altogether qualified. In theory, nothing guarantees that his definition of what is news will establish proper priorities among the important events of government. In practice, the priorities of the press can be decisive, even reshaping the priorities of government itself. Those involved in politics at the higher levels develop acute sensitivity to the interplay between the reality and the image, between policy formulation and the publicizing of it. It has led toward what might be called government by publicity in which a continuing preoccupation of the policy-makers is how the news is managed.

Communication has developed into a massive and complex industry in Washington. The old stereotype of the reporter as a seedy character operating with a hunch and a hangover no longer fits the corps of craftsmen, now estimated at more than twelve hundred, who serve the high consumption needs of a highly specialized business. News is sought out, transmitted, packaged, and delivered in many different ways. Reporters vary widely in their assignments, from the leg man for the wire service covering a departmental beat to the columnist or commentator who encompasses the world's affairs in his daily perspective. Government bureaucracy is cross-hatched by the press bureaucracy. Separate corps concentrate on the political, the economic, the military, and, with increasing zest, the scientific communities in Washington. There are reporters who communicate by the printed word and others who use audio and video apparatus. Together they constitute, in effect, a separate and quasi-official branch of government in Washington holding substantial power over the processes of ratification and veto.*

Recognizing this role, one can better assess the various arrangements which have evolved to maintain relations between government and the press in Washington. Starting at the White House, there has been vast change since the time when Woodrow Wilson, asserting that "news is the atmosphere of public affairs," inaugurated the regular Presidential news conference. Today, the news conference has grown from an intimate gathering into a mammoth ceremony simultaneously shared with the viewing public. The press serves as constant consort to a President during his working day, and is in attendance whenever he travels. Press deadlines play a large part in setting the schedule of a President's responses to the events crowding in on him.

Many critics within and without government are appalled by this relationship. They argue that it encourages a President to speak offhandedly about matters of great moment— that he is hustled by routines not of his own choosing. The ready reply is that a President has no choice. If he values his leadership, he must play front and center stage in the drama of government. Otherwise, rival actors in Congress and elsewhere are eager to claim the spotlight.

Similar dispute rages over congressional dealings with the press. The legislators have resorted increasingly to their investigatory power as an instrument of influence in Wash-

---

* See the author's book, *The Fourth Branch of Government* (Boston: Houghton Mifflin Company, 1959), for a more detailed analysis of the role of the press in Washington.

ington. The accusation is made that many of these investigations are staged simply to attract the mass media. Any reporter who has covered the hearings on Capitol Hill is aware of this orientation. The committee chairman displays skill in the techniques and timing of news. An inquiry is often paced to gather the maximum harvest of headlines.

Some, among the victims particularly, grow irate when they witness these spectaculars in Congress. But the fact must be noted that the congressmen are affected by the same publicity compulsions as the President. Generating news is an important way to assert their own order of priorities. By such means, they hope to capture the attention not merely of the general public but of Congress itself.

A third arrangement for generating news arouses continuing concern in Washington. It involves the subterranean channels of the "leak" which flow most actively during the periods when government is involved in crisis. As domestic or foreign trouble deepens, the reader is aware of a peculiar change in the news he receives. He continues to be informed about what policy-makers are contemplating but there is no indication of the origins of this information. What has happened is that the reporter has made himself party to a conspiracy in which he engages in compulsory plagiarism. He reports official attitudes as if he had made them up himself.

Critics charge that the practice of cloaking the news provides an inducement to irresponsibility. By permitting the official to pass along information which he does not have to endorse publicly, it benefits those who seek to use news as a propaganda weapon. By allowing the press to report without attribution, it permits the more sensationalist reporters to add their own special twist. Any veteran of background conferences can cite numerous instances of both kinds of news fabrication.

But again the realist finds it impossible to join forces with the prohibitionists who would abolish the practice. He recognizes that leakage serves a necessary function if there is to be communication during crisis periods. Handled in a responsible way, cloaked news can help prevent the orgy of wild rumor which occurs when official government spokesmen go silent.

The continuing debate between government and the press has not been much advanced by doctrinaire arguments. Too many of the zealous spokesmen for the public's "right to know" sound as if all government business should be conducted in the newspaper headlines. Too many in government who decry the "irresponsibility" of the press are prone to judge news less for accuracy than for personal embarrassment. Neither concept has much relevance to the workaday world of the Washington correspondent.

Still, a more realistic assessment of the managerial problems of news does raise troublesome dilemmas. Man has come a long way since that distant time when, by projecting a series of photographs at a certain speed, the illusion of movement was created for the human eye, giving birth to the magic of the motion picture industry. Today, much is known about creating illusions in the minds of people. Politicians faced with intractable problems constantly are tempted to employ the publicity resources of government to project images that do not correspond to reality.

The most glaring example of such image-making was provided by the late Senator Joseph McCarthy (R., Wis.). McCarthy was a demagogue of the mass media. Unlike earlier types, he was not proficient in the stump speech or the impassioned filibuster; rather, he was a master at creating headlines—in timing his pseudo-news to distract a nationwide audience over a prolonged period. Almost solely by publicity, he built political power that permitted him to disrupt the important business of government, until he was felled by his own weapons. Though McCarthyism has passed on, its basic evil—the cynical use of communication for deception rather than enlightenment—still crops up in Congress and elsewhere.

Complaints that a President was tinkering with images was raised against even so phlegmatic a man as Calvin Coolidge. But the coincidental growth of the modern Presidency and mass media communication has added new anxieties about news management at the White House level. The accusation was made that Eisenhower, both as candidate and President, benefited from techniques borrowed from Madison Avenue. As evidence, critics pointed out that his press secretary, James Hagerty, employed enormous creative skill in press relations in order to convey the impression of activity at the White House even during periods when the President suffered the enforced idleness of serious illness; that Eisenhower aides peddled catchy slogans to reassure citizens and the press that more defense was being bought for less money, even while forces were being cut back; that Attorney General Herbert Brownell, by a clever "numbers game," pretended to be purging the government of security risks in order to appease McCarthyite sentiment in the nation.

This suspicion of image-manipulation did not depart with Kennedy's arrival at the White House. The late President brought a personal attitude toward the press quite different from the aloofness of Eisenhower. Coming of political age in Washington, Kennedy had long maintained intimate contact with reporters. According to one wry observation, if Eisenhower was disposed not to read newspapers enough, Kennedy had a disposition to read them too much. As President, he began to set a radically new pattern both by his own accessibility to the press and by swiftly responding to stories that aroused his interest. Reporters and government officials alike soon grew accustomed to White House follow-ups after each news break.

Unlike Eisenhower, Kennedy showed a shrewd understanding of the production needs of the press, particularly the mass media. He quite regularly encouraged the purveying of the "inside dope" which commands the media's priority attention. His associates were inclined to boast that never before has government information flowed so abundantly—and this was confirmed by a poll of leading Washington correspondents, who voted thirty-one to four that they enjoyed more access to news sources in the Kennedy than in the Eisenhower Administration.[3]

Nevertheless, the suspicion began to mount that there were sinister aspects to this new era of government-press relations. The same poll of correspondents, in response to the question, which Administration "worked harder at news management," voted twenty-nine for Kennedy to six for Eisenhower.

In part, this developing estrangement was a familiar phenomenon. Leo Rosten, writing more than a quarter of a century ago, made an assessment of a condition that affects all occupants of the White House:

> Newspapermen greet [a newly elected President] with the hope that here, at last, is the great man incarnate. . . . The great man's talents are sung, over-sung in the struggle for journalistic existence. Then "incidents" occur, a political compromise of not admirable hue, a political setback, attacks from the opposition. The newspapermen begin to see the pedal clay. They have been "taken in." Their faith has been outraged. How did they ever "fall for the stuff"? The demon on the desk in the home office sends them sarcastic reminders of their first euphoria. Other newspapermen, columnists, editors, publishers cry that the press corps was hamstrung by phrases. The correspondents are hurt; they are irritated; and they feel guilty. The breaking of the myth begins, by the very men who erected it.[4]

Not all the difficulty, however, lies in this cyclical pattern. There has also been the growing feeling that the traditional devices by which government and the press keep in touch are inadequate for the needs. The heavy reliance on background briefings permits an administration to chronicle its triumphs and play down its shortcomings. After successful exploits—such as the Cuban quarantine—the

White House encourages post mortems which purport to give a play-by-play account of what happened. (The technique can produce unplanned embarrassments—as when a *Saturday Evening Post* article about the quarantine, co-authored by two journalist friends of Kennedy, derogated the role of U.N. Ambassador Stevenson. The White House was forced to issue a denial that this was a Presidential hatchet job.) After less happy exploits, such as the abortive Bay of Pigs invasion, the press finds Administration sources are more discreet.

Suspicion toward cloaked news has also been stirred by administration efforts to improve "co-ordination." There was a loud outcry against directives issued by the Departments of State and Defense requiring employees to submit regular accountings of their conversations with reporters. Information officers in these departments protested vainly that this was merely a routine precaution to keep track of the news flow. But reporters claimed that the directives represented a diabolical effort to cut off a major source of "unmanaged" news—their meticulous probings among subordinates in government who do not always agree with the official line.

Part of the frustration for those who worry about news management arises from the increasing sterility of their on-the-record contacts with the government. Department heads and, not least, the Secretary of State, have held their news conferences much too sporadically to be of interpellative value. And the Presidential news conference simply has grown too big. The influx of participants does not permit systematic follow-up of any line of inquiry. The invasion of the television camera, its red eyes aglow, has brought stiffness and staginess to the proceedings. Questions and answers are apt to be phrased to be understandable to the mass viewing audience rather than to probe deeply into a complicated issue.

Both Eisenhower and Kennedy did achieve a tranquillity at the news conference alien to its tradition. By steadfast re-

liance on the generalities, Eisenhower was able to parry
most of the thrusts that came his way. Kennedy followed
the contrary technique by reciting a parade of specifics
which, the reporter recognized afterward did not always
provide a pertinent answer. Seldom was there the lively
exchange, much less the controversy, that characterized the
conference during Truman's time.

The dilemma of news management has acquired an extra
dimension with the effort to add "national security" to the
criteria by which news is to be judged. During wartime, the
government set the standards for semi-voluntary censorship of the press. Now, during a permanent condition of
Cold War, there is not even agreement in defining the nature of the dilemma. Some officials have offered definitions
with a notable lack of success. Eisenhower's deputy for national security matters, Robert Cutler, proposed a drastic
solution in 1955: "Until the President has acted, until he
has approved a policy recommendation made to him by the
National Security Council, *nothing has happened. . . .*"
[Italics mine.] According to Cutler's view, reporters have no
business delving into security matters during the deliberative stages, or, in certain areas, even after a President has
acted. Rather than requiring government to defend its secrecy, Cutler suggested that members of the press "must
make clear how they will contribute to our survival; they
must prove to us that the widespread, public disclosure of
our secret projects will make the free world stronger, and
the neutrals better disposed; will rally the subject peoples,
and will put the Communist regimes at disadvantage." [5]
Cutler was concerned with suppressing security information. More recently, the suggestion has been made that national security may require positive measures in government's handling of news. After the Cuban quarantine,
Kennedy's Assistant Secretary of Defense for Public Affairs,
Arthur Sylvester, agreed with reporters that the crisis had
posed more difficulties for them than during wartime. Syl-

vester, formerly a newspaperman, defended Pentagon news policies with the argument: "I cannot think of a comparable situation, but in the kind of world we live in the generation of news by the government becomes one weapon in a strained situation. The results, in my opinion, justify the methods we used." [6] For many advocates of freedom of information, this was confirmation of their worst fears.

All three postwar Presidents have worried publicly about the leakage of security information to the press. Truman once claimed that "ninety-five per cent of our secret information has been published by newspapers and slick magazines." In a press conference in 1955, Eisenhower said: "For some two years and three months I have been plagued by inexplicable undiscovered leaks in this Government." But Kennedy carried the argument a bit further when, soon after the failure of the Bay of Pigs invasion, he addressed the Publishers Association and declared, "If the press is waiting for a declaration of war before it imposes the self-discipline of combat conditions, then I can only say that no war ever posed a greater threat to our security." Kennedy argued that while passing judgment on a story's news value, editors must also decide whether its publication would be in "the nation's interest."

Kennedy's Press Secretary, Pierre Salinger, denied that the late President was advocating voluntary censorship. According to his own description:

"What [Kennedy] was seeking was a constructive dialogue on this subject. I must report that no such constructive dialogue took place. A subsequent meeting with a group of top news executives must be labeled as a failure. The President proposed that the newspapers of the country select a representative of their own who could challenge the government whenever any newspaper felt that secrecy was being unduly imposed over any information. The government on its part under the President's plan would make available to this person in whom the newspapers of the country had trust any and all information needed to make an independent judgment on the efficacy of information being withheld. The assembled editors and publishers rejected this proposal as infeasible in peace time despite the fact the President advanced the premise that the United States was and will be for a number of years involved in an international struggle of an unprecedented nature in our nation's history. Subsequent events continue to vindicate the President's view—the Berlin crisis, the situation in Laos and South Viet Nam and the Cuban crisis have all served to underline his point." * 7

The issue that Kennedy had posed is not likely to be settled at the negotiating table. The separation of powers underlying the problem is too deep and too indigenous to our system of government. Still, the reporter recognizes that on occasion he must operate in a no-man's-land where news and national security come into conflict. In the absence of official censorship, he somehow must make judgments about which news is *not* fit to print—at least for the time being. Every Washington newsman knows that there have been concrete instances of disclosures damaging to the nation's interests. An item about unsuccessful Soviet missile launchings compromised U. S. intelligence and necessitated costly alterations in our detection mechanisms. The prior disclosure of the U. S. position at international conferences has, like exposure of a poker player's hand, undermined our bargaining power before debate began. Within the government, premature revelation of new policies aborning—such as the sensationalized account of Secretary Rusk's memorandum cited in an earlier chapter—has disrupted the policy-making process and embarrassed relations with allies.

But it would be idle to lay all the blame at the reporter's doorstep. He does not operate alone in the communication process. As William S. White, a veteran correspondent, has written, "The leak of an exclusive story is rarely an example of a reporter's persistence or skill. More often it is simply an

* Excerpts from remarks at Silver Guild Awards Banquet, Hilton Hotel, Pittsburgh, Pa. Press release dated December 5, 1962.

evidence of the harassed necessity of some official to put a situation before the public with a spurious sense of drama in order to gain attention for it." [8] The intense competition for publicity as a means of power makes it difficult to draw a hard-and-fast line distinguishing matters of national security. Cutler's thesis that nothing has happened until a President has acted simply does not take account of realities in a government of separated powers where policies often flourish or wane without crossing the President's desk.

The attempt to articulate dogmas about the handling of "the news" can be a self-defeating proposition. Certainly news is bound to be regarded as a weapon by officials who are involved in struggles of statecraft. But they are foolish if they expect to say so out loud and get away with it. Certainly the press has the duty to suspect, to challenge, and to try to get round the blockades erected against access to the news. But to evolve a theory about "freedom of information" is to assume mistakenly that getting the important story can ever be made resistance-proof.

A free press and a purposeful government are destined always to be involved in a war of sorts. The fact that recent administrations have become increasingly sophisticated in the usages of publicity only makes this more inevitable. What the protagonists ought to be seeking is not total disarmament of their opponents, but at least limited agreement on weapons control. The objective, often forgotten in the conflict, is to preserve that communication of essential truth which makes democratic government possible.

VI

The Struggle
to Govern

THE STRUGGLE TO GOVERN

"One is startled by the thought of what might befall this huge yet delicate fabric of laws and commerce and social institutions were the foundations it has rested on to crumble away . . . The more democratic republics become, the more the masses grow conscious of their own power, the more do they need to live, not only by patriotism, but by reverence and self-control, and the more essential to their well-being are those sources whence reverence and self-control flow.

JAMES BRYCE[1]

"Every political constitution in which different bodies share the supreme power is only enabled to exist by the forebearance of those among whom this power is distributed."

JOHN RUSSELL[2]

To judge from the fictional accounts of politics in Washington, few holds are barred during its lusty power struggles. In one recent novel, the President cavalierly disregards the perjury committed by his Secretary of State-designate, shanghais a government witness about to give damaging testimony, and callously blackmails an obstinate Senator, causing him to commit suicide. A recent play on Broadway depicts two Presidential candidates engaged in reciprocal skullduggery until one, failing to reconcile his scruples with his ambition, resolves the power struggle by retiring from it.

The novelist's President is described as "utterly removed from the normal morality that holds society together" the playwright's ex-President remarks incredulously, "An immoral President? They hardly come in any other size." [3]

It is an old American custom to suspect the worst about the motives and morals of our politicians. Our image of government in America—of the democratic system, which we esteem, and of those involved professionally in it, whom often as not we eschew—is curiously ambivalent. We are prone to be always examining the moral plight of the politician caught up in bitter conflict; we weigh his dilemma as he balances conscience against conviction, moral restraint against personal ambition, the means against the ends.

The distribution of power in Washington makes for this kind of drama. Because of the highly fragmented power structure, because no one—not even the President—has an unyielding mandate to exercise the decisive power, the business of government requires the continual clash of politicians testing each other's strength and purpose. This continually raises the question of how far will the politician go as he grapples to gain or hold a precarious perch.

Starting with such a premise, the novelist sees nothing wrong in giving free rein to his imagination when creating the saga of Washington. Why not suggest that our political leaders become imbued with a vague immorality or superman morality? Why not believe that Presidents use their power callously and cruelly to destroy those who stand in their way; that Supreme Court Justices filch documents; that Cabinet officials lie under oath; that Senators get involved in predicaments from which suicide is the only escape; that Presidential candidates take dossiers to each other's hotel suites and threaten each other with "exposure"?

The only answer that can be given is that except in rare and isolated instances things do not happen this way. It is unrealistic to employ the lingo of politics without recognizing that there are limits to the power struggle as it is waged at the higher levels of government. Creating hyperbolical plots serves merely to stretch the moral dilemma out of proportion; it results in caricature rather than convincing commentary.

In this writer's observation, there are three quite unnovel conditions of politics in Washington running contrary to the fictional myths. The first is that the public dialogue is usually more ferocious than the private one. The politicians feel compelled to stage a blood-and-guts spectacle even when, behind the scenes, they are prepared to arrive amicably at arrangements. Though there is an uncharted no-man's-land lying between the President and Congress, it is a fact that the two manage to test their respective powers without reaching ultimate showdowns. On the contrary, their private communications are marked by a civility that has survived even in those periods when the two branches of government have been controlled by opposite parties. A great deal of the public noise results from the fact that politicians, like professional wrestlers, know that grunts and groans are expected of them.

A second condition running contrary to fiction is that the important battles in Washington are seldom merely clashes of personality; they are clashes in which policy and personality have become inextricably mixed. This phenomenon may not always be apparent even to the participants. Now and again petty politicians do engage in wholly personal battles, more successfully than in a parliamentary system of government. As the late Senator Joseph McCarthy demonstrated, a petty politician with a lust for power can sometimes manage to stage a big battle.

But political warfare usually enlists the politician on a larger battlefield. To describe it exclusively in terms of individual power drives without reference to the broader struggle, as novelists are inclined to, is like Stendhal's description of the Battle of Waterloo—lively fiction but greatly distorted military history.

Why is it that the political power struggle has not raged on unchecked until the very pillars of government are pulled down amid the melee? This leads to a third, more mysterious aspect of political life. When one considers the extraordinary interests and ambitions that congregate in Washington, it is remarkable how rare and how relatively petty have been the instances of genuine corruption. There exists what might be called a *constitutional morality* that has set limits to the power struggle. It has made the American form of government a workable proposition without bringing leaders to the top who are immoral or amoral in their attitudes toward the use of power. Indeed, so far it has managed to screen out the corrupt politician before he can get to the very top. This reality of politics should not be ignored. We recollect in our history strong Presidents and weak Presidents, but we rarely think of *good* Presidents and *evil* Presidents for the simple reason that we have never had an evil President. White House politics has been played on a higher level than courthouse politics, even when the occupant of the White House was formerly a courthouse politician.

A great deal of serious literature has been dedicated to the proposition that the real power in Washington is not what meets the eye—that there exist hidden repositories and unseen manipulators. A recent magazine article described "The Invisible Men Who Run Congress," reaching the conclusion that, "Of all the sources of power in Washington today, the most nearly invisible—yet in some ways the most influential—is the Congressional staff." The article contained a description of one veteran careerist on Capitol Hill, Colin Stam, who heads the staff of the Joint Committee on Internal Revenue Taxation. In the estimate of an admirer, Stam has been "the godfather of our whole tax structure. He has nursed it through the depression, through two wars and through the postwar period. If there is a pattern or a science to the tax structure today, Stam is its author more than any other American." [4]

Even Stam's detractors are not likely to dispute his influence, though they disagree heartily with his notions about the science of the tax structure. During a session of the Senate Finance Committee in 1962, when Stam produced a series of revenue amendments printed under his own name, one Senator asked caustically which of the states he represented. Stam, equally caustically, replied that he represented "the United States." "Where is your certificate of election?" the Senator snapped. The fact is that this congressional bureaucrat obtained his credentials largely through the support of Senate Finance Chairman Byrd and other committee conservatives. Like a good many other staffers on Capitol Hill, however, he has acquired seniority and expertise which have made him hard to challenge. The role played by these careerists is immeasurable. They count service by decades in a city where most appointed officials come and go after a few brief years.

Similar literature, particularly in the daily journal of politics, the *Congressional Record*, is addressed to the role of the bureaucrats of the Executive branch, the civil servants. Rarely a day passes that a member of Congress fails to challenge their anonymous yet arrogant use of power. Unlike the British Parliament, which freely fastens responsibility on the cabinet minister for misdeeds committed within his bureaucracy, Congress is seldom satisfied merely to blame the boss. A substantial part of the continuing battle between Legislative power and Executive privilege is devoted to this issue of accountability by the careerists.

Civil servants of the upper echelons certainly do play a powerful part in a government grown big and specialized. When the turnover of political executives is swift and the statutes vest uncertain authority, the career executive is often thrust into decision-making beyond his proper competence. But despite its regular complaints, Congress has done little to strengthen the top level civil service. While lesser government employees fare pretty well in salary and working conditions, those higher up the ladder have lagged considerably behind their counterparts in private industry. More important than their pay has been the failure to recognize the necessity of raising their capacities. A Brookings Institution study of the three thousand or more "career executives" who head the various bureaus and divisions of the federal government found that this critically important group was "predominantly inbred." Many had started in government careers at a very low level, progressing up through the ranks by concentrating on specialties. Few ever had opportunity to master the functions they were being called upon to perform as top executives. The conclusion of the Brookings study was that the training programs provided by the government were woefully inadequate.

The portrait of the government bureaucrat which emerged from this and other studies was less that of a man grown arrogant in power than of one who has striven to isolate and insulate himself against the battering of the political process. He has tended to concentrate on his particular bureau and program, frequently remaining indifferent to the larger problems of government. Nothing in his experience has encouraged him to involve himself more deeply.

As a former Chairman of the Civil Service Commission put it, "The idea of Civil Service has outgrown the physical dimensions of a 'corps of clerks.' " Belated efforts are being made to prepare the career executive for the power he is obliged to wield. The Brookings Institution, aided by a Ford Foundation grant, now conducts regular conferences for top- and middle-level government employees. More recently, the Civil Service Commission has launched a program of its own and there has been pressure in Congress to establish a permanent Civil Service Academy.

So far, the military have maintained a clear lead in the field of career development. The National War College, the Air University, and other training meccas are among the country's most advanced educational institutions, permitting the officer to explore matters often only distantly related to battlefield strategies. But the civilian careerist has been victim of the unresolved debate over his rightful role in a democratic system of government. Harboring fear that he will intrude on decision-making that properly belongs to the politician, Congress has been reluctant to recognize that the dividing line cannot always be sharp and clear-cut. There has been a failure to see that even though the career executive should not become involved in partisan politics, he must be deeply involved in the politics of policy. Unless he is, there is likely to be a breakdown in planning and performance despite the best efforts of the politicians. The civil servant's role demands that he become something more than the convenient whipping boy when government gets into trouble.[5]

"Power in America seems to me situational and mercurial," wrote David Riesman in *The Lonely Crowd*. "It resists attempts to locate it the way a molecule, under the Heisenberg principle, resists attempts simultaneously to locate it and time its velocity." [6] Since the publication of Riesman's book in 1950 others have disputed his diagnosis. It has become the fashion to speculate whether there now exists in America something approximating an Establishment to be defined as "a more or less closed and self-sustaining institution that holds a preponderance of power." This idea of a ruling elite, which has long been accepted in British politics, runs counter to our more egalitarian presumptions. Delving into the subject, Richard Rovere, of *The New Yorker*, felt constrained to treat *The American Establishment* with considerable chariness. Though arguing with apparent seriousness that "most fair-minded and objective authorities" concede the existence of such an Establishment, Rovere thrusts his tongue firmly in cheek and proceeds to spoof his subject by describing an Establishment board of directors, citing mythical data about its activities. He thus avoids commitment on a question deserving more serious examination.[7]

One who did attempt such an examination was the late sociologist, C. Wright Mills. During the mid-fifties, Mills concluded that there is, indeed, a "power elite" in America which is "unprecedentedly powerful and increasingly unified and willful." Mills dismissed scornfully those like Riesman who cling to theories of "romantic pluralism" in the power structure. In the running of government, he maintained, "Neither professional party politicians, nor professional bureaucrats are now at the centers of decision. Those centers are occupied by the political directorate of the power elite." The power elite, by his definition, is composed of the "political directorate," the "corporate rich," and the "ascendant military." These three form "an intricate set of overlapping cliques [which] share decisions having at least national consequences. Insofar as national events are decided, the power elite are those who decide them." [8]

According to Mills' analysis, the "middle levels" of elected representatives and civil servants constitute "a drifting set of stalemated, balancing forces. . . ." Beneath them lie the practically powerless general publics. "The rise of the power elite . . . rests upon, and in some ways is part of, the transformation of the publics of America into a mass society," Mills wrote, arguing that the citizenry has lost all hope of influencing the course of government. He characterized his ruling elite as ". . . selected and formed by the means of power, the sources of wealth, the mechanics of celebrity . . . not men selected by a civil service that is linked with the world of knowledge and sensibility . . . not men shaped by nationally responsible parties . . . not men held in check by a plurality of voluntary associations." Mills concluded pessimistically about his elite: "Commanders of power unequalled in human history, they have succeeded within the American system of organized irresponsibility."

This writer, who perhaps has stood overly close to the daily jousting, is doubtful about the validity of such a theory about the ultimate repositories of power in America. It is too pat to be convincing. One can agree with Mills that the growth of leviathan power groups—the corporation, the labor union, the military-industrial complex—has transformed the old power structure in which political parties and voluntary associations once served as basic underpinnings. Likewise, it can be observed that a recognizable group of skilled operatives shuttles back and forth between private enterprise and the key posts of foreign policy, defense, and finance. For evidence, a diligent scholar would do well to delve into the role of the purely unofficial Council on Foreign Relations in the care and breeding of an incipient American Establishment.

But it would be difficult to document the thesis that an elite really rules on matters of national consequence. Mills himself failed noticeably to provide any specific examples of such decision-making. He also neglected to note that the growth of giant organizations has not brought cumulatively greater power to the individuals who head them. On the contrary, the best evidence is that power within each of these groupings has become less coherent. Large-scale enterprise seems to acquire a direction and a momentum which subsumes the energies of those who direct it. The swaggering tycoons of business and labor unions no longer exist to dictate their demands to the subservient politicians. A former DuPont president reflected the new mode of corporate enterprise when he declared, "The more effective an executive, the more his own identity and personality blend into the background of his organization." [9] If this describes the organization man's rule over his own enterprise, it is even more true when he is dealing with the

R

government. Unless defined to include a congeries so diverse and so transient as to lack meaning, Mills' concept of a sinister and cynical power elite hardly seems applicable to decision-making in Washington today.

What of the future? More than the past, it raises forebodings about the workability of a government of fragmented powers. The awesome dimension of the hydrogen bomb tempts the prophet to exaggerated fears when addressing himself to the political problems of the age. How, for example, can such a system of government, necessarily open in its workings, cope with the task of maintaining a closed intelligence system operating on a world-wide basis? The grim enterprises of the Central Intelligence Agency involving Eisenhower's Administration in the U-2 overflight of the Soviet Union and Kennedy's in the Cuban Bay of Pigs invasion prompted bitter questions about whether our government was in control of itself. Though neither enterprise proved to be CIA sorties behind the President's back, there has remained the dilemma of holding rein on this secret bureaucracy numbering tens of thousands of employees whose careers depend on keeping busy. The converse dilemma is whether such an intelligence system, if held in check, can display the initiative to be a suitable adversary of the one employed by the Soviets.

Other areas of government present comparable problems. Even after fifteen years' experience, the handling of foreign aid remains an enigma. In a version of governmental gamesmanship, its bureaucracy has been shuffled and reshuffled with yearly regularity, its agency named and renamed. Pointing out the record of *ten* different administrators holding an average tenure of eighteen months since Paul Hoffman started the program in 1948, its former deputy head, Dr. D. A. Fitzgerald, has remarked despairingly, "Here is a program which for size, complexity, and difficulty of administration is clearly in a class by itself. It dwarfs even the biggest businesses in the United States.

Where would General Motors or AT&T or Standard Oil of New Jersey be if these companies changed their chief executives every year and a half. . . ." Fitzgerald has argued that this drastic treatment was dictated "not by any fundamental weaknesses in the existing organization, but by a mistaken belief that persistent and intractable problems of substance could be resolved by a radical change in the form of the organization." [10] A more basic explanation is that foreign aid seems congenitally unable, despite widespread public acceptance according to the opinion polls, to build a political power base in Washington which can permit it to become a stable program.

Amid the ups and downs of the various programs—often launched ambitiously one year, slashed drastically the next —it is not possible to chart with precision the long-range course government is taking. The legislative box score— kept so religiously by reporters—on Presidential requests sent to the Hill is not always a useful measuring device, particularly when piddling programs are accorded the same emphasis as major ones. Merely counting the dollar expenditures hardly serves for comparisons with the past. A better measure was offered by Congressman Morris K. Udall in replying to those who complain that government is moving inexorably toward the Welfare State. He pointed out that in 1939, forty-four cents of the budget dollar was spent for labor, health, education, and other welfare programs—whereas in 1963, only seven cents of the budget dollar went for these purposes. Based on the 1939 dollar, federal welfare expenditures have shrunk from thirty dollars per citizen to sixteen dollars.[11] "The fact is that for the last fifteen years the federal government—also the federal debt—and also the federal bureaucracy—have grown less rapidly than the economy as a whole," declared the late President Kennedy at Yale, in June, 1962.

The incessant thrust of science has raised still another bothersome question about the future of government. In his farewell address, Eisenhower alluded to this when he warned that ". . . we must also be alert to the . . . danger that public policy could itself become the captive of a scientific-technological elite." While it is doubtful that Eisenhower meant to promote fears of a cabal of mad scientists taking over the organs of government, there is room for concern that government increasingly may find itself dancing to science's tune. One observer has prophesied: "For we are rapidly becoming a society whose outlines are determined by the leverage provided by science . . . Our future society will have a new power base. Those who are able to control the flow of the new type of power will have within their hands a potential for 'despotism' similar to that exercised by the more traditional despots of the past . . . the organization and control of science, whether governmental, quasi-governmental, or private, will provide the agency through which the most important overall decisions are taken . . . The process of scientific innovation will provide the establishment of a new (and once established, most potent) 'legislature.' " [12]

Military and space enterprises are not the only ones caught in the breakneck pace of scientific innovation. A case was when President Kennedy overruled an earlier veto to launch a near billion-dollar investment in developing a supersonic commercial aircraft. Pentagon leaders had refused to give a military justification to this decision which apparently was provoked by fear of competition from the western Europeans rather than the Soviets. It will require a complete overhaul of the nation's air facilities, and discommode untold millions who live and work on the ground, while cutting coast-to-coast flight time only by minutes. One may wonder whether the Executive carefully weighed priorities before joining step to this particular march of progress.

One other test of government comes with increasing U. S. involvement in international decision-making. So far, our government has not yet been obliged to put up or shut up in its frequent appeals for closer community action among nations. But the time may be approaching when the demands of multilateralism, whether in the North Atlantic Treaty Organization, the Alliance For Progress or the United Nations itself, may require a different order of commitment. For example, can we work out a way of sharing responsibility with NATO nuclear forces for triggering nuclear warfare? There is likely to be stubborn resistance in Congress to even allowing a foreign finger on the safety catch. Similarly, the European Common Market, the consortia for aiding developing countries, and the countless other multi-nation projects with which we are engaged will hardly permit the interminable bargaining over policy that has always gone on within the U. S. government.

Despite his admiration for the American experiment, de Tocqueville felt obliged to qualify it with a warning: "Foreign politics demand scarcely any of those qualities which are peculiar to a democracy; they require, on the contrary, the perfect use of almost all those in which it is deficient . . . a democracy can only with great difficulty regulate the details of an important undertaking, persevere in a fixed design, and work out its execution in spite of serious obstacles. It cannot combine its measures with secrecy, or await their consequences with patience." [18] De Tocqueville could hardly foresee the time when these same faculties would be needed not simply for foreign politics but for practically every one of the far-flung activities of government.

Yet the extent to which our ancient institutions have managed to adapt to new situations is remarkable. One purpose of this book has been to attempt to trace some of these adaptations: how power has shifted in the roles of the Executive and Congress; how it has been parcelled out within the branches; how it has coalesced in various new groupings. This rearranging of power has been inevitable in a government grown so big and complex. Within the Constitution's separations, the rearrangements have been an unavoidable consequence of the need to keep government functioning.

Working at its best, the competition bred by a fragmented power structure has given vitality to American government and vigor to its leaders. Not all the surface confusion connotes weakness, even if it does distract a great many observers at home and abroad. Only when lesser and local priorities outweigh the greater, when short-term interests crowd out the long-term, when the subgovernments grow unruly and create stalemate, has the competition gotten out of bounds.

These are facts of life with which the students of politics must reckon. Those who wring their hands despairingly over departures from *the* Constitution ignore reality, just as do those who, in their impatient quest for more effective government, would disregard the Constitution. Both are apt to forget that government has been shaped by basic forces in the body politic. Our institutions are not easily tinkered with, and the very act of tinkering can produce bizarre results. It is doubtful whether any of the basic institutions which exercise power—Presidency, Congress, parties, pressure groups, press—can be reformed by fiat or made to perform a markedly different role than the one it has come to play.

Still, the struggle to govern requires a continuing effort to make power more responsive and responsible. For the fact is that all the institutions examined in these pages show disturbing evidence of power being exercised in unresponsive and irresponsible ways. They have inadequate standards of accountability; they fall short when measured against the colossal task of governing.

This present disarray in our institutions of government helps in turn condition those who become adept in the uses of power in Washington. It tends to accentuate the role of the tacticians—the operators skilled in daily maneuver, in whipping together transient coalitions, and in triggering instant objectives. It tends to diminish the role of the long-term strategists—those who try to live by the governmental standard urged by George Washington: "For the more combined and distant things are seen, the more likely they are to be turned to advantage." In the capital named after the first President there is too much tendency to see things close up and in part.

To elevate the art of governing must require the existence of a power elite—not of the cynical or sinister, but comprising those who by distant vision and capacity to see things whole come to play a superior role. In an age of mammoth organization, the future still depends on individuals dedicated to this higher calling of politics, whether professionals or amateurs, working in Washington or elsewhere. By their genius and ethic, by the purpose and self-restraint with which they exercise power, they will determine whether a government of separated powers can continue to endure.

NOTES

I. THE CONSTITUTION

Chapter 1. *The Living vs. the Literal*

1. Thomas Paine, *Common Sense*, (1776). In *The People Shall Judge*. Chicago: University of Chicago Press, 1949. Vol. I, p. 184.
2. Woodrow Wilson, *Congressional Government*. Boston: Houghton Mifflin Company, 1885. p. 7.
3. Robert H. Jackson, *The Struggle for Judicial Supremacy*. New York: Random House, 1941. p. xi.
4. John W. Finney, "Rocket Setbacks Spur House Study," *New York Times*, May 15, 1962, p. 1.
5. "M'Namara Faces Fight on Carrier," *New York Times*, November 4, 1963, p. 22.
6. Richard E. Neustadt, *Presidential Power*. New York: John Wiley & Sons, 1960. p. 33.
7. Louis J. Hector, Testimony before Senate Subcommittee on Administrative Practice and Procedure, December 1, 1960.
8. Wilson, *op. cit.*, p. 10.
9. Sidney Hyman, "The War of Presidential Succession," *The Reporter*, June 25, 1959, p. 11.
10. Robert Engler, *The Politics of Oil*. New York: The Macmillan Company, 1961. p. 132.
11. Wilson, *op. cit.*, p. 10.
12. Robert H. Jackson, *The Supreme Court in the American System of Government*. Cambridge, Mass.: Harvard University Press, 1955.

Chapter 2. On the Nature of Subgovernments:
The Military-Industrial Complex

1. Neil MacNeil, *The Forge of Democracy: The House of Representatives.* New York: David McKay Company, 1963. p. 170.
2. Fletcher Knebel and Charles W. Bailey II, "Military Control: Can It Happen Here?" *Look*, September 11, 1962, p. 20.
3. Fred J. Cook, *The Warfare State.* New York: The Macmillan Company, 1962.
4. Leonard D. White, *The Federalists, A Study in Administrative History.* New York: The Macmillan Company, 1956. p. 147.
5. *Ibid.*, p. 150. (Original source: July 22, 1792, Hamilton, *Works* [Hamilton ed.] IV, 226.)
6. *Ibid.*, p. 156. (Original source: *Annals of Congress*, IV, 434, February 6, 1794.)
7. *Ibid.*, p. 157. (Original source: *Annals of Congress*, VIII, 1548, April 25, 1778.)
8. *Ibid.*, p. 158. (Original source: *Ibid.*, 1553.)
9. *Ibid.*, p. 158. (June 23, 1789, *Sewanee Review*, 1906, XIV, 96.)
10. William Manchester. See his "The Department of Defense," *Holiday*, May, 1963, p. 78. Reprinted by special permission from *Holiday*, copyright 1963, by the Curtis Publishing Co.
11. James Real, "The Politics of Science" in the Report, *Science and Democratic Government.* Center for Study of Democratic Institutions, January, 1963.
12. Manchester, *op. cit.*, p. 141.
13. *Congressional Quarterly*, XIX, March 24, 1961. Study by Defense Procurement Subcommittee of the Joint Economic Committee, 1960. p. 464.
14. Editorial in *Science*, 140, 3564, April 19, 1963, 267.
15. Real, *op. cit.*
16. Manchester, *op. cit.*, p. 145.
17. Hearings, House Armed Services Committee, Executive Session, May 2, 1961.
18. *Congressional Quarterly, loc. cit.*, p. 466.

19. *Ibid.*, p. 464.
20. *Ibid.*
21. *Ibid.*, p. 466.
22. *Ibid.*, p. 467.
23. Editorial, *The Oregonian*, April 28, 1962.
24. Report to the Congress of the United States, *Review of Manned Aircraft Nuclear Propulsion Program Atomic Energy Commission and Department of Defense*, by the Comptroller General of the United States, February, 1963, cover letter.
25. Rep. Jamie L. Whitten (D., Miss.) before the Joint Economic Committee's Defense Procurement Subcommittee, January 29, 1960.
26. Richard Austin Smith, "The $7-Billion Contract That Changed The Rules," *Fortune*, March, 1963, p. 184.
27. *Ibid.*
28. Joseph Alsop, "Matter of Fact—The Attack on McNamara," *New York Herald Tribune*, May 2, 1963.
29. Smith, *op. cit.*, p. 186.

II. THE PRESIDENCY

Chapter 3. The Shaping Role of the Selection Process

1. James Bryce, *The American Commonwealth*. New York: The Macmillan Company, 1893. Vol. I, p. 79.
2. Anthony Lewis, "The Case Against Electoral Reform," *The Reporter*, December 8, 1960.
3. Alexander Hamilton, *The Federalist*, Number 68, March 12, 1788, p. 1. In Jacob E. Cooke, Ed., *The Federalist*, Middletown, Conn.: Wesleyan University Press, 1961.
4. Hugh Gaitskill, Speech to American Society of Newspaper Editors, Spring, 1960.
5. Sidney Kraus, *The Great Debates*. Bloomington: Indiana University Press, 1962. p. 109.
6. *Ibid.*, p. 102.
7. *Ibid.*, pp. 173, 190.
8. *Ibid.*, p. 200.

9. *Ibid.*, p. 211.
10. Richard M. Nixon, *Six Crises*. New York: Doubleday & Company, 1962. p. 355.
11. Lewis, *op. cit.*
12. Bryce, *op. cit.*, p. 80.

Chapter 4. The Do-It-Yourself Nature of Presidential Power

1. James Fenimore Cooper, *The American Democrat*. Cooperstown, N. Y.: H & E Phinney, 1838.
2. Alistair Cooke, *The Listener*, LXIX, 1775, Thursday, 4 April 1963.
3. Richard E. Neustadt, *Presidential Power*. New York: John Wiley & Sons, 1960. p. 5.
4. *Ibid.*, p. 10.
5. Grant McConnell, *The Steel Seizure of 1952*. (Inter-University Case Program.) Tuscaloosa: University of Alabama Press, 1960. ICP Case Series 52, p. 53.
6. President Kennedy's Address at Yale University, June 11, 1962. Text from *The Wall Street Journal*, Tuesday, June 12, 1962, p. 20.
7. Tom Wicker, "President Feels West Gained in '61 But Sees Danger," *New York Times*, Sunday, December 31, 1961, p. 1.

Chapter 5. The Lonely Job in a Crowded White House

1. Jacob E. Cooke, *op. cit.*, (Hamilton, Number 70).
2. Theodore C. Sorensen, *Decision-Making in the White House*; (The Gino Speranza Lectures). New York: Columbia University Press, 1963. p. 71.
3. William Hillman, *Mr. President*. New York: Farrar, Straus & Company, 1952. p. 13.
4. "Inside Story—How Ike Makes the Big Decisions," *U. S. News & World Report*, Copyright, April 20, 1956, p. 32.
5. Douglass Cater, "Loneliest Job in a Crowded White House," *The Reporter*, June 25, 1959, p. 14.
6. Robert J. Donovan, *Eisenhower: The Inside Story*. New York: Harper & Brothers, 1956. p. 71.
7. Committee Print, Eighty-Sixth Congress, Second Session:

Organizing for National Security, "The National Security Council." Study submitted to the Committee on Government Operations, United States Senate by its Subcommittee on National Policy Machinery. December 12, 1960, p. 4.

8. *Ibid.*, "Super-Cabinet Officers and Superstaffs," November 16, 1960, p. 23.
9. *Ibid.*, "The National Security Council," pp. 5-9.
10. *Ibid.*, "Super-Cabinet Officers and Superstaffs," p. 5.
11. Laurin L. Henry, "The Transition: The New Administration," *The Presidential Election and Transition 1960-61.* Paul T. David, Ed. Washington, D. C.: Brookings Institution, 1961. p. 256.
12. Hans J. Morgenthau, "Failure and Challenge," *The New Leader,* July 3, 1961.
13. Arthur Krock, "In the Nation," *New York Times,* Friday, June 30, 1961.
14. Joseph Alsop, "Matter of Fact," *New York Herald Tribune,* October 18, 1961.
15. Author's interview with President Kennedy, May 9, 1961.
16. President's News Conference, June 28, 1961, as recorded in the *New York Times,* June 29, 1961, p. L12.
17. Letter to the author from Richard Neustadt, December 15, 1961.

Chapter 6. The Dilemmas of Being Heard

1. Bryce, *op. cit.*, Vol. II, p. 358.
2. Sorensen, *op. cit.*, p. 45.
3. Neustadt, *op. cit.*, p. 103. (Franklin D. Roosevelt to Ray Stannard Baker, March 20, 1935. This letter is included in the Roosevelt Library collection at Hyde Park, New York.)
4. C. P. Snow, *Science and Government*; (The Godkin Lectures). Cambridge, Mass.: Harvard University Press, 1961. p. 64.
5. Address by President Kennedy at Yale University, June 11, 1962. Text from *The Wall Street Journal,* June 12, 1962, p. 20.

III. THE CONGRESS

Chapter 7. The Conditioning of Congressmen
1. Bryce, *op. cit.*, Vol. I, p. 192.

Chapter 8. The Search for Role
1. Clem Miller, *Member of the House, Letters of a Congressman,* John W. Baker, Ed. New York: Charles Scribner's Sons, 1962. Letter from William W. Broom to Congressman Miller, pp. 63-64.
2. *Ibid.*, p. 52.
3. *Ibid.*, p. 67.
4. *Ibid.*, pp. 61-62.
5. Wilson, *op. cit.*, pp. 62-63.
6. Miller, *op. cit.*, pp. 104-105.
7. *Ibid.*, p. 91.
8. Jerry Landauer, "Debate's Decline," *The Wall Street Journal,* February 7, 1963, p. 16.
9. *Ibid.*
10. Byron L. Johnson, "Congress and the Executive." Address delivered at Annual Meeting of the American Political Science Association, Washington, D. C., 1962, p. 17.
11. "The Shame of Congress," *Printers' Ink,* August 19, 1960, Part I.
12. Letter to the author from Congressman Jack Brooks (D., Texas), August 12, 1959.
13. Lewis A. Dexter, "Congress and the Formation of Military Policy." Paper delivered at the American Association for the Advancement of Science, Washington, D. C., December 31, 1958, p. 4.
14. Congressman Mendel Rivers (D., S. C.), "The Defense Appropriations Rider," *Case Studies in American Government,* Edwin Bock and Alan Campbell, Eds., (Inter-University Case Program). Englewood Cliffs, N. J.: Prentice-Hall, 1962. ICP Case Series 2, p. 60.

15. Joseph P. Harris, "The Legislative Veto of Executive Actions." Speech delivered at the annual meeting of The American Political Science Association, Washington, D. C., September, 1959, p. 16.
16. Senator Eugene McCarthy, "The Eighty-Seventh Congress." Brookings Institution Lecture, February, 1961. *Loc. cit.* (*See* note 5-11), p. 287.
17. Senator Henry M. Jackson, "Congress and the Atom," 290 *Annals of the American Political Science Association* 77, 1953.
18. Harold P. Green and Alan Rosenthal in *The Joint Committee on Atomic Energy: A Study in Fusion of Governmental Power.* Washington, D. C.: The National Law Center of the George Washington University, 1961. p. 288.
19. *Ibid.,* p. 295.

Chapter 9. *The Nature of Baronial Power*

1. Wilson, *op. cit.,* p. 92.
2. Miller, *op. cit.,* p. 112.
3. *Congressional Quarterly,* XIX, 36, September 8, 1961, p. 1554.
4. Rowland Evans, Jr., "Louisiana's Passman: The Scourge of Foreign Aid." © 1963, by Harper & Row, Publishers, Incorporated. Reprinted from *Harper's Magazine* by the Author's Permission.
5. John Stuart Mill, *Autobiography.* New York: Henry Holt & Co., 1873. pp. 264-265.
6. Wilson, *op. cit.,* p. 69.
7. Dean Acheson, *A Citizen Looks at Congress.* New York: Harper & Brothers, 1956. p. 26.
8. Richard F. Fenno, Jr., "The House Appropriations Committee as a Political System: The Problem of Integration," *The American Political Science Review,* LVI, June, 1962, pp. 310-324.
9. George Galloway, *History of the House of Representatives.* New York: Thomas Y. Crowell, 1961. p. 67.
10. *Ibid.,* p. 71.
11. Wilson, *op. cit.,* p. 102.

12. George Galloway, *The Legislative Process in Congress*. New York: Thomas Y. Crowell, 1953. p. 289.
13. *Congressional Record*, Eighty-Third Congress, Second Session, Vol. 100, Part 2, February 8, 1954, p. 1476.
14. George Goodwin, Jr., "Subcommittees: The Miniature Legislatures of Congress," *The American Political Science Review*, LVI, September, 1962.
15. Charles O. Jones, "Representatives in Congress: The Case of the House Agriculture Committee," *The American Political Science Review*, LV, June, 1961.
16. *Congressional Record*, Eighty-Fourth Congress, Second Session, Vol. 102, Part 3, March 2, 1956, p. 3822.

Chapter 10. Leadership and Reform
1. *Congressional Record*, Eighty-Eighth Congress, First Session, Vol. 109, No. 24. February 19, 1963, p. 2413.
2. *Congressional Record*, Eighty-Eighth Congress, First Session, Vol. 109, No. 28. February 25, 1963, p. 2771.
3. Roscoe Drummond, "Congress Must Reform," *Saturday Evening Post*, January 9, 1963.
4. Homer D. Babbidge, Jr., and Robert M. Rosenzweig, *The Federal Interest in Higher Education*. New York: McGraw-Hill, 1962. p. 70.

IV.   THE PARTIES

Chapter 11. The Loss of Role
1. Sorensen, *op. cit.*, pp. 32-33.
2. Speech delivered by Senator John F. Kennedy at National Press Club, January 14, 1960. Text in the *New York Times*, January 15, 1960, p. 14.
3. Donovan, *op. cit.*, pp. 151-152.
4. James MacGregor Burns, *The Deadlock of Democracy*. Englewood Cliffs, N. J.: Prentice-Hall, 1963. p. 265.
5. *Ibid.*, p. 276.
6. *Ibid.*, pp. 338-339.

7. William G. Carleton, "The Cult of Personality Comes to the White House." © 1961, by Harper & Row, Publishers, Incorporated. Reprinted from *Harper's Magazine* by the Author's Permission.

V. OUTSIDERS ON THE INSIDE

Chapter 12. *The Subtle Art of Pressure*

1. Jacob E. Cooke, *op. cit.*, (Madison, Number 10).
2. Robert Luce, *Congress*; (The Godkin Lectures). Cambridge, Mass.: Harvard University Press, 1926.
3. General Interim Report, House Select Committee on Lobbying Activities, Eighty-First Congress, Second Session, House Report 3138, 1950.
4. Karl Schriftgiesser, *The Lobbyists*. Boston: Atlantic-Little, Brown and Company, 1951. pp. 5-7.
5. Rep. Emanuel Celler, "Pressure Groups in Congress," *Annals of the American Academy of Political and Social Science*, 319, Philadelphia, September, 1958. Issue subtitled: *Unofficial Government: Pressure Groups and Lobbies*. p. 4.
6. House Report No. 113, Sixty-Third Congress, Second Session, p. 5.
7. Dayton D. McKean, *Party and Pressure Politics*. Boston: Houghton Mifflin Company, 1949.
8. Richard W. Gable, "NAM: Influential Lobby or Kiss of Death?" *Journal of Politics*, Vol. 15, May, 1953.
9. Lester W. Milbrath, "Lobbying as a Communication Process," *Public Opinion Quarterly*, Spring, 1960.
10. Donald C. Blaisdell, *Annals of the American Academy of Political and Social Science, loc. cit.* Philadelphia, September, 1958, p. ix.
11. Tad Szulc, "Igor Cassini Indicted as Failing to Register as Trujillo Agent," *New York Times*, February 9, 1963, p. 8.
12. *Ibid.*
13. Douglass Cater and Walter Pincus, "Foreign Legion of

U. S. Public Relations," *The Reporter*, December 22, 1960, pp. 15-22.

14. Celler, *op. cit.*, p. 3.

15. A. F. Bentley, *The Process of Government*, 1908. Cited by R. M. MacIver, *The Web of Government*. New York: The Macmillan Company, 1947. p. 220.

16. Clement E. Vose, "Litigation as a Form of Pressure Group Activity," *Annals of the American Academy of Political and Social Science, loc. cit.*, pp. 22-23.

17. Miller, *op. cit.*, pp. 131-140.

18. Al Toffler, "How Congressmen Make Up Their Minds," *Redbook*, February, 1962, p. 131.

Chapter 13. The News Managers

1. Speech delivered by Pierre Salinger at the Women's Press Club, Washington, D. C. Reported in the *New York Times*, March 23, 1963.

2. Statement by Arthur Sylvester to reporters, October 30, 1962. Reported in the *New York Herald Tribune*, November 1, 1962.

3. Poll conducted by *Newsweek*, and reported in issue of April 8, 1963.

4. Leo Rosten, *The Washington Correspondents*. New York: Harcourt, Brace, 1937, p. 254.

5. Speech by Robert Cutler to Harvard alumni, May, 1955.

6. Richard Frykland, "Control of Cuban News Seen as U. S. 'Weapon,' " *Washington Star*, October 29, 1962.

7. Excerpts from remarks by Pierre Salinger at Silver Guild Awards Banquet, Hilton Hotel, Pittsburgh, Pa. Press release dated December 5, 1962.

8. William S. White, "Trying to Find the Shape—If Any— of the News in Washington." © 1963, by Harper & Row, Publishers, Incorporated. Reprinted from *Harper's Magazine* by the Author's Permission.

VI. THE STRUGGLE TO GOVERN

Chapter 14. Power in Washington: Fact and Fiction
1. Bryce, *op. cit.*, Vol. II, pp. 793-794.
2. Wilson, *op. cit.*, p. 242.
3. Douglass Cater, "Advice and Dissent About the Best Man," the *New York Times Magazine*, Sunday, May 22, 1960, quoting Allen Drury (*Advise and Consent*) and Gore Vidal (*The Best Man*).
4. Rowland Evans, Jr., "The Invisible Men Who Run Congress," *Saturday Evening Post*, June 8, 1963, p. 13.
5. See the author's report, "Developing Leadership in Government." The Brookings Institution Center for Advanced Study, 1960.
6. David Riesman with Nathan Glazer and Reuel Denney, *The Lonely Crowd: A Study of the Changing American Character*. New Haven: Yale University Press, 1950. p. 252.
7. Richard Rovere, *The American Establishment and Other Reports, Opinions, and Speculations*. New York: Harcourt, Brace and World, 1962. p. 3.
8. C. Wright Mills, *The Power Elite*. New York: Oxford University Press, 1956. p. 18.
9. Crawford Greenewalt, *The Uncommon Man*. New York: McGraw-Hill, 1959. p. 72.
10. Felix Belair, Jr., "White House Accused of Retarding Foreign Aid Program by Interference," *New York Times*, Sunday, November 18, 1962, p. 59.
11. Morris K. Udall, "Where's the Welfare State?" *New Republic*, October 1, 1962, p. 13.
12. Harvey Wheeler, Jr., "The Politics of Science," included in the study *Science and Democratic Government*, published by the Center for the Study of Democratic Institutions, January, 1963.
13. Alexis de Tocqueville, *Democracy in America*. New York: Alfred A. Knopf, 1945. Vol. I, pp. 234-235.

INDEX